CASEBOOK

GENERAL EDITO

Shakespeare: *Julius Caesar* PETER URE
Shakespeare: *King Lear* FRANK KERMODE
Shakespeare: *Macbeth* JOHN WAIN
Shakespeare: *Measure for Measure* G. K. STEAD
Shakespeare: *The Merchant of Venice* JOHN WILDERS
Shakespeare: *Othello* JOHN WAIN
Shakespeare: *Richard II* NICHOLAS BROOKE
Shakespeare: *The Tempest* D. J. PALMER
Shakespeare: *Troilus and Cressida* PRISCILLA MARTIN
Shakespeare: *Twelfth Night* D. J. PALMER
Shakespeare: *The Winter's Tale* KENNETH MUIR
Shelley: *Shorter Poems and Lyrics* PATRICK SWINDEN
Spenser: *The Faerie Queene* PETER BAYLEY
Swift: *Gulliver's Travels* RICHARD GRAVIL
Tennyson: *In Memoriam* JOHN DIXON HUNT
Webster: *'The White Devil' and 'The Duchess of Malfi'*
R. V. HOLDSWORTH
Virginia Woolf: *To the Lighthouse* MORRIS BEJA
Wordsworth: *Lyrical Ballads* ALUN R. JONES AND WILLIAM
TYDEMAN
Wordsworth: *The Prelude* W. J. HARVEY AND RICHARD GRAVIL
Yeats: *Last Poems* JON STALLWORTHY

TITLES IN PREPARATION INCLUDE

George Eliot: *'The Mill on the Floss' and 'Silas Marner'* R. P. DRAPER
T. S. Eliot: *'Prufrock', 'Gerontion', 'Ash Wednesday' and Other Shorter Poems*
B. C. SOUTHAM
Farquhar: *'The Beaux' Stratagem' and 'The Recruiting Officer'* RAY
ANSELMENT
Jonson: *'Every Man in His Humour' and 'The Alchemist'*
R. V. HOLDSWORTH
Shakespeare: *Coriolanus* B. A. BROCKMAN
Shakespeare: *'Much Ado about Nothing' and 'As You Like It'*
JENNIFER SEARLE
Shakespeare: *Sonnets* PETER JONES
Sheridan: *'The Rivals', 'The School for Scandal' and 'The Critic'*
WILLIAM RUDDICK
Thackeray: *Vanity Fair* ARTHUR POLLARD

The Evolution of Novel Criticism STEPHEN HAZELL
The Romantic Imagination JOHN S. HILL

Shakespeare

Henry IV
Parts I and II

A CASEBOOK

EDITED BY

G. K. HUNTER

Selection and editorial matter © G. K. Hunter 1970

All rights reserved. No part of this publication
may be reproduced or transmitted, in any form
or by any means, without permission.

First edition 1970
Reprinted 1977

Published by
THE MACMILLAN PRESS LTD
London and Basingstoke
Associated companies in New York Dublin
Melbourne Johannesburg and Madras

ISBN 0 333 06747 9

Printed in Hong Kong by
Shanghai Printing Press Ltd

CONTENTS

ACKNOWLEDGEMENTS

A. C. Bradley, *Oxford Lectures on Poetry* (the executors of the late A. C. Bradley); H. B. Charlton, *Shakespeare, Politics, and Politicians* (Mrs E. F. Charlton); J. Dover Wilson, *The Fortunes of Falstaff* (Cambridge University Press); E. M. W. Tillyard, *Shakespeare's History Plays* (Chatto & Windus Ltd and Barnes & Noble Inc.); J. I. M. Stewart, *Character and Motive in Shakespeare* (Longmans, Green & Co. Ltd); William Empson, 'Falstaff and Mr Dover Wilson', from the *Kenyon Review* (Spring 1953) (© Kenyon College 1953); Harold Jenkins, *The Structural Problem in Shakespeare's Henry IV* (Methuen & Co. Ltd); L. C. Knights, *Some Shakespearean Themes* (Chatto & Windus Ltd and Stanford University Press; © L. C. Knights 1959); W. H. Auden, 'The Fallen City', from *Encounter*, XIII (1959) 21–31 (Curtis Brown Ltd, London and New York); C. L. Barber, 'Rule and Misrule in *Henry IV*', from *Shakespeare's Festive Comedy* (© Princeton University Press 1959); Paul A. Jorgensen, 'Redeeming Time', from *Tennessee Studies in Literature*, v, ed. Alwin Thaler and Richard Beale Davis (© the University of Tennessee Press 1960).

GENERAL EDITOR'S PREFACE

GENERAL EDITOR'S PREFACE

EACH of this series of Casebooks concerns either one well-known and influential work of literature or two or three closely linked works. The main section consists of critical readings, mostly modern, brought together from journals and books. A selection of reviews and comments by the author's contemporaries is also included, and sometimes comments from the author himself. The Editor's Introduction charts the reputation of the work from its first appearance until the present time.

What is the purpose of such a collection? Chiefly, to assist reading. Our first response to literature may be, or seem to be, 'personal'. Certain qualities of vigour, profundity, beauty or 'truth to experience' strike us, and the work gains a foothold in our mind. Later, an isolated phrase or passage may return to haunt or illuminate. Where did we hear that? we wonder – it could scarcely be better put.

In these and similar ways appreciation begins, but major literature prompts to very much more. There are certain facts we need to know if we are to understand properly. Who were the author's original readers, and what assumptions did he share with them? What was his theory of literature? Was he committed to a particular historical situation, or to a set of beliefs? We need historians as well as critics to help us with this. But there are also more purely literary factors to take account of: the work's structure and rhetoric; its symbols and archetypes; its tone, genre and texture; its use of language; the words on the page. In all these matters critics can inform and enrich our individual responses by offering imaginative recreations of their own.

For the life of a book is not, after all, merely 'personal'; it is more like a tripartite dialogue, between a writer living 'then', a reader living 'now', and whatever forces of survival and honour link the two. Criticism is the public manifestation of this dialogue, a witness to the continuing power of literature to arouse and excite. It illuminates the possibilities and rewards of the dialogue, pushing 'interpretation' as far forward as it can go.

And here, indeed, is the rub: how far can it go? Where does 'interpretation' end and nonsense begin? Why is one interpretation superior to another, and why does each age need to interpret for itself? The critic knows that his insights have value only in so far as they serve the text, and that he must take account of views differing sharply from his own. He knows that his own writing will be judged as well as the work he writes about, so that he cannot simply assert inner illumination or a differing taste.

The critical forum is a place of vigorous conflict and disagreement, but there is nothing in this to cause dismay. What is attested is the complexity of human experience and the richness of literature, not any chaos or relativity of taste. A critic is better seen, no doubt, as an explorer than as an 'authority', but explorers ought to be, and usually are, well equipped. The effect of good criticism is to convince us of what C. S. Lewis called 'the enormous extension of our being which we owe to authors'. A Casebook will be justified only if it helps to promote the same end.

A single volume can represent no more than a small selection of critical opinions. Some critics have been excluded for reasons of space, and it is hoped that readers will follow up the further suggestions in the Select Bibliography. Other contributions have been severed from their original context, to which some readers may wish to return. Indeed, if they take a hint from the critics represented here, they certainly will.

A. E. DYSON

INTRODUCTION

The 'History Play'

THE most obvious feature of Shakespeare's 'history plays' is their variety; nowhere is this more obvious or more important than in the two parts of *Henry IV*. The immense and continuous popularity of these plays is largely dependent on the rich variety of theatrical and literary stimulus which they provide. Even if one removes the great attractiveness of Falstaff, the plays still abound in dramatic interest; the guilt and sorrow of the king himself, the youthful fire of Hotspur, the Celtic romanticism of Glendower, the politic anguish of Northumberland, the provincial smugness of Shallow, the political and personal virtuosity of Hal – these give riches enough to keep a company of brilliant actors and a nation of attentive play-goers diversely occupied. The fullness of life depicted and the variousness of the methods used to depict it have always, however, raised critical difficulties. The plays resist attempts to describe them simply as Comedy or Tragedy; and if they succeed in unifying their material the question then arises whether or not they do so in terms of some other generic discipline. Is there a discipline attached to the *genre* of the 'history play'? Certainly when Shakespeare's fellow actors and first editors – Heminge and Condell – called the First Folio of 1623 'Mr William Shakespeare's Comedies, Histories and Tragedies' they implied that three distinct kinds of plays were to be found in that famous collection.

Of course we may assume that the distinction in the minds of Heminge and Condell was based on content, not on form. A 'history play' would then be a play about the history of the people who formed its original audience, so that English history produces history plays in England; but under the same circumstances Roman history (as in *Coriolanus*, *Julius Caesar*,

Antony and Cleopatra) produces tragedies. But if we assume that
the name describes content and not form, the aesthetic power of
the history play must probably be limited to something like the
level of a military pageant – appealing mainly to patriotism by
showing nationally significant episodes from the past ('The
historical plays of Shakespeare', says Dryden, 'are rather so
many chronicles of Kings'; they are 'full-length portraits of the
Kings of England' says Edward Dowden), with perhaps a few
knockabout low-life scenes for contrast or light relief. The phrase
'chronicle-history' is sometimes used to give objective-seeming
validity to this derogatory view of the art of the history play, and
a number of plays, ruder than Shakespeare's (such as *The Famous
Victories of Henry the Fifth*), are cited to explain the roots of this
mode of writing. The earliest writers on Shakespeare certainly
seem to have taken the view that these plays did not have the
critical importance that warranted reference to *The Rules*.
Charles Gildon in his 'Remarks on the plays of Shakespeare',
published in Rowe's edition of Shakespeare (1709), says that they
'mix comic and tragic, and, being histories, contain no fable or
design'. Dr Johnson (1765) says that 'Shakespeare's histories,
being neither tragedies nor comedies, are not subject to any of
their laws'. Mrs Montagu, in her *Essay on the writings and genius
of Shakespeare* (1769), allows the general truth of the condemna-
tion and pleads only that the Rules may be waived in the case of a
play as entertaining as *Henry IV*: 'But if the pedantry of learning
could ever recede from its dogmatical rules, I think this play
[*Henry IV*] instead of being condemned for being of that species,
would obtain favour for the species itself.'

Modern critics, with less tendency to measure excellence by
The Rules, and with more willingness to accept forms outside
the *genres* of tragedy and comedy, do not raise these same objec-
tions to *Henry IV* (though even Coleridge felt himself obliged
to define it as a 'mixed drama' because 'in the purely historical
plays, the history *informs* the plot, in the mixed it *directs* it'); but
the discipline of the historical kind, the focus of our identification
with the play – which is the essential matter that the Rules sought
to codify – remains a problem. With whom or what are we sup-

posed to sympathise in plays like *Henry IV*? The name-role is
not here (as in the tragedies) that of the hero through whose eyes
the major action must be seen. F. S. Boas speaks for many when
he says (*Shakspere and his Predecessors*, 1896) that 'the per-
sonages in the historical plays are wanting in the infinite complexity of the tragic creations. . . . Their dramatic dignity and
value spring rather from the width of radius within which they
operate than from their own inherent force.' The implication
that breadth of interest will somehow compensate for lack of
depth or intensity is one that has considerable importance in
German criticism. Shakespeare seemed different from, even
better than, Greek and French classics because he was in touch
with the *Volksgeist*, the national spirit. In this wide sense, says
Herder (writing in 1771), *all* his plays are history plays. Ulrici
(writing in 1847) says that 'historical drama, dealing with the life
of nations, acquires a greater and more significant beauty than
comedy or tragedy'. Via Georg Brandes, the late nineteenth-
century Danish critic, these ideas became important in the work
of the most notable modern writer of history plays – August
Strindberg – who admired, and sought to reproduce, precisely
this 'polyphonic effect' of court and tavern, the 'realism' of
people in their greatness and their triviality. In Shakespeare's
play, Henry of Bolingbroke, later Henry IV, is the limiting condition upon the play that bears his name rather than its hero.
Hall's Chronicle, presumably Shakespeare's principal source for
the overall design of his history plays, refers to 'the unquiet time
of Henry IV'; and the play uses the King's name to indicate this
quality of life, as something everyone in the play has to cope
with, but does not explore in any sense the inner landscape of his
individual mind. The 'realism' of these plays is often praised, and
justly; but the fidelity to experience given by details cannot take
one very far in defence, when the charge made is that they lack
unifying vision. None the less the point of the richness, copious-
ness and splendour of Shakespeare's writing in this period must
not be overlooked.

Henry IV is usually dated 1597 (Part I) and 1598 (Part II) –
that is, in the period of writing immediately preceding the turn

to tragedy, and immediately after the plays of fanciful delight in poetry-making (*A Midsummer-Night's Dream, Romeo and Juliet, Richard II*). The work of this intermediate period (not only the *Henry IV* plays, but such comedies as *Much Ado about Nothing, The Merchant of Venice*, or *As You Like It*) is characterized by the easy strength, assurance, command of the writing, by the generous flow of sympathy over wide areas of human experience, by what we may think of as effortless maturity. But these qualities do not necessarily overwhelm criticism, especially in an age like ours more accustomed to nervous intensity than to dispersed grandeur, and anxious to find the organic oneness behind the disparate appearances.

Some critics (Tillyard and Dover Wilson for example) suppose that the plays are unified round the audience's identification with England, with *Respublica*, rather than with any character in the play. Certainly 'the state of England' is a recurrent concern of Shakespeare's history plays; but it is hard to know how this mode of identification should work in either part of *Henry IV* (whether taken in isolation or together). We desire peace and honour for the country, of course; but cannot care much, I suggest, how these good effects are produced. On the other hand, we know that the rebels *were* defeated and that Hal *did* become Henry V; and this points to another distinctive feature of the history plays – the sense of inevitability, even stasis, in the story-line.

Ethical and Political Focus

History plays do not seem to press forward to their dénouement with the urgency of tragedies; but rather explore various partial ways of coping with a static national situation. Neither the inside of a hero's mind, nor the excitement of progressive revelation provides the focus for plays like *Henry IV*. Sometimes it is suggested that it is patriotism that provides such focus, that the original audience flocked to the theatre for 'such stimulus as visible reminders of England's past could give' (H. B. Charlton); 'the great use of the historic drama', says Coleridge, is 'familiarizing men to the great names of the country, and exciting patriotism'. This view, however, seems to bear little relation to the realities of plays like *Henry IV* or *Henry VI*, neither of which could have given much stimulus even to the most virulent of patriots. Patriotism, like other forms of sentimentality, can only simplify; and *Henry IV* is fairly resistant to such simplifications.

Shakespeare, most modern students would suggest, was a conformist, anxious to retire to half-timbered respectability in Stratford. The plays suggest no desire to reform, to shock or even to argue. The official homilies, especially concerned with obedience to the Crown, are echoed again and again. J. F. Danby tells us in his *Shakespeare's Doctrine of Nature* (1949) that the *Henry IV* plays have 'only the external order to fall back on, the officialese of Elizabeth's Homilies to be repeated, with their non-theology that maintains Tudor possession at all costs, their no-morality that claims rebellion is always wicked'. Officially, of course, this is what the plays say; but could the effect of *Henry IV* ever have been simple king-and-country moralizing? Do we not find ourselves too deeply involved in the lives of Northumberland and Hotspur and their fellows to be happy about their defeat, let alone the betrayal at Gaultree forest – though the result is a royal victory?

The assumption that Shakespeare was simply the loud-speaker of the Tudor propaganda machine raises natural resistance in modern anti-absolutists, crude rebuttal on the part of G. B. Shaw, more dainty critical ameliorations in such diverse critics as John Palmer (*Political Characters of Shakespeare*), H. B. Charlton and L. C. Knights. Knights makes the point that Shakespeare's political judgment is always taken to the bar of individual living experience. Our response to the political *situation* of the history play is determined by the human involvement with sympathetic individuals inside that situation. Hal may be a political hero, but, says Knights, we do not find him so if he impresses us as cold and egotistical. If politics can only achieve its successes by sacrificing living individuality, Shakespeare's plays can be seen to condemn politics.

A more historically oriented view is sometimes advanced to save the substance of patriotism and make it more compatible with ethics. The History-of-Ideas approach, descending from

Lovejoy's *The Great Chain of Being* through Hardin Craig's
The Enchanted Glass to Tillyard and others, shows Tudor political ideals to be concerned with Order, conceived religiously,
metaphysically and psychologically as well as socially. The
political stance of the Homilies is thus no mere propaganda for
Tudor absolutism, but a statement of part of a noble total
explanation of life. The rephrasing of *Henry IV*'s political substance in these terms saves the appearances, but not without some
sacrifice of dramatic merit. Individual life tends to drain out of
characters and is replaced by capital-lettered abstraction. In the
formalized versions of Tillyard and Dover Wilson Hal becomes
The Prince, Hotspur 'Excess of Honour', the Lord Chief Justice
becomes Justice Incarnate. Falstaff is the particular victim of this
approach; he is *Riot*, or the *Miles Gloriosus*, or the Vice, or the
Parasite. In any case he ceases to be the fully rounded individual
we have all felt at home with, and the human critique he brings
to the world of Lancastrian politics is explained out of the play.
An extreme form of this substitution of the idea for the man
appears in the attempts of Richard Simpson (in *Transactions of
the New Shakspere Society*, 1874) and Lily B. Campbell, *Shakespeare's Histories, Mirrors of Elizabethan Policy* (1947) to turn the
histories into cautionary tales for Elizabethan statesmen. The
Percy rebellion in *Henry IV* becomes a mirror of the Elizabethan
rebellion of 1569; even in an appendix sealed off from the rest of
the book Miss Campbell's Falstaff still has to earn his moral keep
by illustrating the conditions of Elizabethan soldiership.

Starting from a post-war mid-European point of view, Jan
Kott's *Shakespeare Our Contemporary* (1964) formalizes the
material of the histories in slightly different terms. He shares
with other critics the conception that 'in Shakespeare's world
there is a contradiction between the order of action and the moral
order'. But he endorses as 'real' not the moral order but the
'grand mechanism', 'the system' by which History cancels out
its individuals. Kott has not applied this in detail to *Henry IV*,
but he has noted – and the note may be taken as a significant
pointer to the range of his sympathies – that the two best scenes
in the play are (1) Falstaff on Shrewsbury battlefield and (2)

Falstaff with the recruits ('this entire scene might have been put, as it stands, into a play by Brecht'). Recent productions of the play (as those at Stratford in 1964) give importance to Kott by showing how far the 'epic' theatre of Brecht and the 'theatre of cruelty' derived from Artaud can be drawn on to display Kott's interpretations, illustrating the violence and meaninglessness, and so the theatrical contemporaneity of *Henry IV* and the other history plays.

The Structure of the two parts of 'Henry IV'

It is presumably no accident that the critics who seek to describe the *Henry IV* plays in terms of the abstract patterns they contain are the same critics who prefer to think of the individual plays as mere fragments of a vast historical 'epic of England'. This is often seen as designed by Shakespeare to stretch across eight or even ten plays, carrying the pattern of political sin and retribution from the deposition of Richard II to the arrival of Richmond, the Tudor saviour, at the end of *Richard III*. It is assumed that Shakespeare based his whole 'epic' on the Chronicle of Edward Hall, covering the same period from the death of Edward III to the coming of the Tudor dynasty. The relationship between one history play and another is of course bound to be closer than the relationship between one tragedy and another; and since Shakespeare (for whatever reason) chose to work mainly in the limited historical period of the Lancastrian usurpation, his plays inevitably fit together with some continuity. Each play, however, achieves meaning on its own account; and this poses a problem of interpretation for all the plays, and for the two parts of *Henry IV* in particular. Dr Johnson thought of the *Henry IV* plays as continuous, 'two only because they are too long for one'; similarly Dr Dover Wilson finds a 'normal dramatic curve' extending through ten acts rather than five, and Dr Tillyard finds Part I 'patently incomplete'. Others (e.g. Edmund Malone in the eighteenth century, M. A. Shaaber and Harold Jenkins in ours) believe that they are separate plays, the second being designed some time after the first, and using up such material as was left in the sources after the first selection was completed. They suppose that Part II was probably prompted by the success of Falstaff on the stage. Harold Jenkins's treatment is the most subtle of these. He detects a change of direction in Part I, believing that the play begins with a structure in which the overthrow of Hotspur and the overthrow of Falstaff will be parallel; but that Shakespeare abandons the original plan in Act IV, postpones the battle of Shrewsbury from Act IV to Act V and the death of the King from Act V to the end of Part II. G. K. Hunter has proposed a compromise between these positions, supposing that Part II may have been an afterthought which yet contributed to a unified structure, like that of a diptych.

Recent theatrical experiments in tandem productions of the *Henry IV* plays have not always met with critical acclaim. But the problem posed by using one cast of actors for both parts of *Henry IV* is obviously much less serious than the problem posed by one actor's performance of both Bolingbroke and Henry IV or both Hal and Henry V.

Falstaff

For the theatre-goer, if not for the scholar, the *Henry IV* plays are above all the plays with Falstaff in them. It is clear from *The Shakspere Allusion-Book* and from G. E. Bentley's *Shakespeare and Jonson* (1945) that Falstaff very quickly established himself as 'the most famous of all the characters of Shakespeare and Jonson in the seventeenth century'. Falstaff collects 131 references, while Othello (the next highest), even with Rymer's *Short View* included in the count, scores only 55. The note added to the index of the *Shakspere Allusion-Book* makes the same point: 'For the purposes of this Index, Falstaff is treated as a work.'

Falstaff seemed to the seventeenth century to be the extreme example of that god-like power given to Shakespeare to *originate* human beings, which had to be set against his *lack of art* or ignorance of The Rules. Generations who looked to the stage rather than the study for their essential Shakespeare gave continuous witness to their living relationship with the 'merry fat gentleman who lived in days of yore' (as Rochester calls him). Dryden refers to him as 'the best of Comical Characters, Falstaff . . . not properly one humour, but a Miscellany of Humours or Images, drawn from so many several men'. His adventures were part of the national scene, and his English historical status made him seem part of the national heritage to a degree that more obviously fictional or remote inventions could hardly claim.

In addition, Falstaff was fascinating to this period as the possessor of one of its most prized qualities – wit. Could *wit* coexist with other, socially disagreeable, characteristics? or did it cause those disagreeables to evaporate? Falstaff seemed to prove that it could be so. As Rowe remarks, 'he [Shakespeare] has given him so much wit as to make him almost too aggreeable'; or, as Carlyn Morris says (1744): 'for the sake of his wit, you forgive his cowardice, or rather are fond of his cowardice for the occasion it gives to his wit.' Dr Johnson, on the other hand, drew the moral that 'no man is more dangerous than he that with a will to corrupt hath the power to please; and neither wit nor honesty ought to think themselves safe with such a companion when they see *Henry* seduced by *Falstaff*'.

This sense of the paradox in Falstaff may seem to lead up to the famous and excellent essay of Maurice Morgann, published in 1777. This takes up the same paradoxical coexistence of lewdness and wit that the earlier authors had noted, but pursues the paradox into the inner life of Falstaff: if wit and cowardice do not coexist in real people perhaps they do not coexist in Falstaff; perhaps he is not a coward. Morgann was well aware of the enormity of his undertaking, and pursues it selfconsciously in the spirit of paradox. 'The vindication of Falstaff's courage is truly no otherwise the object [of the essay] than some fantastic oak or grotesque rock may be the object of a morning's ride; yet being proposed as such, may serve to limit the distance and shape the course: the real object is exercise.' Morgann is often viewed as a precursor of the Romantic critics who treat dramatic characters as if they were real-life people; certainly if we deduct the element of *paradox*, this seems a tenable assumption. But Morgann finds no need to develop his paradox to the Romantic extent of preferring Falstaff to Hal, as in Hazlitt's 'Falstaff is the better man of the two', or to involve Shakespeare in the preference. The 'Rejection of Falstaff' does not seem to have been *the* critical issue for any critic before Bradley; but since Bradley's essay it has been a recurrent topic of discussion and dispute. The viewpoint of the whole action of the play has been shifted in Bradley's essay from the moral to the aesthetic; and though Falstaff is admitted to be immoral, he makes us share in his happiness; and this is where the central focus is supposed to lie for those who have ears to hear and hearts to respond.

The aesthetic and the moral focuses have continued, since Bradley's time, to collect supporters, often carrying strange banners. E. E. Stoll has subjected Falstaff (like most other Shakespearian characters) to a *theatrical* (rather than literary) scrutiny and found him (like them) to be a conventional figure, a bundle of commonplaces. J. W. Spargo (1922), and J. Dover Wilson (1943) have sought morality in other conventions, especially those of the Medieval Vice-figure, the tempter of the Prince.

On the other hand J. Middleton Murry and E. K. Chambers find Falstaff to be a symbol of the Shakespearian or Elizabethan spontaneity and naturalness. H. B. Charlton has linked this sense of animal delight with what he detects in Shakespeare's handling of politicians – that he came increasingly to dislike and distrust the man whose virtue was his power to direct the lives of other men. Hence Falstaff and Hotspur are two touchstones of the spontaneous vitality that politicians cannot afford to possess or at least to show.

At a middle point between those who wish to label Falstaff a coward or a mere theatrical convenience, and those who wish to endorse him as a totally attractive man lies the position of A. J. A. Waldock (*RES* xxiii (1947)), who points out that Falstaff's role is not monolithic, but flexible enough (in the mode that S. L. Bethell misleadingly labelled 'the popular dramatic tradition') to allow him to assume (however temporarily) the role of the vaudeville comedian. He *knows* that he is controlling the joke, but this does not imply that Falstaff the quasi-man *really* knew that the two rogues in buckram were the Prince and

Poins. The distinction between the vital Falstaff of the *Henry IV* plays and the lay-figure of the *Merry Wives of Windsor* seems to depend principally upon this capacity to change role which is given to the greater Falstaff of the history plays.

Falstaff and Hal

It is probably as difficult (or impossible) to separate the figures of Falstaff and Hal as to separate those of Othello and Iago. Like a couple of Henry Moore 'standing figures' these Shakespearian roles offer a different relationship as we walk round the pedestal. It seems proper to suppose that in such cases the two figures were not conceived separately, but by the same impulse of generation; and only separated later, when the necessity of expressing their complementary natures became paramount. When both are looked at in this way different views of each begin to emerge. Certainly if irresponsible gaiety, the tune of the human heart, is allowed to be the touchstone, we must praise Falstaff and dispraise Hal. But what are we to think of responsibility for effective government, rational control of the processes of action and rational use made of the time-sequence? Do these not matter to audiences of *Henry IV*?

A point that must have been obvious to Elizabethans is that one of the group – Hal – is a prince, and the other is not. Hal has a destiny ahead of him which matters enormously; and he must be prepared for it. As recently as the beginning of this century the concept of the gentleman 'sowing his wild oats' was perfectly acceptable; this was not hooliganism but 'training'. It is in these terms that Dostoevsky calls chapter 2 of *The Devils*, 'Prince Harry' – Stavrogin's early violences are excused as 'the first riotous effervescence of a too richly endowed nature'; they do not necessarily imply any failure in the future. But Falstaff has no destiny ahead of him for which he can train, as we are told repeatedly in the play. Opportunities like the King's commission to impress are treated as occasions for immediate exploitation. His function is to live in the present, and to appeal to all those hedonistic elements in all of us which bid us do the same. The relationship between the two characters is not conceptual and static, but dramatic or dynamic. The play does not tell us what to prefer; it implicates us in the action of preferring; and this is the heart of the dramatic experience.

What the most modern phase of Falstaff criticism has done is to stress the interdependence of the two figures, on the ritualistic level of the play. Falstaff, as scapegoat, or as substitute father (see J. I. M. Stewart), as *shamanized* man (as Wyndham Lewis calls him), or as Carnival King (in C. L. Barber's essay), has a ritual role to play, which affects the whole structure of meaning in this world. This can be held responsible for the effect he makes on audiences even in these unarchetypal times. Barber shows effectively how Falstaff's world is neither a real escape nor a real *criticism* of the court world of responsibility, but is continuously related to it as holiday to work-day. The fact that Falstaff is a gentleman as well as a buffoon keeps the tension between responsibility and irresponsibility the more strongly stretched, as it is in the main plot between loyalty and rebellion. But Falstaff at Shrewsbury with a bottle in place of his pistol does not devalue those who prefer pistols and honour to sack and safety. The two figures of Hal and Falstaff are at perfect equipoise at the end of Part I – each at the limits of his assertion (though one opposite to the other) and yet both closely connected with one another. At the end of Part II it turns out in fact that Hal, left alone by the dismissal of Falstaff, cannot command the world of the play, is not satisfactory as a free-standing figure. Patriotism and chivalry can be admired still (even today) while their opposite is allowed to exist. When that base note is removed their assertion sounds strident. The variousness of *Henry IV* – the point at which this essay began – is the basic condition of our assent to it.

G. K. HUNTER

PART ONE
Earlier Critics

Samuel Johnson

A NOTE ON *HENRY IV* (1765)

NONE of Shakespeare's plays are more read than the first and second parts of *Henry IV*. Perhaps no authour has ever in two plays afforded so much delight. The great events are interesting, for the fate of kingdoms depends upon them; the slighter occurrences are diverting, and, except one or two, sufficiently probable; the incidents are multiplied with wonderful fertility of invention, and the characters diversified with the utmost nicety of discernment, and the profoundest skill in the nature of man.

The prince, who is the hero both of the comick and tragick part, is a young man of great abilities and violent passions, whose sentiments are right, though his actions are wrong; whose virtues are obscured by negligence, and whose understanding is dissipated by levity. In his idle hours he is rather loose than wicked, and when the occasion forces out his latent qualities, he is great without effort, and brave without tumult. The trifler is roused into a hero, and the hero again reposes in the trifler. This character is great, original, and just.

Piercy is a rugged soldier, cholerick, and quarrelsome, and has only the soldier's virtues, generosity and courage.

But Falstaff unimitated, unimitable Falstaff, how shall I describe thee? Thou compound of sense and vice; of sense which may be admired but not esteemed, of vice which may be despised, but hardly detested. Falstaff is a character loaded with faults, and with those faults which naturally produce contempt. He is a thief, and a glutton, a coward, and a boaster, always ready to cheat the weak, and prey upon the poor; to terrify the timorous and insult the defenceless. At once obsequious and malignant, he satirises in their absence those whom he lives by flattering. He is familiar with the prince only as an agent of vice, but of this

familiarity he is so proud as not only to be supercilious and
haughty with common men, but to think his interest of importance to the duke of Lancaster. Yet the man thus corrupt, thus
despicable, makes himself necessary to the prince that despises
him, by the most pleasing of all qualities, perpetual gaiety, by
an unfailing power of exciting laughter, which is the more freely
indulged, as his wit is not of the splendid or ambitious kind, but
consists in easy escapes and sallies of levity, which make sport but
raise no envy. It must be observed that he is stained with no
enormous or sanguinary crimes, so that his licentiousness is not
so offensive but that it may be borne for his mirth.

The moral to be drawn from this representation is, that no
man is more dangerous than he that with a will to corrupt, hath
the power to please; and that neither wit nor honesty ought to
think themselves safe with such a companion when they see
Henry seduced by Falstaff.

(from *Shakespeare's Works*, 1765)

Maurice Morgann

AN ESSAY ON THE DRAMATIC
CHARACTER OF SIR JOHN FALSTAFF
(1777)*

THE ideas which I have formed concerning the Courage and
Military Character of the Dramatic Sir John Falstaff are so different from those which I find generally to prevail in the world, that
I shall take the liberty of stating my sentiments on the subject;
in hope that some person, as unengaged as myself, will either
correct and reform my error in this respect; or, joining himself to
my opinion, redeem me from, what I may call, the reproach of
singularity.

I am to avow, then, that I do not clearly discern that Sir John
Falstaff deserves to bear the character so generally given him of
an absolute Coward; or, in other words, that I do not conceive
Shakespeare ever meant to make Cowardice an essential part of
his constitution.

I know how universally the contrary opinion prevails; and I
know what respect and deference are due to the public voice. But
if to the avowal of this singularity, I add all the reasons that have
led me to it, and acknowledge myself to be wholly in the judgment of the public, I shall hope to avoid the censure of too much
forwardness or indecorum.

It must, in the first place, be admitted that the appearances in
this case are singularly strong and striking; and so they had need

---

* [*Editor's note*.] Samuel Johnson's comment on Maurice Morgann's
Essay on the Dramatic Character of Sir John Falstaff (quoted under the
year 1783 in Boswell's *Life of Johnson*). 'Johnson being asked his
opinion of this Essay, answered, "Why, Sir, we shall have the man
come forth again; and as he has proved Falstaff to be no coward he
may prove Iago to be a very good character".'

be, to become the ground of so general a censure. We see this extraordinary Character, almost in the first moment of our acquaintance with him, involved in circumstances of apparent dishonour; and we hear him familiarly called Coward by his most intimate companions. We see him, on occasion of the robbery at Gads-Hill, in the very act of running away from the Prince and Poins; and we behold him, on another of more honourable obligation, in open day light, in battle, and acting in his profession as a Soldier, escaping from Douglas even out of the world as it were; counterfeiting death, and deserting his very existence; and we find him on the former occasion, betrayed into those lies and braggadocioes which are the usual concomitants of Cowardice in Military men, and pretenders to valour. These are not only in themselves strong circumstances, but they are moreover thrust forward, prest upon our notice as the subject of our mirth, as the great business of the scene: No wonder, therefore, that the word should go forth that Falstaff is exhibited as a character of Cowardice and dishonour.

What there is to the contrary of this, it is my business to discover. Much, I think, will presently appear; but it lies so dispersed, is so latent, and so purposely obscured, that the reader must have some patience whilst I collect it into one body, and make it the object of a steady and regular contemplation.

But what have we to do, may my readers exclaim, with principles so latent, so obscured? In Dramatic composition the Impression is the Fact; and the Writer, who, meaning to impress one thing, has impressed another, is unworthy of observation.

It is a very unpleasant thing to have, in the first setting out, so many and so strong prejudices to contend with. All that one can do in such case, is, to pray the reader to have a little patience in the commencement; and to reserve his censure, if it must pass, for the conclusion. Under his gracious allowance, therefore, I presume to declare it as my opinion, that Cowardice is not the Impression which the whole character of Falstaff is calculated to make on the minds of an unprejudiced audience; tho' there be, I confess, a great deal of something in the composition likely enough to puzzle, and consequently to mislead the Understanding. – The reader will perceive that I distinguish between mental Impressions and the Understanding. – I wish to avoid every thing that looks like subtlety and refinement; but this is a distinction which we all comprehend. – There are none of us unconscious of certain feelings or sensations of mind which do not seem to have passed thro' the Understanding; the effects, I suppose, of some secret influences from without, acting upon a certain mental sense, and producing feelings and passions in just correspondence to the force and variety of those influences on the one hand, and to the quickness of our sensibility on the other. Be the cause, however, what it may, the fact is undoubtedly so; which is all I am concerned in. And it is equally a fact, which every man's experience may avouch, that the Understanding and those feelings are frequently at variance. The latter often arise from the most minute circumstances, and frequently from such as the Understanding cannot estimate, or even recognize; whereas the Understanding delights in abstraction, and in general propositions; which, however true considered as such, are very seldom, I had like to have said never, perfectly applicable to any particular case. And hence, among other causes, it is, that we often condemn or applaud characters and actions on the credit of some logical process, while our hearts revolt, and would fain lead us to a very different conclusion.

The Understanding seems for the most part to take cognizance of actions only, and from these to infer motives and character; but the sense we have been speaking of proceeds in a contrary course; and determines of actions from certain first principles of character, which seem wholly out of the reach of the Understanding. We cannot indeed do otherwise than admit that there must be distinct principles of character in every distinct individual: The manifest variety even in the minds of infants will oblige us to this. But what are these first principles of character? Not the objects, I am persuaded, of the Understanding; and yet we take as strong Impressions of them as if we could compare and assort them in a syllogism. We often love or hate at first sight; and indeed, in general, dislike or approve by some secret reference to these principles; and we judge even of conduct, not from any idea of

abstract good or evil in the nature of actions, but by referring
those actions to a supposed original character in the man himself.
I do not mean that we talk thus; we could not indeed, if we would,
explain ourselves in detail on this head; we can neither account
for Impressions and passions, nor communicate them to others
by words: Tones and looks will sometimes convey the passion
strangely, but the Impression is incommunicable. The same
causes may produce it indeed at the same time in many, but it is
the separate possession of each, and not in its nature transferable:
It is an imperfect sort of instinct, and proportionably dumb. –
We might indeed, if we chose it, candidly confess to one another
that we are greatly swayed by these feelings, and are by no means
so *rational* in all points as we could wish; but this would be a
betraying of the interests of that high faculty, the Understanding,
which we so value ourselves upon, and which we more peculiarly
call our own. This, we think, must not be; and so we huddle up
the matter, concealing it as much as possible, both from ourselves
and others. In Books indeed, wherein character, motive, and
action, are all alike subjected to the Understanding, it is generally
a very clear case; and we make decisions compounded of them
all: And thus we are willing to approve of Candide, tho' he kills
my Lord the Inquisitor, and runs thro' the body the Baron of
Thunder-ten-tronckh the son of his patron and the brother of
his beloved Cunégonde: But in real life, I believe, my Lords the
Judges would be apt to inform the Gentlemen of the Jury that
my Lord the Inquisitor was ill killed; as Candide did not proceed
on the urgency of the moment, but on the speculation only of
future evil. And indeed this clear perception, in Novels and
Plays, of the union of character and action not seen in nature,
is the principal defect of such compositions, and what renders
them but ill pictures of human life, and wretched guides of
conduct.

But if there was one man in the world who could make a more
perfect draught of real nature, and steal such Impressions on his
audience, without their special notice, as should keep their hold
in spite of any error of their Understanding, and should thereupon venture to introduce an apparent incongruity of character

and action, for ends which I shall presently endeavour to explain; such an imitation would be worth our nicest curiosity and attention. But in such a case as this, the reader might expect that he should find us all talking the language of the Understanding only; that is, censuring the action with very little conscientious investigation even of that; and transferring the censure, in every odious colour, to the actor himself; how much soever our hearts and affections might secretly revolt: For as to the Impression, we have already observed that it has no tongue; nor is its operation and influence likely to be made the subject of conference and communication.

It is not to the Courage only of Falstaff that we think these observations will apply: No part whatever of his character seems to be fully settled in our minds; at least there is something strangely incongruous in our discourse and affections concerning him. We all like Old Jack; yet, by some strange perverse fate, we all abuse him, and deny him the possession of any one single good or respectable quality. There is something extraordinary in this: It must be a strange art in Shakespeare which can draw our liking and good will towards so offensive an object. He has wit, it will be said; chearfulness and humour of the most characteristic and captivating sort. And is this enough? Is the humour and gaiety of vice so very captivating? Is the wit, characteristic of baseness and every ill quality, capable of attaching the heart and winning the affections? Or does not the apparency of such humour, and the flashes of such wit, by more strongly disclosing the deformity of character, but the more effectually excite our hatred and contempt of the man? And yet this is not our feeling of Falstaff's character. When he has ceased to amuse us, we find no emotions of disgust; we can scarcely forgive the ingratitude of the Prince in the new-born virtue of the King, and we curse the severity of that poetic justice which consigns our old good-natured companion to the custody of the warden, and the dishonours of the Fleet.

I am willing, however, to admit that if a Dramatic writer will but preserve to any character the qualities of a strong mind, particularly Courage and ability, that it will be afterwards no very difficult task (as I may have occasion to explain) to discharge that *disgust* which arises from vicious manners; and even to attach us (if such character should contain any quality productive of chearfulness and laughter) to the cause and subject of our mirth with some degree of affection.

But the question which I am to consider is of a very different nature: It is a question of fact, and concerning a quality which forms the basis of every respectable character; a quality which is the very essence of a Military man; and which is held up to us, in almost every Comic incident of the Play, as the subject of our observation. It is strange then that it should now be a question, whether Falstaff is or is not a man of Courage; and whether we do in fact contemn him for the want, or respect him for the possession of that quality: And yet I believe the reader will find that he has by no means decided this question, even for himself. – If then it should turn out that this difficulty has arisen out of the Art of Shakespeare, who has contrived to make secret Impressions upon us of Courage, and to preserve those Impressions in favour of a character which was to be held up for sport and laughter on account of actions of apparent Cowardice and dishonour, we shall have less occasion to wonder, as Shakespeare is a Name which contains All of Dramatic artifice and genius.

If in this place the reader shall peevishly and prematurely object that the observations and distinctions I have laboured to establish are wholly unapplicable; he being himself unconscious of ever having received any such Impression; what can be done in so nice a case, but to refer him to the following pages; by the number of which he may judge how very much I respect his objection, and by the variety of those proofs which I shall employ to induce him to part with it; and to recognize in its stead certain feelings, concealed and covered over perhaps, but not erazed, by time, reasoning, and authority?

In the mean while, it may not perhaps be easy for him to resolve how it comes about, that, whilst we look upon Falstaff as a character of the like nature with that of Parolles or of Bobadil, we should preserve for him a great degree of respect and goodwill, and yet feel the highest disdain and contempt of the others, tho' they are all involved in similar situations. The reader, I believe, would wonder extremely to find either Parolles or Bobadil possess himself in danger: What then can be the cause that we are not at all surprized at the gaiety and ease of Falstaff under the most trying circumstances; and that we never think of charging Shakespeare with departing, on this account, from the truth and coherence of character? Perhaps, after all, the real character of Falstaff may be different from his apparent one; and possibly this difference between reality and appearance, whilst it accounts at once for our liking and our censure, may be the true point of humour in the character, and the source of all our laughter and delight. We may chance to find, if we will but examine a little into the nature of those circumstances which have accidentally involved him, that he was intended to be drawn as a character of much Natural courage and resolution; and be obliged thereupon to repeal those decisions which may have been made upon the credit of some general tho' unapplicable propositions; the common source of error in other and higher matters. A little reflection may perhaps bring us round again to the point of our departure, and unite our Understandings to our instinct. – Let us then for a moment suspend at least our decisions, and candidly and coolly inquire if Sir John Falstaff be, indeed, what he has so often been called by critic and commentator, male and female, – a Constitutional Coward.

It will scarcely be possible to consider the Courage of Falstaff as wholly detached from his other qualities: But I write not professedly of any part of his character, but what is included under the term, Courage; however, I may incidentally throw some lights on the whole. – The reader will not need to be told that this Inquiry will resolve itself of course into a Critique on the genius, the arts, and the conduct of Shakespeare: For what is Falstaff, what Lear, what Hamlet, or Othello, but different modifications of Shakespeare's thought? It is true that this Inquiry is narrowed almost to a single point: But general criticism is as uninstructive as it is easy: Shakespeare deserves to be considered in detail; – a task hitherto unattempted. . . .

Let us then examine, as a source of very authentic information,

what Impressions Sir John Falstaff had made on the characters of
the Drama; and in what estimation he is supposed to stand with
mankind in general as to the point of Personal Courage. But the
quotations we make for this or other purposes, must, it is con-
fessed, be lightly touched, and no particular passage strongly
relied on, either in his favour or against him. Every thing which
he himself says, or is said of him, is so phantastically discoloured
by humour, or folly, or jest, that we must for the most part look
to the spirit rather than the letter of what is uttered, and rely at
last only on a combination of the whole.

We will begin then, if the reader pleases, by inquiring what
Impression the very Vulgar had taken of Falstaff. If it is not that
of Cowardice, be it what else it may, that of a man of violence, or
a Ruffian in years, as Harry calls him, or any thing else, it answers
my purpose; how insignificant soever the characters or incidents
to be first produced may otherwise appear; – for these Impressions must have been taken either from personal knowledge and
observation; or, what will do better for my purpose, from common fame. Altho' I must admit some part of this evidence will
appear so weak and trifling that it certainly ought not to be
produced but in proof Impression only.

The Hostess Quickly employs two officers to arrest Falstaff:
On the mention of his name, one of them immediately observes,
'that it may chance to cost some of them their lives, for that he
will stab.' – 'Alas a day,' says the hostess, 'take heed of him, he
cares not what mischief he doth; if his weapon be out, he will
foin like any devil; He will spare neither man, woman, or child.'
Accordingly, we find that when they lay hold on him he resists to
the utmost of his power, and calls upon Bardolph, whose arms
are at liberty, to draw. 'Away, varlets, draw Bardolph, cut me off
the villain's head, throw the quean in the kennel.' The officers
cry, a rescue, a rescue! But the Chief Justice comes in and the
scuffle ceases. In another scene, his wench Doll Tearsheet asks
him 'when he will leave fighting . . . and patch up his old body
for heaven.' This is occasioned by his drawing his rapier, on
great provocation, and driving Pistol, who is drawn likewise,
down stairs, and hurting him in the shoulder. To drive Pistol

was no great feat; nor do I mention it as such; but upon this occasion it was necessary. 'A Rascal bragging slave,' says he, 'the rogue fled from me like quicksilver': Expressions which, as they remember the cowardice of Pistol, seem to prove that Falstaff did not value himself on the adventure. Even something may be drawn from Davy, Shallow's serving man, who calls Falstaff, in ignorant admiration, the man of war. I must observe here, and I beg the reader will notice it, that there is not a single expression dropt by these people, or either of Falstaff's followers, from which may be inferred the least suspicion of Cowardice in his character; and this is I think such an implied negation as deserves considerable weight. . . .

It will be needless to shew, which might be done from a variety of particulars, that Falstaff was known and had consideration at Court. Shallow cultivates him in the idea that a friend at Court is better than a penny in purse: Westmorland speaks to him in the tone of an equal: Upon Falstaff's telling him that he thought his lordship had been already at Shrewsbury, Westmorland replies, – 'Faith Sir John, 'tis more than time that I were there, and you too; the King I can tell you looks for us all; we must away all tonight.' – 'Tut,' says Falstaff, 'never fear me, I am as vigilant as a cat to steal cream.' – He desires, in another place, of my lord John of Lancaster, 'that when he goes to Court, he may stand in his good report.' His intercourse and correspondence with both these lords seem easy and familiar. 'Go,' says he to the page, 'bear this to my Lord of Lancaster, this to the Prince, this to the Earl of Westmorland, and this (for he extended himself on all sides) to old Mrs Ursula,' whom, it seems, the rogue ought to have married many years before. – But these intimations are needless: We see him ourselves in the Royal Presence; where, certainly, his buffooneries never brought him; never was the Prince of a character to commit so high an indecorum, as to thrust, upon a solemn occasion, a mere Tavern companion into his father's Presence, especially in a moment when he himself deserts his looser character, and takes up that of a Prince indeed. – In a very important scene, where Worcester is expected with proposals from Percy, and wherein he is re-

ceived, is treated with, and carries back offers of accommodation
from the King, the King's attendants upon the occasion are the
Prince of Wales, Lord John of Lancaster, the Earl of Westmorland, Sir Walter Blunt, and Sir John Falstaff. – What shall
be said to this? Falstaff is not surely introduced here in vicious
indulgence to a mob audience; – he utters but one word, a buffoon
one indeed, but aside, and to the Prince only. Nothing, it should
seem, is wanting, if decorum would here have permitted, but
that he should have spoken one sober sentence in the Presence
(which yet we are to suppose him ready and able to do if occasion
should have required; or his wit was given him to little purpose)
and Sir John Falstaff might be allowed to pass for an established
Courtier and counsellor of state. 'If I do grow great,' says he,
'I'll grow less, purge and leave sack, and live as a nobleman
should do.' Nobility did not then appear to him at an unmeasur-
able distance; it was, it seems, in his idea, the very next link in
the chain. . . .

I cannot foresee the temper of the reader, nor whether he be
content to go along with me in these kind of observations. Some
of the incidents which I have drawn out of the Play may appear
too minute, whilst yet they refer to principles which may seem
too general. Many points require explanation; something should
be said of the nature of Shakespeare's Dramatic characters;* by

* The reader must be sensible of something in the composition of
Shakespeare's characters, which renders them essentially different from
those drawn by other writers. The characters of every Drama must
indeed be grouped; but in the groupes of other poets the parts which
are not seen do not in fact exist. But there is a certain roundness and
integrity in the forms of Shakespeare, which give them an independence
as well as a relation, insomuch that we often meet with passages which,
tho' perfectly felt, cannot be sufficiently explained in words, without
unfolding the whole character of the speaker: And this I may be
obliged to do in respect to that of Lancaster, in order to account for
some words spoken by him in censure of Falstaff. – Something which
may be thought too heavy for the text, I shall add here, as a conjecture
concerning the composition of Shakespeare's characters: Not that they
were the effect, I believe, so much of a minute and laborious attention,
as of a certain comprehensive energy of mind, involving within itself
all the effects of system and of labour.

Bodies of all kinds, whether of metals, plants, or animals, are supposed to possess certain first principles of being, and to have an existence independent of the accidents which form their magnitude or growth: Those accidents are supposed to be drawn in from the surrounding elements, but not indiscriminately; each plant and each animal imbibes those things only which are proper to its own distinct nature, and which have besides such a secret relation to each other as to be capable of forming a perfect union and coalescence: But so variously are the surrounding elements mingled and disposed, that each particular body, even of those under the same species, has yet some peculiar of its own. Shakespeare appears to have considered the being and growth of the human mind as analogous to this system: There are certain qualities and capacities which he seems to have considered as first principles; the chief of which are certain energies of courage and activity, according to their degrees; together with different degrees and sorts of sensibilities, and a capacity, varying likewise in degree, of discernment and intelligence. The rest of the composition is drawn in from an atmosphere of surrounding things; that is, from the various influences of the different laws, religions and governments in the world; and from those of the different ranks and inequalities in society; and from the different professions of men, encouraging or repressing passions of particular sorts, and inducing different modes of thinking and habits of life; and he seems to have known intuitively what those influences in particular were which this or that original constitution would most freely imbibe and which would most easily associate and coalesce. But all these things being, in different situations, very differently disposed, and those differences exactly discerned by him, he found no difficulty in marking every individual, even among characters of the same sort, with something peculiar and distinct. – Climate and complexion demand their influence; 'Be thus when thou art dead, and I will kill thee, and love thee after,' is a sentiment characteristic of, and fit only to be uttered by a Moor.

But it was not enough for Shakespeare to have formed his characters with the most perfect truth and coherence; it was further necessary that he should possess a wonderful facility of compressing, as it were, his own spirit into these images, and of giving alternate animation to the forms. This was not to be done from without; he must have felt every varied situation, and have spoken thro' the organ he had formed. Such an intuitive comprehension of things and such a facility must unite to produce a Shakespeare. The reader will not now be surprised if I affirm that those characters in Shakespeare, which are seen only in part, are yet capable of being unfolded and understood in the whole; every part being in fact relative, and inferring all the rest. It is true that the point of action or sentiment, which we are most concerned in, is always what arts they were formed, and wherein they differ from those of other writers; something likewise more professedly of Shakespeare himself, and of the peculiar character of his genius. After such a review we may not perhaps think any consideration arising out of the Play, or out of general nature, either as too minute or too extensive. . . .

Shakespeare is a name so interesting, that it is excusable to stop a moment, nay it would be indecent to pass him without the tribute of some admiration. He differs essentially from all other writers: Him we may profess rather to feel than to understand; and it is safer to say, on many occasions, that we are possessed by him, than that we possess him. And no wonder; – He scatters the seeds of things, the principles of character and action, with so cunning a hand, yet with so careless an air, and, master of our feelings, submits himself so little to our judgment, that every thing seems superior. We discern not his course, we see no connection of cause and effect, we are rapt in ignorant admiration, and claim no kindred with his abilities. All the incidents, all the parts, look like chance, whilst we feel and are sensible that the whole is design. His Characters not only act and speak in strict conformity to nature, but in strict relation to us; just so much is shewn as is requisite, just so much is impressed; he commands every passage to our heads and to our hearts, and

---

held out for our special notice. But who does not perceive that there is a peculiarity about it, which conveys a relish of the whole? And very frequently, when no particular point presses, he boldly makes a character act and speak from those parts of the composition which are inferred only, and not distinctly shewn. This produces a wonderful effect; it seems to carry us beyond the poet to nature itself, and gives an integrity and truth to facts and character, which they could not otherwise obtain: And this is in reality that art in Shakespeare which, being withdrawn from our notice, we more emphatically call nature. A felt propriety and truth from causes unseen, I take to be the highest point of Poetic composition. If the characters of Shakespeare are thus whole, and as it were original, while those of almost all other writers are mere imitation, it may be fit to consider them rather as Historic than Dramatic beings; and, when occasion requires, to account for their conduct from the whole of character, from general principles, from latent motives, and from policies not avowed.

moulds us as he pleases, and that with so much ease, that he never betrays his own exertions. We see these Characters act from the mingled motives of passion, reason, interest, habit, and complection, in all their proportions, when they are supposed to know it not themselves; and we are made to acknowledge that their actions and sentiments are, from those motives, the necessary result. He at once blends and distinguishes every thing; – every thing is complicated, every thing is plain. I restrain the further expressions of my admiration lest they should not seem applicable to man; but it is really astonishing that a mere human being, a part of humanity only, should so perfectly comprehend the whole; and that he should possess such exquisite art, that whilst every woman and every child shall feel the whole effect, his learned Editors and Commentators should yet so very frequently mistake or seem ignorant of the cause. A sceptre or a straw are in his hands of equal efficacy; he needs no selection; he converts every thing into excellence; nothing is too great, nothing is too base. Is a character efficient like Richard, it is every thing we can wish: Is it otherwise, like Hamlet, it is productive of equal admiration: Action produces one mode of excellence, and inaction another: The Chronicle, the Novel, or the Ballad; the king, or the beggar, the hero, the madman, the sot, or the fool; it is all one; – nothing is worse, nothing is better: The same genius pervades and is equally admirable in all. Or, is a character to be shewn in progressive change, and the events of years comprized within the hour; – with what a Magic hand does he prepare and scatter his spells! The Understanding must, in the first place, be subdued; and lo! how the rooted prejudices of the child spring up to confound the man! The Weird sisters rise, and order is extinguished. The laws of nature give way, and leave nothing in our minds but wildness and horror. No pause is allowed us for reflection: Horrid sentiment, furious guilt and compunction, air-drawn daggers, murders, ghosts, and inchantment, shake and possess us wholly. In the mean time the process is completed. Macbeth changes under our eye, the milk of human kindness is converted to gall; he has supped full of horrors, and his May of life is fallen into the sear, the yellow leaf; whilst we,

the fools of amazement, are insensible to the shifting of place
and the lapse of time, and, till the curtain drops, never once wake
to the truth of things, or recognize the laws of existence. – On
such an occasion, a fellow, like Rymer, waking from his trance,
shall lift up his Constable's staff, and charge this great Magician,
this daring practicer of arts inhibited, in the name of Aristotle,
to surrender; whilst Aristotle himself, disowning his wretched
Officer, would fall prostrate at his feet and acknowledge his
supremacy. – O supreme of Dramatic excellence! (might he say)
not to me be imputed the insolence of fools. The bards of Greece
were confined within the narrow circle of the Chorus, and hence
they found themselves constrained to practice, for the most part,
the precision, and copy the details of nature. I followed them, and
knew not that a larger circle might be drawn, and the Drama
extended to the whole reach of human genius. Convinced, I see
that a more compendious nature may be obtained; a nature of
effects only, to which neither the relations of place, or continuity
of time, are always essential. Nature, condescending to the
faculties and apprehensions of man, has drawn through human
life a regular chain of visible causes and effects: But Poetry
delights in surprise, conceals her steps, seizes at once upon the
heart, and obtains the Sublime of things without betraying the
rounds of her ascent: True Poesy is magic, not nature; an effect
from causes hidden or unknown. To the Magician I prescribed
no laws; his law and his power are one; his power is his law.
Him, who neither imitates, nor is within the reach of imitation,
no precedent can or ought to bind, no limits to contain. If his
end is obtained, who shall question his course? Means, whether
apparent or hidden, are justified in Poesy by success; but then
most perfect and most admirable when most concealed.* But

* These observations have brought me so near to the regions of
Poetic magic (using the word here in its strict and proper sense, and
not loosely as in the text), that, tho' they lie not directly in my course,
I yet may be allowed in this place to point the reader that way. A felt
propriety, or truth of art, from an unseen, tho' supposed adequate
cause, we call nature. A like feeling of propriety and truth, supposed
without a cause, or as seeming to be derived from causes inadequate,
fantastic, and absurd, – such as wands, circles, incantations, and so

forth, – we call by the general name magic, including all the train of superstition, witches, ghosts, fairies, and the rest. – Reason is confined to the line of visible existence; our passions and our fancy extend far beyond into the obscure; but however lawless their operations may seem, the images they so wildly form have yet a relation to truth, and are the shadows at least, however fantastic, of reality. I am not investigating but passing this subject, and must therefore leave behind me much curious speculation. Of Personifications however we should observe that those which are made out of abstract ideas are the creatures of the Understanding only: Thus, of the mixed modes, virtue, beauty, wisdom and others, – what are they but very obscure ideas of qualities considered as abstracted from any subject whatever? The mind cannot steadily contemplate such an abstraction: What then does it do? – Invent or imagine a subject in order to support these qualities; and hence we get the Nymphs or Goddesses of virtue, of beauty, or of wisdom; the very obscurity of the ideas being the cause of their conversion into sensible objects, with precision both of feature and of form. But as reason has its personifications, so has passion. – Every passion has its Object, tho' often distant and obscure; – to be brought nearer then, and rendered more distinct, it is personified; and Fancy fantastically decks, or aggravates the form, and adds 'a local habitation and a name'. But passion is the dupe of its own artifice and realises the image it had formed. The Grecian theology was mixed of both these kinds of personification. Of the images produced by passion it must be observed that they are the images, for the most part, not of the passions themselves, but of their remote effects. Guilt looks through the medium, and beholds a devil; fear, spectres of every sort; hope, a smiling cherub; malice and envy see hags, and witches, and inchanters dire; whilst the innocent and the young behold with fearful delight the tripping fairy, whose shadowy form the moon gilds with its softest beams. – Extravagant as all this appears, it has its laws so precise that we are sensible both of a local and temporary and of an universal magic; the first derived from the general nature of the human mind, influenced by particular habits, institutions, and climate; and the latter from the same general nature abstracted from those considerations: Of the first sort the machinery in *Macbeth* is a very striking instance; a machinery, which, however exquisite at the time, has already lost more than half its force; and the Gallery now laughs in some places where it ought to shudder: – But the magic of the *Tempest* is lasting and universal.

There is besides a species of writing for which we have no term of art, and which holds a middle place between nature and magic; I mean where fancy either alone, or mingled with reason, or reason assuming the appearance of fancy, governs some real existence; but the whole of this art is pourtrayed in a single Play; in the real madness of Lear, in whither am I going! This copious and delightful topic has drawn me far beyond my design; I hasten back to my subject, and am guarded, for a time at least, against any further temptation to digress.

I was considering the dignity of Falstaff so far as it might seem connected with or productive of military merit, and I have assigned him reputation at least, if not fame, noble connection, birth, attendants, title, and an honourable pension; every one of them presumptive proofs of Military merit, and motives of action. What deduction is to be made on these articles, and why they are so much obscured may, perhaps, hereafter appear.

I have now gone through the examination of all the Persons

---

the assumed wildness of Edgar, and in the Professional Fantasque of the Fool, all operating to contrast and heighten each other. There is yet another feat in this kind, which Shakespeare has performed; – he has personified malice in his Caliban; a character kneaded up of three distinct natures, the diabolical, the human, and the brute. The rest of his preternatural beings are images of effects only, and cannot subsist but in a surrounding atmosphere of those passions from which they are derived. Caliban is the passion itself, or rather a compound of malice, servility, and lust, substantiated; and therefore best shewn in contrast with the lightness of Ariel and the innocence of Miranda. – Witches are sometimes substantial existences, supposed to be possessed by, or allyed to the unsubstantial: but the Witches in *Macbeth* are a gross sort of shadows, 'bubbles of the earth', as they are finely called by Banquo. – Ghosts differ from other imaginary beings in this, that they belong to no element, have no specific nature or character, and are effects, however harsh the expression, supposed without a cause; the reason of which is that they are not the creation of the poet, but the servile copies or transcripts of popular imagination, connected with supposed reality and religion. Should the poet assign the true cause, and call them the mere painting or coinage of the brain, he would disappoint his own end, and destroy the being he had raised. Should he assign fictitious causes, and add a specific nature, and a local habitation, it would not be endured; or the effect would be lost by the conversion of one being into another. The approach to reality in this case defeats all the arts and managements of fiction. – The whole play of the *Tempest* is of so high and superior a nature that Dryden, who had attempted to imitate in vain, might well exclaim that

– Shakespeare's magic could not copied be,
Within that circle none durst walk but He.

of the Drama from whose mouths any thing can be drawn relative to the Courage of Falstaff, excepting the Prince and Poins,
whose evidence I have begged leave to reserve, and excepting a
very severe censure passed on him by Lord John of Lancaster,
which I shall presently consider: But I must first observe that,
setting aside the jests of the Prince and Poins, and this censure of
Lancaster, there is not one expression uttered by any character
in the Drama that can be construed into any impeachment of
Falstaff's Courage; – an observation made before as respecting
some of the Witnesses; – it is now extended to all: And though
this silence be a negative proof only, it cannot, in my opinion,
under the circumstances of the case, and whilst uncontradicted
by facts, be too much relied on. If Falstaff had been intended for
the character of a Miles Gloriosus, his behaviour ought and
therefore would have been commented upon by others. Shakespeare seldom trusts to the apprehensions of his audience; his
characters interpret for one another continually, and when we
least suspect such artful and secret management: The conduct of
Shakespeare in this respect is admirable, and I could point out a
thousand passages which might put to shame the advocates of a
formal Chorus, and prove that there is as little of necessity as
grace in so mechanic a contrivance.* But I confine my censure of
the Chorus to its supposed use of comment and interpretation
only. . . .

But as yet we have dealt principally in parole and circum-
stantial evidence, and have referred to Fact only incidentally. But
Facts have a much more operative influence: They may be produced, not as arguments only, but Records; not to dispute alone,
but to decide. – It is time then to behold Falstaff in actual service
as a soldier, in danger, and in battle. We have already displayed
one fact in his defence against the censure of Lancaster; a fact
extremely unequivocal and decisive. But the reader knows I have
others, and doubtless goes before me to the action at Shrewsbury.
In the midst and in the heat of battle we see him come forwards;
– what are his words? 'I have led my Rag-o-muffians where they

* Ænobarbus, in *Anthony and Cleopatra*, is in effect the Chorus of
the Play; as Menenius Agrippa is of *Coriolanus*.

are peppered; there's not three of my hundred and fifty left alive.' But to whom does he say this? To himself only; he speaks in soliloquy. There is no questioning the fact, he had led them; they were peppered; there were not three left alive. He was in luck, being in bulk equal to any two of them, to escape unhurt. Let the author answer for that, I have nothing to do with it: He was the Poetic maker of the whole Corps, and he might dispose of them as he pleased. Well might the Chief justice, as we now find, acknowledge Falstaff's services in this day's battle; an acknowledgment which amply confirms the fact. A Modern officer, who had performed a feat of this kind, would expect, not only the praise of having done his duty, but the appellation of a hero. But poor Falstaff has too much wit to thrive: In spite of probability, in spite of inference, in spite of fact, he must be a Coward still. He happens unfortunately to have more Wit than Courage, and therefore we are maliciously determined that he shall have no Courage at all. But let us suppose that his modes of expression, even in soliloquy, will admit of some abatement; – how much shall we abate? Say that he brought off fifty instead of three; yet a Modern captain would be apt to look big after an action with two-thirds of his men, as it were, in his belly. Surely Shakespeare never meant to exhibit this man as a Constitutional coward; if he did, his means were sadly destructive of his end. We see him, after he had expended his Rag-o-muffians, with sword and target in the midst of battle, in perfect possession of himself, and replete with humour and jocularity. He was, I presume, in some immediate personal danger, in danger also of a general defeat; too corpulent for flight; and to be led a prisoner was probably to be led to execution; yet we see him laughing and easy, offering a bottle of sack to the Prince instead of a pistol, punning, and telling him, 'there was that which would sack a city'. – 'What, is it a time', says the Prince 'to jest and dally now?' No, a sober character would not jest on such an occasion, but a Coward could not; he would neither have the inclination, or the power. And what could support Falstaff in such a situation? Not principle; he is not suspected of the Point of honour; he seems indeed fairly to renounce it. 'Honour cannot set a leg or an arm; it has no skill in surgery: – What is it? a word only; meer air. It is insensible to the dead; and detraction will not let it live with the living.' What then but a strong natural constitutional Courage, which nothing could extinguish or dismay? – In the following passages the true character of Falstaff as to Courage and Principle is finely touched, and the different colours at once nicely blended and distinguished. 'If Percy be alive, I'll pierce him. If he do come in my way, so: – If he do not, if I come in his willingly, let him make a Carbonado of me. I like not such grinning honour as Sir Walter hath; give me life; which if I can save, so; if not, honour comes unlook'd for, and there's an end.' One cannot say which prevails most here, profligacy or courage; they are both tinged alike by the same humour, and mingled in one common mass; yet when we consider the superior force of Percy, as we must presently also that of Douglas, we shall be apt, I believe, in our secret heart, to forgive him. These passages are spoken in soliloquy and in battle: If every soliloquy made under similar circumstances were as audible as Falstaff's, the imputation might perhaps be found too general for censure. These are among the passages that have impressed on the world an idea of Cowardice in Falstaff; – yet why? He is resolute to take his fate: If Percy do come in his way, so; – if not, he will not seek inevitable destruction; he is willing to save his life, but if that cannot be, why, – 'honour comes unlook'd for, and there's an end'. This surely is not the language of Cowardice: It contains neither the Bounce or Whine of the character; he derides, it is true, and seems to renounce that grinning idol of Military zealots, Honour. But Falstaff was a kind of Military free-thinker, and has accordingly incurred the obloquy of his condition. He stands upon the ground of natural Courage only and common sense, and has, it seems, too much wit for a hero. – But let me be well understood; – I do not justify Falstaff for renouncing the point of honour; it proceeded doubtless from a general relaxation of mind, and profligacy of temper. Honour is calculated to aid and strengthen natural courage, and lift it up to heroism; but natural courage, which can act as such without honour, is natural courage still; the very quality I wish to maintain to Falstaff. And if, without the aid of honour, he can act with firmness, his portion is only the more eminent and distinguished. In such a character, it is to his actions, not his sentiments, that we are to look for conviction. But it may be still further urged in behalf of Falstaff, that there may be false honour as well as false religion. It is true; yet even in that case candour obliges me to confess that the best men are most disposed to conform, and most likely to become the dupes of their own virtue. But it may however be more reasonably urged that there are particular tenets both in honour and religion, which it is the grossness of folly not to question. To seek out, to court assured destruction, without leaving a single benefit behind, may be well reckoned in the number: And this is precisely the very folly which Falstaff seems to abjure; – nor are we, perhaps, intitled to say more, in the way of censure, than that he had not virtue enough to become the dupe of honour, nor prudence enough to hold his tongue. I am willing however, if the reader pleases, to compound this matter, and acknowledge, on my part, that Falstaff was in all respects the old soldier; that he had put himself under the sober discipline of discretion, and renounced, in a great degree at least, what he might call the Vanities and Superstitions of honour; if the reader will, on his part, admit that this might well be, without his renouncing, at the same time, the natural firmness and resolution he was born to.

But there is a formidable objection behind. Falstaff counterfeits basely on being attacked by Douglas; he assumes, in a cowardly spirit, the appearance of death to avoid the reality. But there was no equality of force; not the least chance for victory, or life. And is it the duty then, think we still, of true Courage, to meet, without benefit to society, certain death? Or is it only the phantasy of honour? – But such a fiction is highly disgraceful; – true, and a man of nice honour might perhaps have grinned for it. But we must remember that Falstaff had a double character; he was a wit as well as a soldier; and his Courage, however eminent, was but the accessary; his wit was the principal; and the part, which, if they should come in competition, he had the greatest interest in maintaining. Vain indeed were the licentiousness of his principles, if he should seek death like a bigot, yet without the meed of honour; when he might live by wit, and encrease the reputation of that wit by living. But why do I labour this point? It has been already anticipated, and our improved acquaintance with Falstaff will now require no more than a short narrative of the fact.

Whilst in the battle of Shrewsbury he is exhorting and encouraging the Prince who is engaged with the Spirit Percy – 'Well said Hal, to him Hal,' – he is himself attacked by the Fiend Douglas. There was no match; nothing remained but death or stratagem; grinning honour, or laughing life. But an expedient offers, a mirthful one, – Take your choice Falstaff, a point of honour, or a point of drollery. – It could not be a question; – Falstaff falls, Douglas is cheated, and the world laughs. But does he fall like a Coward? No, like a buffoon only; the superior principle prevails, and Falstaff lives by a stratagem growing out of his character, to prove himself no counterfeit, to jest, to be employed, and to fight again. That Falstaff valued himself, and expected to be valued by others, upon this piece of saving wit, is plain. It was a stratagem, it is true; it argued presence of mind; but it was moreover, what he most liked, a very laughable joke; and as such he considers it; for he continues to counterfeit after the danger is over, that he may also deceive the Prince, and improve the event into more laughter. He might, for ought that appears, have concealed the transaction; the Prince was too earnestly engaged for observation; he might have formed a thousand excuses for his fall; but he lies still and listens to the pronouncing of his epitaph by the Prince with all the waggish glee and levity of his character. The circumstance of his wounding Percy in the thigh, and carrying the dead body on his back like luggage, is indecent but not cowardly. The declaring, though in jest, that he killed Percy, seems to me idle, but it is not meant or calculated for imposition; it is spoken to the Prince himself, the man in the world who could not be, or be supposed to be, imposed on. . . .

The first observation then which strikes us, as to his braggadocioes, is, that they are braggadocioes after the fact. In other cases we see the Coward of the Play bluster and boast for a time, talk of distant wars, and private duels, out of the reach of know-

ledge and of evidence; of storms and stratagems, and of falling in
upon the enemy pell-mell and putting thousands to the sword;
till, at length, on the proof of some present and apparent fact,
he is brought to open and lasting shame; to shame I mean as a
Coward; for as to what there is of lyar in the case, it is considered
only as accessory, and scarcely reckoned into the account of
dishonour. – But in the instance before us, every thing is reversed:
The Play opens with the Fact; a Fact, from its circumstances as
well as from the age and inactivity of the man, very excusable
and capable of much apology, if not of defence. This Fact is
preceded by no bluster or pretence whatever; – the lyes and
braggadocioes follow; but they are not general; they are confined
and have reference to this one Fact only; the detection is immediate; and after some accompanying mirth and laughter, the
shame of that detection ends; it has no duration, as in other cases;
and, for the rest of the Play, the character stands just where it did
before, without any punishment or degradation whatever.

To account for all this, let us only suppose that Falstaff was a
man of natural Courage, though in all respects unprincipled; but
that he was surprized in one single instance into an act of real
terror; which, instead of excusing upon circumstances, he endeavours to cover by lyes and braggadocio; and that these lyes
become thereupon the subject, in this place, of detection. Upon
these suppositions the whole difficulty will vanish at once, and
every thing be natural, common, and plain. The Fact itself will
be of course excusable; that is, it will arise out of a combination
of such circumstances as, being applicable to one case only, will
not destroy the general character: It will not be preceded by any
braggadocio, containing any fair indication of Cowardice; as
real Cowardice is not supposed to exist in the character. But the
first act of real or apparent Cowardice would naturally throw a
vain unprincipled man into the use of lyes and braggadocio; but
these would have reference only to the Fact in question, and not
apply to other cases or infect his general character, which is not
supposed to stand in need of imposition. Again, – the detection
of Cowardice, as such, is more diverting after a long and various
course of Pretence, where the lye of character is preserved, as it

were, whole, and brought into sufficient magnitude for a burst of discovery; yet, mere occasional lyes, such as Falstaff is hereby supposed to utter, are, for the purpose of sport, best detected in the telling; because, indeed, they cannot be preserved for a future time; the exigence and the humour will be past: But the shame arising to Falstaff from the detection of mere lyes would be temporary only; his character as to this point, being already known, and tolerated for the humour. Nothing, therefore, could follow but mirth and laughter, and the temporary triumph of baffling a wit at his own weapons, and reducing him to an absolute surrender: After which, we ought not to be surprized if we see him rise again, like a boy from play, and run another race with as little dishonour as before.

What then can we say, but that it is clearly the lyes only, not the Cowardice, of Falstaff which are here detected: Lyes, to which what there may be of Cowardice is incidental only, improving indeed the Jest, but by no means the real Business of the scene. – And now also we may more clearly discern the true force and meaning of Poins's prediction. 'The Jest will be', says he 'the incomprehensible Lyes that this fat rogue will tell us: How thirty at least he fought with: – and in the reproof of this lyes the jest'; That is, in the detection of these lyes simply; for as to Courage, he had never ventured to insinuate more than that Falstaff would not fight longer than he saw cause: Poins was in expectation indeed that Falstaff would fall into some dishonour on this occasion; an event highly probable: But this was not, it seems, to be the principal ground of their mirth, but the detection of those incomprehensible lyes, which he boldly predicts, upon his knowledge of Falstaff's character, this fat rogue, not Coward, would tell them. This prediction therefore, and the completion of it, go only to he impeachment of Falstaff's veracity, and not of his Courage. 'These lyes,' says the Prince, 'are like the father of them, gross as a mountain, open, palpable. – Why, thou clay-brained gutts, thou knotty-pated fool; how couldst thou know these men in Kendal Green, when it was so dark thou couldst not see thy hand? Come, tell us your reason.'

Poins. 'Come, your reason, Jack, your reason.'

Again, says the Prince, 'Hear how a plain Tale shall put you down – What trick, what device, what starting hole canst thou now find out to hide thee from this open and apparent shame?'

Poins. 'Come, let's hear, Jack, what trick hast thou now?'

All this clearly refers to Falstaff's lyes only as such; and the objection seems to be, that he had not told them well, and with sufficient skill and probability. Indeed nothing seems to have been required of Falstaff at any period of time but a good evasion. The truth is, that there is so much mirth, and so little of malice or imposition in his fictions, that they may for the most part be considered as mere strains of humour and exercises of wit, impeachable only for defect, when that happens, of the quality from which they are principally derived. Upon this occasion Falstaff's evasions fail him; he is at the end of his invention; and it seems fair that, in defect of wit, the law should pass upon him, and that he should undergo the temporary censure of that Cowardice which he could not pass off by any evasion whatever. The best he could think of, was instinct: He was indeed a Coward upon instinct; in that respect like a valiant lion, who would not touch the true Prince. It would have been a vain attempt, the reader will easily perceive, in Falstaff, to have gone upon other ground, and to have aimed at justifying his Courage by a serious vindication: This would have been to have mistaken the true point of argument: It was his lyes, not his Courage, which was really in question. There was besides no getting out of the toils in which he had entangled himself: If he was not, he ought at least, by his own shewing, to have been at half-sword with a dozen of them two hours together; whereas, it unfortunately appears, and that too evidently to be evaded, that he had run with singular celerity from two, after the exchange of a few blows only. This precluded Falstaff from all rational defence in his own person; – but it has not precluded me, who am not the advocate of his lyes, but of his Courage. . . .

Tho' I have considered Falstaff's character as relative only to one single quality, yet so much has been said, that it cannot escape the reader's notice that he is a character made up by Shakespeare wholly of incongruities; – a man at once young and old, enterprizing and fat, a dupe and a wit, harmless and wicked, weak in principle and resolute by constitution, cowardly in appearance and brave in reality; a knave without malice, a lyar without deceit; and a knight, a gentleman, and a soldier, without either dignity, decency, or honour: This is a character, which, though it may be de-compounded, could not, I believe, have been formed, nor the ingredients of it duly mingled, upon any receipt whatever: It required the hand of Shakespeare himself to give to every particular part a relish of the whole, and of the whole to every particular part; – alike the same incongruous, identical Falstaff, whether to the grave Chief Justice he vainly talks of his youth, and offers to caper for a thousand; or cries to Mrs Doll, 'I am old, I am old,' though she is seated on his lap, and he is courting her for busses. How Shakespeare could furnish out sentiment of so extraordinary a composition, and supply it with such appropriated and characteristic language, humour and wit, I cannot tell; but I may, however, venture to infer, and that confidently, that he who so well understood the uses of incongruity, and that laughter was to be raised by the opposition of qualities in the same man, and not by their agreement or conformity, would never have attempted to raise mirth by shewing us Cowardice in a Coward unattended by Pretence, and softened by every excuse of age, corpulence, and infirmity: And of this we cannot have a more striking proof than his furnishing this very character, on one instance of real terror, however excusable, with boast, braggadocio, and pretence, exceeding that of all other stage Cowards the whole length of his superior wit, humour, and invention.

What then upon the whole shall be said but that Shakespeare has made certain Impressions, or produced certain effects, of which he has thought fit to conceal or obscure the cause? How he has done this, and for what special ends, we shall now presume to guess. – Before the period in which Shakespeare wrote, the fools and Zanys of the stage were drawn out of the coarsest and cheapest materials: Some essential folly, with a dash of knave and coxcomb, did the feat. But Shakespeare, who delighted in difficulties, was resolved to furnish a richer repast, and to give to one eminent buffoon the high relish of wit, humour, birth, dignity, and Courage. But this was a process which required the nicest hand, and the utmost management and address: These enumerated qualities are, in their own nature, productive of respect; an Impression the most opposite to laughter that can be. This Impression then, it was, at all adventures, necessary to with-hold; which could not perhaps well be without dressing up these qualities in fantastic forms, and colours not their own; and thereby cheating the eye with shews of baseness and of folly, whilst he stole as it were upon the palate a richer and a fuller *goût*. To this end, what arts, what contrivances, has he not practised! How has he steeped this singular character in bad habits for fifty years together, and brought him forth saturated with every folly and with every vice not destructive of his essential character, or incompatible with his own primary design! For this end, he has deprived Falstaff of every good principle; and for another, which will be presently mentioned, he has concealed every bad one. He has given him also every infirmity of body that is not likely to awaken our compassion, and which is most proper to render both his better qualities and his vices ridiculous: he has associated levity and debauch with age, corpulence and inactivity with courage, and has roguishly coupled the gout with Military honours, and a pension with the pox. He has likewise involved this character in situations, out of which neither wit nor Courage can extricate him with honour. The surprize at Gads-Hill might have betrayed a hero into flight, and the encounter with Douglas left him no choice but death or stratagem. If he plays an after-game, and endeavours to redeem his ill fortune by lies and braggadocio, his ground fails him; no wit, no evasion will avail: Or is he likely to appear respectable in his person, rank, and demeanour, how is that respect abated or discharged! Shakespeare has given him a kind of state indeed; but of what is it composed? Of that fustian cowardly rascal Pistol, and his yoke-fellow of few words, the equally deedless Nym; of his cup-bearer the fiery Trigon, whose zeal burns in his nose, Bardolph; and of the boy, who bears the purse with seven groats and two-pence; – a boy who was given him on purpose to set him off, and whom he walks before, according to his own description, 'like a sow that had overwhelmed all her litter but one'.

But it was not enough to render Falstaff ridiculous in his figure, situations, and equipage; still his respectable qualities would have come forth, at least occasionally, to spoil our mirth; or they might have burst the intervention of such slight impediments, and have every where shone through: It was necessary then to go farther, and throw on him that substantial ridicule, which only the incongruities of real vice can furnish; of vice, which was to be so mixed and blended with his frame as to give a durable character and colour to the whole.

But it may here be necessary to detain the reader a moment in order to apprize him of my further intention; without which, I might hazard that good understanding, which I hope has hitherto been preserved between us.

I have 'till now looked only to the Courage of Falstaff, a quality which, having been denied, in terms, to belong to his constitution, I have endeavoured to vindicate to the Understandings of my readers; the Impression on their Feelings (in which all Dramatic truth consists) being already, as I have supposed, in favour of the character. In the pursuit of this subject I have taken the general Impression of the whole character pretty much, I suppose, like other men; and, when occasion has required, have so transmitted it to the reader; joining in the common Feeling of Falstaff's pleasantry, his apparent freedom from ill principle, and his companionable wit and good humour: With a stage character, in the article of exhibition, we have nothing more to do; for in fact what is it but an Impression; an appearance, which we are to consider as a reality, and which we may venture to applaud or condemn as such, without further inquiry or investigation? But if we would account for our Impressions, or for certain sentiments or actions in a character, not derived from its apparent principles, yet appearing, we know not why, natural, we are then compelled to look farther, and examine if there be not something more in the character than is shewn; something inferred, which is not brought under our special notice: In short, we must look to the art of the writer, and to the principles of

human nature, to discover the hidden causes of such effects. –
Now this is a very different matter. – The former considerations
respected the Impression only, without regard to the Understanding; but this question relates to the Understanding alone.
It is true that there are but few Dramatic characters which will
bear this kind of investigation, as not being drawn in exact conformity to those principles of general nature to which we must
refer. But this is not the case with regard to the characters of
Shakespeare; they are struck out whole, by some happy art
which I cannot clearly comprehend, out of the general mass of
things, from the block as it were of nature: And it is, I think, an
easier thing to give a just draught of man from these Theatric
forms, which I cannot help considering as originals, than by
drawing from real life, amidst so much intricacy, obliquity, and
disguise. If therefore, for further proofs of Falstaff's Courage, or
for the sake of curious speculation, or for both, I change my
position, and look to causes instead of effects, the reader must not
be surprized if he finds the former Falstaff vanish like a dream,
and another, of more disgustful form, presented to his view; one
whose final punishment we shall be so far from regretting, that
we ourselves shall be ready to consign him to a severer doom.

The reader will very easily apprehend that a character, which
we might wholly disapprove of, considered as existing in human
life, may yet be thrown on the stage into certain peculiar situations, and be compressed by external influences into such temporary appearances, as may render such character for a time highly
acceptable and entertaining, and even more distinguished for
qualities, which on this supposition would be accidents only,
than another character really possessing those qualities, but which,
under the pressure of the same situation and influences, would be
distorted into a different form, or totally left in timidity and weakness. If therefore the character before us will admit of this kind
of investigation, our Inquiry will not be without some dignity,
considered as extending to the principles of human nature, and
to the genius and arts of him, who has best caught every various
form of the human mind, and transmitted them with the greatest
happiness and fidelity. . . .

A character really possessing the qualities which are on the stage imputed to Falstaff, would be best shewn by its own natural energy; the least compression would disorder it, and make us feel for it all the pain of sympathy: It is the artificial condition of Falstaff which is the source of our delight; we enjoy his distresses, we gird at him ourselves, and urge the sport without the least alloy of compassion; and we give him, when the laugh is over, undeserved credit for the pleasure we enjoyed. If any one thinks that these observations are the effect of too much refinement, and that there was in truth more of chance in the case than of management or design, let him try his own luck; – perhaps he may draw out of the wheel of fortune a Macbeth, an Othello, a Benedict, or a Falstaff.

Such, I think, is the true character of this extraordinary buffoon; and from hence we may discern for what special purposes Shakespeare has given him talents and qualities, which were to be afterwards obscured, and perverted to ends opposite to their nature; it was clearly to furnish out a Stage buffoon of a peculiar sort; a kind of Game-bull which would stand the baiting thro' a hundred Plays, and produce equal sport, whether he is pinned down occasionally by Hal or Poins, or tosses such mongrils as Bardolph, or the Justices, sprawling in the air. There is in truth no such thing as totally demolishing Falstaff; he has so much of the invulnerable in his frame that no ridicule can destroy him; he is safe even in defeat, and seems to rise, like another Antæus, with recruited vigour from every fall; in this, as in every other respect, unlike Parolles or Bobadil: They fall by the first shaft of ridicule, but Falstaff is a butt on which we may empty the whole quiver, whilst the substance of his character remains unimpaired. His ill habits, and the accidents of age and corpulence, are no part of his essential constitution; they come forward indeed on our eye, and solicit our notice, but they are second natures, not first; mere shadows, we pursue them in vain; Falstaff himself has a distinct and separate subsistence; he laughs at the chace, and when the sport is over, gathers them with unruffled feather under his wing: And hence it is that he is made to undergo not one detection only, but a series of detections;

that he is not formed for one Play only, but was intended originally at least for two; and the author, we are told, was doubtful if he should not extend him yet farther, and engage him in the wars with France. This he might well have done, for there is nothing perishable in the nature of Falstaff: He might have involved him, by the vicious part of his character, in new difficulties and unlucky situations, and have enabled him, by the better part, to have scrambled through, abiding and retorting the jests and laughter of every beholder. . . .

But whatever be the question, or whatever the character, the curtain must not only be dropt before the eyes, but over the minds of the spectators, and nothing left for further examination and curiosity. – But how was this to be done in regard to Falstaff? He was not involved in the fortune of the Play; he was engaged in no action which, as to him, was to be compleated; he had reference to no system, he was attracted to no center; he passes thro' the Play as a lawless meteor, and we wish to know what course he is afterwards likely to take: He is detected and disgraced, it is true; but he lives by detection, and thrives on disgrace; and we are desirous to see him detected and disgraced again. The Fleet might be no bad scene of further amusement; – he carries all within him, and what matter where, if he be still the same, possessing the same force of mind, the same wit, and the same incongruity. This, Shakespeare was fully sensible of, and knew that this character could not be compleatly dismissed but by death. – 'Our author', says the Epilogue to the Second Part of *Henry IV*, 'will continue the story with Sir John in it, and make you merry with fair Catherine of France; where, for any thing I know, Falstaff shall dye of a sweat, unless already he be killed with your hard opinions.' If it had been prudent in Shakespeare to have killed Falstaff with hard opinion, he had the means in his hand to effect it; – but dye, it seems, he must, in one form or another, and a sweat would have been no unsuitable catastrophe. However we have reason to be satisfied as it is; – his death was worthy of his birth and of his life: 'He was born', he says, 'about three o'clock in the afternoon, with a white head, and something a round belly.' But if he came into the world in the evening with

these marks of age, he departs out of it in the morning in all the
follies and vanities of youth; – 'He was shaked' (we are told)
'of a burning quotidian tertian; – the young King had run bad
humours on the knight; – his heart was fracted and corroborate;
and a' parted just between twelve and one, even at the turning
of the tide, yielding the crow a pudding, and passing directly
into Arthur's bosom, if ever man went into the bosom of Arthur.'
– So ended this singular buffoon; and with him ends an Essay,
on which the reader is left to bestow what character he pleases:
An Essay professing to treat of the Courage of Falstaff, but
extending itself to his Whole character; to the arts and genius
of his Poetic-Maker, Shakespeare; and thro' him sometimes, with
ambitious aim, even to the principles of human nature itself.

(from *An Essay on the Dramatic Character
of Sir John Falstaff*, 1777)

A. C. Bradley

THE REJECTION OF FALSTAFF (1909)[1]

OF the two persons principally concerned in the rejection of
Falstaff, Henry, both as Prince and as King, has received, on the
whole, full justice from readers and critics. Falstaff, on the other
hand, has been in one respect the most unfortunate of Shakespeare's famous characters. All of them, in passing from the
mind of their creator into other minds, suffer change; they tend
to lose their harmony through the disproportionate attention
bestowed on some one feature, or to lose their uniqueness by
being conventionalised into types already familiar. But Falstaff
was degraded by Shakespeare himself. The original character is
to be found alive in the two parts of *Henry IV*, dead in *Henry V*,
and nowhere else. But not very long after these plays were composed, Shakespeare wrote, and he afterwards revised, the very
entertaining piece called *The Merry Wives of Windsor*. Perhaps
his company wanted a new play on a sudden; or perhaps, as
one would rather believe, the tradition may be true that Queen
Elizabeth, delighted with the Falstaff scenes of *Henry IV*, expressed a wish to see the hero of them again, and to see him in
love. Now it was no more possible for Shakespeare to show his
own Falstaff in love than to turn twice two into five. But he
could write in haste – the tradition says, in a fortnight – a comedy
or farce differing from all his other plays in this, that its scene is
laid in English middle-class life, and that it is prosaic almost to
the end. And among the characters he could introduce a disreputable fat old knight with attendants, and could call them
Falstaff, Bardolph, Pistol, and Nym. And he could represent this
knight assailing, for financial purposes, the virtue of two matrons,
and in the event baffled, duped, treated like dirty linen, beaten,
burnt, pricked, mocked, insulted, and, worst of all, repentant

and didactic. It is horrible. It is almost enough to convince one that Shakespeare himself could sanction the parody of Ophelia in the *Two Noble Kinsmen*. But it no more touches the real Falstaff than Ophelia is degraded by that parody. To picture the real Falstaff befooled like the Falstaff of the *Merry Wives* is like imagining Iago the gull of Roderigo, or Becky Sharp the dupe of Amelia Osborne. Before he had been served the least of these tricks he would have had his brains taken out and buttered, and have given them to a dog for a New Year's gift. I quote the words of the imposter, for after all Shakespeare made him and gave to him a few sentences worthy of Falstaff himself. But they are only a few – one side of a sheet of notepaper would contain them. And yet critics have solemnly debated at what period in his life Sir John endured the gibes of Master Ford, and whether we should put this comedy between the two parts of *Henry IV*, or between the second of them and *Henry V*. And the Falstaff of the general reader, it is to be feared, is an impossible conglomerate of two distinct characters, while the Falstaff of the mere playgoer is certainly much more like the imposter than the true man.

The separation of these two has long ago been effected by criticism, and is insisted on in almost all competent estimates of the character of Falstaff. I do not propose to attempt a full account either of this character or of that of Prince Henry, but shall connect the remarks I have to make on them with a question which does not appear to have been satisfactorily discussed – the question of the rejection of Falstaff by the Prince on his accession to the throne. What do we feel, and what are we meant to feel, as we witness this rejection? And what does our feeling imply as to the characters of Falstaff and the new King?

I

Sir John, you remember, is in Gloucestershire, engaged in borrowing a thousand pounds from Justice Shallow; and here Pistol, riding helter-skelter from London, brings him the great news that the old King is as dead as nail in door, and that Harry the Fifth is the man. Sir John, in wild excitement, taking any man's

horses, rushes to London; and he carries Shallow with him, for he
longs to reward all his friends. We find him standing with his
companions just outside Westminster Abbey, in the crowd that
is waiting for the King to come out after his coronation. He
himself is stained with travel and has had no time to spend any
of the thousand pounds in buying new liveries for his men. But
what of that? This poor show only proves his earnestness of
affection, his devotion, how he could not deliberate or remember
or have patience to shift himself, but rode day and night,
thought of nothing else but to see Henry, and put all affairs else
in oblivion, as if there were nothing else to be done but to see
him. And now he stands sweating with desire to see him, and
repeating and repeating this one desire of his heart – 'to see him'.
The moment comes. There is a shout within the Abbey like the
roaring of the sea, and a clangour of trumpets, and the doors open
and the procession streams out.

> *Fal.* God save thy grace, King Hal! my royal Hal!
> *Pist.* The heavens thee guard and keep, most royal imp of
>   fame!
> *Fal.* God save thee, my sweet boy!
> *King.* My Lord Chief Justice, speak to that vain man.
> *Ch. Just.* Have you your wits? Know you what 'tis you
>   speak?
> *Fal.* My King! my Jove! I speak to thee, my heart!
> *King.* I know thee not, old man: fall to thy prayers;
>   How ill white hairs become a fool and jester!
>   I have long dream'd of such a kind of man,
>   So surfeit-swell'd, so old and so profane;
>   But being awaked I do despise my dream.
>   Make less thy body hence, and more thy grace;
>   Leave gormandizing; know the grave doth gape
>   For thee thrice wider than for other men.
>   Reply not to me with a fool-born jest:
>   Presume not that I am the thing I was;
>   For God doth know, so shall the world perceive,
>   That I have turn'd away my former self;
>   So will I those that kept me company.
>   When thou dost hear I am as I have been,

Approach me, and thou shalt be as thou wast,
The tutor and the feeder of my riots:
Till then, I banish thee, on pain of death,
As I have done the rest of my misleaders,
Not to come near our person by ten mile.
For competence of life I will allow you,
That lack of means enforce you not to evil:
And, as we hear you do reform yourselves,
We will, according to your strength and qualities,
Give you advancement. Be it your charge, my lord,
To see perform'd the tenour of our word.
Set on.

The procession passes out of sight, but Falstaff and his friends remain. He shows no resentment. He comforts himself, or tries to comfort himself – first, with the thought that he has Shallow's thousand pounds, and then, more seriously, I believe, with another thought. The King, he sees, must look thus to the world; but he will be sent for in private when night comes, and will yet make the fortunes of his friends. But even as he speaks, the Chief Justice, accompanied by Prince John, returns, and gives the order to his officers:

Go, carry Sir John Falstaff to the Fleet;
Take all his company along with him.

Falstaff breaks out, 'My lord, my lord,' but he is cut short and hurried away; and after a few words between the Prince and the Chief Justice the scene closes, and with it the drama.

What are our feelings during this scene? They will depend on our feelings about Falstaff. If we have not keenly enjoyed the Falstaff scenes of the two plays, if we regard Sir John chiefly as an old reprobate, not only a sensualist, a liar, and a coward, but a cruel and dangerous ruffian, I suppose we enjoy his discomfiture and consider that the King has behaved magnificently. But if we *have* keenly enjoyed the Falstaff scenes, if we have enjoyed them as Shakespeare surely meant them to be enjoyed, and if, accordingly, Falstaff is not to us solely or even chiefly a reprobate and ruffian, we feel, I think, during the King's speech, a good deal of

pain and some resentment; and when, without any further offence
on Sir John's part, the Chief Justice returns and sends him to
prison we stare in astonishment. These, I believe, are, in greater or
less degree, the feelings of most of those who really enjoy the
Falstaff scenes (as many readers do not). Nor are these feelings
diminished when we remember the end of the whole story, as
we find it in *Henry V*, where we learn that Falstaff quickly died,
and, according to the testimony of persons not very sentimental,
died of a broken heart.[2] Suppose this merely to mean that he
sank under the shame of his public disgrace, and it is pitiful
enough: but the words of Mrs Quickly, 'The king has killed his
heart'; of Nym, 'The king hath run bad humours on the knight;
that's the even of it'; of Pistol,

> Nym, thou hast spoke the right,
> His heart is fracted and corroborate,

assuredly point to something more than wounded pride; they
point to wounded affection, and remind us of Falstaff's own
answer to Prince Hal's question, 'Sirrah, do I owe you a thousand
pound?' 'A thousand pound, Hal? a million: thy love is worth a
million: thou owest me thy love.'

Now why did Shakespeare end his drama with a scene which,
though undoubtedly striking, leaves an impression so unpleasant?
I will venture to put aside without discussion the idea that he
meant us throughout the two plays to regard Falstaff with disgust or indignation, so that we naturally feel nothing but pleasure
at his fall; for this idea implies that kind of inability to understand Shakespeare with which it is idle to argue. And there is
another and a much more ingenious suggestion which must
equally be rejected as impossible. According to it, Falstaff,
having listened to the King's speech, did not seriously hope to
be sent for by him in private; he fully realised the situation at
once, and was only making game of Shallow; and in his immediate
turn upon Shallow when the King goes out, 'Master Shallow, I
owe you a thousand pound,' we are meant to see his humorous
superiority to any rebuff, so that we end the play with the
delightful feeling that, while Henry has done the right thing,

Falstaff, in his outward overthrow, has still proved himself inwardly invincible. This suggestion comes from a critic who understands Falstaff, and in the suggestion itself shows that he understands him.[3] But it provides no solution, because it wholly ignores, and could not account for, that which follows the short conversation with Shallow. Falstaff's dismissal to the Fleet, and his subsequent death, prove beyond doubt that his rejection was meant by Shakespeare to be taken as a catastrophe which not even his humour could enable him to surmount.

Moreover, these interpretations, even if otherwise admissible, would still leave our problem only partly solved. For what troubles us is not only the disappointment of Falstaff, it is the conduct of Henry. It was inevitable that on his accession he should separate himself from Sir John, and we wish nothing else. It is satisfactory that Sir John should have a competence, with the hope of promotion in the highly improbable case of his reforming himself. And if Henry could not trust himself within ten miles of so fascinating a companion, by all means let him be banished that distance: we do not complain. These arrangements would not have prevented a satisfactory ending: the King could have communicated his decision, and Falstaff could have accepted it, in a private interview rich in humour and merely touched with pathos. But Shakespeare has so contrived matters that Henry could not send a private warning to Falstaff even if he wished to, and in their public meeting Falstaff is made to behave in so infatuated and outrageous a manner that great sternness on the King's part was unavoidable. And the curious thing is that Shakespeare did not stop here. If this had been all we should have felt pain for Falstaff, but not, perhaps, resentment against Henry. But two things we do resent. Why, when this painful incident seems to be over, should the Chief Justice return and send Falstaff to prison? Can this possibly be meant for an act of private vengeance on the part of the Chief Justice, unknown to the King? No; for in that case Shakespeare would have shown at once that the King disapproved and cancelled it. It must have been the King's own act. This is one thing we resent; the other is the King's sermon. He had a right to turn away his former self, and his old companions with it, but he had no right to talk all of a sudden like a clergyman; and surely it was both ungenerous and insincere to speak of them as his 'misleaders', as though in the days of Eastcheap and Gadshill he had been a weak and silly lad. We have seen his former self, and we know that it was nothing of the kind. He had shown himself, for all his follies, a very strong and independent young man, deliberately amusing himself among men over whom he had just as much ascendency as he chose to exert. Nay, he amused himself not only among them, but at their expense. In his first soliloquy – and first soliloquies are usually significant – he declares that he associates with them in order that, when at some future time he shows his true character, he may be the more wondered at for his previous aberrations. You may think he deceives himself here; you may believe that he frequented Sir John's company out of delight in it and not merely with this cold-blooded design; but at any rate he *thought* the design was his one motive. And, that being so, two results follow. He ought in honour long ago to have given Sir John clearly to understand that they must say good-bye on the day of his accession. And, having neglected to do this, he ought not to have lectured him as his misleader. It was not only ungenerous, it was dishonest. It looks disagreeably like an attempt to buy the praise of the respectable at the cost of honour and truth. And it succeeded. Henry *always* succeeded.

You will see what I am suggesting, for the moment, as a solution of our problem. I am suggesting that our fault lies not in our resentment at Henry's conduct, but in our surprise at it; that if we had read his character truly in the light that Shakespeare gave us, we should have been prepared for a display both of hardness and of policy at this point in his career. And although this suggestion does not suffice to solve the problem before us, I am convinced that in itself it is true. Nor is it rendered at all improbable by the fact that Shakespeare has made Henry, on the whole, a fine and very attractive character, and that here he makes no one express any disapprobation of the treatment of Falstaff. For in similar cases Shakespeare is constantly misunderstood. His readers expect him to mark in some distinct way his approval or disapproval of that which he represents; and hence where *they* disapprove and *he* says nothing, they fancy that he does *not* disapprove, and they blame his indifference, like Dr Johnson, or at the least are puzzled. But the truth is that he shows the fact and leaves the judgment to them. And again, when he makes us like a character we expect the character to have no faults that are not expressly pointed out, and when other faults appear we either ignore them or try to explain them away. This is one of our methods of conventionalising Shakespeare. We want the world's population to be neatly divided into sheep and goats, and we want an angel by us to say, 'Look, that is a goat and this is a sheep,' and we try to turn Shakespeare into this angel. His impartiality makes us uncomfortable: we cannot bear to see him, like the sun, lighting up everything and judging nothing. And this is perhaps especially the case in his historical plays, where we are always trying to turn him into a partisan. He shows us that Richard II was unworthy to be king, and we at once conclude that he thought Bolingbroke's usurpation justified; whereas he shows merely, what under the conditions was bound to exist, an inextricable tangle of right and unright. Or, Boling-broke being evidently wronged, we suppose Bolingbroke's statements to be true, and are quite surprised when, after attaining his end through them, he mentions casually on his death-bed that they were lies. Shakespeare makes us admire Hotspur heartily; and accordingly when we see Hotspur discussing with others how large his particular slice of his mother-country is to be, we either fail to recognise the monstrosity of the proceeding, or, recognising it, we complain that Shakespeare is inconsistent. Prince John breaks a tottering rebellion by practising a detestable fraud on the rebels. We are against the rebels, and have heard high praise of Prince John, but we cannot help seeing that his fraud is detestable; so we say indignantly to Shakespeare, 'Why, you told us he was a sheep'; whereas, in fact, if we had used our eyes we should have known beforehand that he was the brave, determined, loyal, cold-blooded, pitiless, unscrupulous son of a usurper whose throne was in danger.

To come, then, to Henry. Both as prince and as king he is

deservedly a favourite, and particularly so with English readers,
being, as he is, perhaps the most distinctively English of all
Shakespeare's men. In *Henry V* he is treated as a national hero.
In this play he has lost much of the wit which in him seems to
have depended on contact with Falstaff, but he has also laid aside
the most serious faults of his youth. He inspires in a high degree
fear, enthusiasm, and affection; thanks to his beautiful modesty
he has the charm which is lacking to another mighty warrior,
Coriolanus; his youthful escapades have given him an understanding of simple folk, and sympathy with them; he is the
author of the saying, 'There is some soul of goodness in things
evil'; and he is much more obviously religious than most of
Shakespeare's heroes. Having these and other fine qualities, and
being without certain dangerous tendencies which mark the
tragic heroes, he is, perhaps, the most *efficient* character drawn
by Shakespeare, unless Ulysses, in *Troilus and Cressida*, is his
equal. And so he has been described as Shakespeare's ideal man
of action; nay, it has even been declared that here for once
Shakespeare plainly disclosed his own ethical creed, and showed
us his ideal, not simply of a man of action, but of a man.

But Henry is neither of these. The poet who drew Hamlet and
Othello can never have thought that even the ideal man of action
would lack that light upon the brow which at once transfigures
them and marks their doom. It is as easy to believe that, because
the lunatic, the lover, and the poet are not far apart, Shakespeare
would have chosen never to have loved and sung. Even poor
Timon, the most inefficient of the tragic heroes, has something
in him that Henry never shows. Nor is it merely that his nature
is limited: if we follow Shakespeare and look closely at Henry,
we shall discover with the many fine traits a few less pleasing.
Henry IV describes him as the noble image of his own youth;
and, for all his superiority to his father, he is still his father's
son, the son of the man whom Hotspur called a 'vile politician'.
Henry's religion, for example, is genuine, it is rooted in his
modesty; but it is also superstitious – an attempt to buy off
supernatural vengeance for Richard's blood; and it is also in part
political, like his father's projected crusade. Just as he went to

war chiefly because, as his father told him, it was the way to keep factious nobles quiet and unite the nation, so when he adjures the Archbishop to satisfy him as to his right to the French throne, he knows very well that the Archbishop *wants* the war because it will defer and perhaps prevent what he considers the spoliation of the Church. This same strain of policy is what Shakespeare marks in the first soliloquy in *Henry IV*, where the prince describes his riotous life as a mere scheme to win him glory later. It implies that readiness to use other people as means to his own ends which is a conspicuous feature in his father; and it reminds us of his father's plan of keeping himself out of the people's sight while Richard was making himself cheap by his incessant public appearances. And if I am not mistaken there is a further likeness. Henry is kindly and pleasant to every one as Prince, to every one deserving as King; and he is so not merely out of policy: but there is no sign in him of a strong affection for any one, such an affection as we recognise at a glance in Hamlet and Horatio, Brutus and Cassius, and many more. We do not find this in *Henry V*, not even in the noble address to Lord Scroop, and in *Henry IV* we find, I think, a liking for Falstaff and Poins, but no more: there is no more than a liking, for instance, in his soliloquy over the supposed corpse of his fat friend, and he never speaks of Falstaff to Poins with any affection. The truth is, that the members of the family of Henry IV have love for one another, but they cannot spare love for any one outside their family, which stands firmly united, defending its royal position against attack and instinctively isolating itself from outside influence.

Thus I would suggest that Henry's conduct in his rejection of Falstaff is in perfect keeping with his character on its unpleasant side as well as on its finer; and that, so far as Henry is concerned, we ought not to feel surprise at it. And on this view we may even explain the strange incident of the Chief Justice being sent back to order Falstaff to prison (for there is no sign of any such uncertainty in the text as might suggest an interpolation by the players). Remembering his father's words about Henry, 'Being incensed, he's flint,' and remembering in *Henry V* his ruthlessness about killing the prisoners when he is incensed, we may imagine that, after he had left Falstaff and was no longer influenced by the face of his old companion, he gave way to anger at the indecent familiarity which had provoked a compromising scene on the most ceremonial of occasions and in the presence alike of court and crowd, and that he sent the Chief Justice back to take vengeance. And this is consistent with the fact that in the next play we find Falstaff shortly afterwards not only freed from prison, but unmolested in his old haunt in Eastcheap, well within ten miles of Henry's person. His anger had soon passed, and he knew that the requisite effect had been produced both on Falstaff and on the world.

But all this, however true, will not solve our problem. It seems, on the contrary, to increase its difficulty. For the natural conclusion is that Shakespeare *intended* us to feel resentment against Henry. And yet that cannot be, for it implies that he meant the play to end disagreeably; and no one who understands Shakespeare at all will consider that supposition for a moment credible. No; he must have meant the play to end pleasantly, although he made Henry's action consistent. And hence it follows that he must have intended our sympathy with Falstaff to be so far weakened when the rejection-scene arrives that his discomfiture should be satisfactory to us; that we should enjoy this sudden reverse of enormous hopes (a thing always ludicrous if sympathy is absent); that we should approve the moral judgment that falls on him; and so should pass lightly over that disclosure of unpleasant traits in the King's character which Shakespeare was too true an artist to suppress. Thus our pain and resentment, if we feel them, are wrong, in the sense that they do not answer to the dramatist's intention. But it does not follow that they are wrong in a further sense. They may be right, because the dramatist has missed what he aimed at. And this, though the dramatist was Shakespeare, is what I would suggest. In the Falstaff scenes he overshot his mark. He created so extraordinary a being, and fixed him so firmly on his intellectual throne, that when he sought to dethrone him he could not. The moment comes when we are to look at Falstaff in a serious light, and the comic hero is to figure as a baffled schemer; but we cannot make the required change, either in our attitude or in our sympathies. We wish Henry a glorious reign and much joy of his crew of hypocritical politicians, lay and clerical; but our hearts go with Falstaff to the Fleet, or, if necessary, to Arthur's bosom or wheresomever he is.[4]

I will try to make this view clear. And to that end we must go back to the Falstaff of the body of the two plays, the immortal Falstaff, a character almost purely humorous, and therefore no subject for moral judgments. I can but draw an outline, and in describing one aspect of this character must be content to hold another in reserve.

II

Up to a certain point Falstaff is ludicrous in the same way as many other figures, his distinction lying, so far, chiefly in the mere abundance of ludicrous traits. *Why* we should laugh at a man with a huge belly and corresponding appetites; at the inconveniences he suffers on a hot day, or in playing the footpad, or when he falls down and there are no levers at hand to lift him up again; at the incongruity of his unwieldy bulk and the nimbleness of his spirit, the infirmities of his age and his youthful lightness of heart; at the enormity of his lies and wiles, and the suddenness of their exposure and frustration; at the contrast between his reputation and his real character, seen most absurdly when, at the mere mention of his name, a redoubted rebel surrenders to him – *why*, I say, we should laugh at these and many such things, this is no place to inquire; but unquestionably we do. Here we have them poured out in endless profusion and with that air of careless ease which is so fascinating in Shakespeare; and with the enjoyment of them I believe many readers stop. But while they are quite essential to the character, there is in it much more. For these things by themselves do not explain why, beside laughing at Falstaff, we are made happy by him and laugh *with* him. He is not, like Parolles, a mere *object* of mirth.

The main reason why he makes us so happy and puts us so entirely at our ease is that he himself is happy and entirely at his ease. 'Happy' is too weak a word; he is in bliss, and we share his glory. Enjoyment – no fitful pleasure crossing a dull life, nor any vacant convulsive mirth – but a rich deep-toned chuckling enjoyment circulates continually through all his being. If you ask *what* he enjoys, no doubt the answer is, in the first place, eating and drinking, taking his ease at his inn, and the company of other merry souls. Compared with these things, what we count the graver interests of life are nothing to him. But then, while we are under his spell, it is impossible to consider these graver interests; gravity is to us, as to him, inferior to gravy; and what he does enjoy he enjoys with such a luscious and good-humoured zest that we sympathise and he makes us happy. And if any one objected, we should answer with Sir Toby Belch, 'Dost thou think, because thou art virtuous, there shall be no more cakes and ale?'

But this, again, is far from all. Falstaff's ease and enjoyment are not simply those of the happy man of appetite;[5] they are those of the humorist, and the humorist of genius. Instead of being comic to you and serious to himself, he is more ludicrous to himself than to you; and he makes himself out more ludicrous than he is, in order that he and others may laugh. Prince Hal never made such sport of Falstaff's person as he himself did. It is *he* who says that his skin hangs about him like an old lady's loose gown, and that he walks before his page like a sow that hath o'erwhelmed all her litter but one. And he jests at himself when he is alone just as much as when others are by. It is the same with his appetites. The direct enjoyment they bring him is scarcely so great as the enjoyment of laughing at this enjoyment; and for all his addiction to sack you never see him for an instant with a brain dulled by it, or a temper turned solemn, silly, quarrelsome, or pious. The virtue it instils into him, of filling his brain with nimble, fiery, and delectable shapes – this, and his humorous attitude towards it, free him, in a manner, from slavery to it; and it is this freedom, and no secret longing for better things (those who attribute such a longing to him are far astray), that makes his enjoyment contagious and prevents our sympathy with it from being disturbed.

The bliss of freedom gained in humour is the essence of Falstaff. His humour is not directed only or chiefly against obvious absurdities; he is the enemy of everything that would interfere with his ease, and therefore of anything serious, and especially of everything respectable and moral. For these things impose limits and obligations, and make us the subjects of old father antic the law, and the categorical imperative, and our station and its duties, and conscience, and reputation, and other people's opinions, and all sorts of nuisances. I say he is therefore their enemy; but I do him wrong; to say that he is their enemy implies that he regards them as serious and recognises their power, when in truth he refuses to recognise them at all. They are to him absurd; and to reduce a thing *ad absurdum* is to reduce it to nothing and to walk about free and rejoicing. This is what Falstaff does with all the would-be serious things of life, sometimes only by his words, sometimes by his actions too. He will make truth appear absurd by solemn statements, which he utters with perfect gravity and which he expects nobody to believe; and honour, by demonstrating that it cannot set a leg, and that neither the living nor the dead can possess it; and law, by evading all the attacks of its highest representative and almost forcing him to laugh at his own defeat; and patriotism, by filling his pockets with the bribes offered by competent soldiers who want to escape service, while he takes in their stead the halt and maimed and the gaol-birds; and duty, by showing how he labours in his vocation − of thieving; and courage, alike by mocking at his own capture of Colvile and gravely claiming to have killed Hotspur; and war, by offering the Prince his bottle of sack when he is asked for a sword; and religion, by amusing himself with remorse at odd times when he has nothing else to do; and the fear of death, by maintaining perfectly untouched, in the face of imminent peril and even while he *feels* the fear of death, the very same power of dissolving it in persiflage that he shows when he sits at ease in his inn. These are the wonderful achievements which he performs, not with the discontent of a cynic, but with the gaiety of a boy. And, therefore, we praise him, we laud him, for he offends none but the virtuous, and denies that life is real

or life is earnest, and delivers us from the oppression of such
nightmares, and lifts us into the atmosphere of perfect freedom.

No one in the play understands Falstaff fully, any more than
Hamlet was understood by the persons round him. They are
both men of genius. Mrs Quickly and Bardolph are his slaves,
bu+ they know not why. 'Well, fare thee well,' says the hostess
whom he has pillaged and forgiven; 'I have known thee these
twenty-nine years, come peas-cod time, but an honester and
truer-hearted man – well, fare thee well.' Poins and the Prince
delight in him; they get him into corners for the pleasure of
seeing him escape in ways they cannot imagine; but they often
take him much too seriously. Poins, for instance, rarely sees, the
Prince does not always see, and moralising critics never see, that
when Falstaff speaks ill of a companion behind his back, or writes
to the Prince that Poins spreads it abroad that the Prince is to
marry his sister, he knows quite well that what he says will be
repeated, or rather, perhaps, is absolutely indifferent whether it
be repeated or not, being certain that it can only give him an
opportunity for humour. It is the same with his lying, and almost
the same with his cowardice, the two main vices laid to his charge
even by sympathisers. Falstaff is neither a liar nor a coward in the
usual sense, like the typical cowardly boaster of comedy. He tells
his lies either for their own humour, or on purpose to get himself
into a difficulty. He rarely expects to be believed, perhaps never.
He abandons a statement or contradicts it the moment it is made.
There is scarcely more intent in his lying than in the humorous
exaggerations which he pours out in soliloquy just as much as
when others are by. Poins and the Prince understand this in
part. You see them waiting eagerly to convict him, not that they
may really put him to shame, but in order to enjoy the greater
lie that will swallow up the less. But their sense of humour lags
behind his. Even the Prince seems to accept as half-serious that
remorse of his which passes so suddenly into glee at the idea of
taking a purse, and his request to his friend to bestride him if he
should see him down in the battle. Bestride Falstaff! 'Hence!
Wilt thou lift up Olympus?'

Again, the attack of the Prince and Poins on Falstaff and the other thieves on Gadshill is contrived, we know, with a view to the incomprehensible lies it will induce him to tell. But when, more than rising to the occasion, he turns two men in buckram into four, and then seven, and then nine, and then eleven, almost in a breath, I believe they partly misunderstand his intention, and too many of his critics misunderstand it altogether. Shakespeare was not writing a mere farce. It is preposterous to suppose that a man of Falstaff's intelligence would utter these gross, palpable, open lies with the serious intention to deceive, or forget that, if it was too dark for him to see his own hand, he could hardly see that the three misbegotten knaves were wearing Kendal green. No doubt, if he *had* been believed, he would have been hugely tickled at it, but he no more expected to be believed than when he claimed to have killed Hotspur. Yet he is supposed to be serious even then. Such interpretations would destroy the poet's whole conception; and of those who adopt them one might ask this out of some twenty similar questions: – When Falstaff, in the men in buckram scene, begins by calling twice at short intervals for sack, and then a little later calls for more and says, 'I am a rogue if I drunk to-day,' and the Prince answers, 'O villain, thy lips are scarce wiped since thou drunk'st last,' do they think that *that* lie was meant to deceive? And if not, why do they take it for granted that the others were? I suppose they consider that Falstaff was in earnest when, wanting to get twenty-two yards of satin on trust from Master Dombledon the silk-mercer, he offered Bardolph as security; or when he said to the Chief Justice about Mrs Quickly, who accused him of breaking his promise to marry her, 'My lord, this is a poor mad soul, and she says up and down the town that her eldest son is like you'; or when he explained his enormous bulk by exclaiming, 'A plague of sighing and grief! It blows a man up like a bladder'; or when he accounted for his voice being cracked by declaring that he had 'lost it with singing of anthems'; or even when he sold his soul on Good-Friday to the devil for a cup of Madeira and a cold capon's leg. Falstaff's lies about Hotspur and the men in buckram do not essentially differ from these statements. There is nothing serious in any of them except the refusal to take anything seriously.

This is also the explanation of Falstaff's cowardice, a subject on which I should say nothing if Maurice Morgann's essay, now more than a century old, were better known. That Falstaff sometimes behaves in what we should generally call a cowardly way is certain; but that does not show that he was a coward; and if the word means a person who feels painful fear in the presence of danger, and yields to that fear in spite of his better feelings and convictions, then assuredly Falstaff was no coward. The stock bully and boaster of comedy is one, but not Falstaff. It is perfectly clear in the first place that, though he had unfortunately a reputation for stabbing and caring not what mischief he did if his weapon were out, he had not a reputation for cowardice. Shallow remembered him five-and-fifty years ago breaking Scogan's head at the court-gate when he was a crack not thus high; and Shallow knew him later a good back-swordsman. Then we lose sight of him till about twenty years after, when his association with Bardolph began; and that association implies that by the time he was thirty-five or forty he had sunk into the mode of life we witness in the plays. Yet, even as we see him there, he remains a person of consideration in the army. Twelve captains hurry about London searching for him. He is present at the Council of War in the King's tent at Shrewsbury, where the only other persons are the King, the two princes, a nobleman and Sir Walter Blunt. The messenger who brings the false report of the battle to Northumberland mentions, as one of the important incidents, the death of Sir John Falstaff. Colvile, expressly described as a famous rebel, surrenders to him as soon as he hears his name. And if his own wish that his name were not so terrible to the enemy, and his own boast of his European reputation, are not evidence of the first rank, they must not be entirely ignored in presence of these other facts. What do these facts mean? Does Shakespeare put them all in with no purpose at all, or in defiance of his own intentions? It is not credible.

And when, in the second place, we look at Falstaff's actions, what do we find? He boldly confronted Colvile, he was quite

ready to fight with him, however pleased that Colvile, like a kind
fellow, gave himself away. When he saw Henry and Hotspur
fighting, Falstaff, instead of making off in a panic, stayed to
take his chance if Hotspur should be the victor. He *led* his hundred
and fifty ragamuffins where they were peppered, he did not *send*
them. To draw upon Pistol and force him downstairs and wound
him in the shoulder was no great feat, perhaps, but the stock
coward would have shrunk from it. When the Sheriff came to the
inn to arrest him for an offence whose penalty was death, Falstaff,
who was hidden behind the arras, did not stand there quaking
for fear, he immediately fell asleep and snored. When he stood
in the battle reflecting on what would happen if the weight of
his paunch should be increased by that of a bullet, he cannot
have been in a tremor of craven fear. He *never* shows such fear;
and surely the man who, in danger of his life, and with no one
by to hear him, meditates thus: 'I like not such grinning honour
as Sir Walter hath. Give me life: which if I can save, so; if not,
honour comes unlooked-for, and there's an end,' is not what we
commonly call a coward.

'Well,' it will be answered, 'but he ran away on Gadshill; and
when Douglas attacked him he fell down and shammed dead.'
Yes, I am thankful to say, he did. For of course he did not want
to be dead. He wanted to live and be merry. And as he had reduced the idea of honour *ad absurdum*, had scarcely any self-
respect, and only a respect for reputation as a means to life,
naturally he avoided death when he could do so without a ruinous
loss of reputation, and (observe) with the satisfaction of playing
a colossal practical joke. For *that* after all was his first object.
If his one thought had been to avoid death he would not have
faced Douglas at all, but would have run away as fast as his legs
could carry him; and unless Douglas had been one of those
exceptional Scotchmen who have no sense of humour, he would
never have thought of pursuing so ridiculous an object as Falstaff running. So that, as Mr Swinburne remarks, Poins is right
when he thus distinguishes Falstaff from his companions in
robbery: 'For two of them, I know them to be as true-bred
cowards as ever turned back; and for the third, if he fight longer

than he sees reason, I'll forswear arms.' And the event justifies this distinction. For it is exactly thus that, according to the original stage-direction, Falstaff behaves when Henry and Poins attack him and the others. The rest run away at once; Falstaff, here as afterwards with Douglas, fights for a blow or two, but, finding himself deserted and outmatched, runs away also. Of course. He saw no reason to stay. *Any* man who had risen superior to all serious motives would have run away. But it does not follow that he would run from mere fear, or be, in the ordinary sense, a coward.[6]

III

The main source, then, of our sympathetic delight in Falstaff is his humorous superiority to everything serious, and the freedom of soul enjoyed in it. But, of course, this is not the whole of his character. Shakespeare knew well enough that perfect freedom is not to be gained in this manner; we are ourselves aware of it even while we are sympathising with Falstaff; and as soon as we regard him seriously it becomes obvious. His freedom is limited in two main ways. For one thing he cannot rid himself entirely of respect for all that he professes to ridicule. He shows a certain pride in his rank: unlike the Prince, he is haughty to the drawers, who call him a proud Jack. He is not really quite indifferent to reputation. When the Chief Justice bids him pay his debt to Mrs Quickly for his reputation's sake, I think he feels a twinge, though to be sure he proceeds to pay her by borrowing from her. He is also stung by any thoroughly serious imputation on his courage, and winces at the recollection of his running away on Gadshill; he knows that his behaviour there certainly looked cowardly, and perhaps he remembers that he would not have behaved so once. It is, further, very significant that, for all his dissolute talk, he has never yet allowed the Prince and Poins to *see* him as they saw him afterwards with Doll Tearsheet; not, of course, that he has any moral shame in the matter, but he knows that in such a situation he, in his old age, must appear contemptible – not a humorist but a mere object of mirth. And, finally, he has affection in him – affection, I think, for Poins and Bardolph, and certainly for the Prince; and that is a thing which he cannot jest out of existence. Hence, as the effect of his rejection shows, he is not really invulnerable. And then, in the second place, since he is in the flesh, his godlike freedom has consequences and conditions; consequences, for there is something painfully wrong with his great toe; conditions, for he cannot eat and drink for ever without money, and his purse suffers from consumption, a disease for which he can find no remedy.[7] As the Chief Justice tells him, his means are very slender and his waste great; and his answer, 'I would it were otherwise; I would my means were greater and my waist slenderer,' though worth much money, brings none in. And so he is driven to evil deeds; not only to cheating his tailor like a gentleman, but to fleecing Justice Shallow, and to highway robbery, and to cruel depredations on the poor woman whose affection he has secured. All this is perfectly consistent with the other side of his character, but by itself it makes an ugly picture.

Yes, it makes an ugly picture when you look at it seriously. But then, surely, so long as the humorous atmosphere is preserved and the humorous attitude maintained, you do not look at it so. You no more regard Falstaff's misdeeds morally than you do the much more atrocious misdeeds of Punch or Reynard the Fox. You do not exactly ignore them, but you attend only to their comic aspect. This is the very spirit of comedy, and certainly of Shakespeare's comic world, which is one of make-believe, not merely as his tragic world is, but in a further sense — a world in which gross improbabilities are accepted with a smile, and many things are welcomed as merely laughable which, regarded gravely, would excite anger and disgust. The intervention of a serious spirit breaks up such a world, and would destroy our pleasure in Falstaff's company. Accordingly through the greater part of these dramas Shakespeare carefully confines this spirit to the scenes of war and policy, and dismisses it entirely in the humorous parts. Hence, if *Henry IV* had been a comedy like *Twelfth Night*, I am sure that he would no more have ended it with the painful disgrace of Falstaff than he ended *Twelfth Night* by disgracing Sir Toby Belch.[8]

But *Henry IV* was to be in the main a historical play, and its chief hero Prince Henry. In the course of it his greater and finer qualities were to be gradually revealed, and it was to end with beautiful scenes of reconciliation and affection between his father and him, and a final emergence of the wild Prince as a just, wise, stern, and glorious King. Hence, no doubt, it seemed to Shakespeare that Falstaff at last must be disgraced, and must therefore appear no longer as the invincible humorist, but as an object of ridicule and even of aversion. And probably also his poet's insight showed him that Henry, as he conceived him, *would* behave harshly to Falstaff in order to impress the world, especially when his mind had been wrought to a high pitch by the scene with his dying father and the impression of his own solemn consecration to great duties.

This conception was a natural and a fine one; and if the execution was not an entire success, it is yet full of interest. Shakespeare's purpose being to work a gradual change in our feelings towards Falstaff, and to tinge the humorous atmosphere more and more deeply with seriousness, we see him carrying out this purpose in the Second Part of *Henry IV*. Here he separates the Prince from Falstaff as much as he can, thus withdrawing him from Falstaff's influence, and weakening in our minds the connection between the two. In the First Part we constantly see them together; in the Second (it is a remarkable fact) only once before the rejection. Further, in the scenes where Henry appears apart from Falstaff, we watch him growing more and more grave, and awakening more and more poetic interest; while Falstaff, though his humour scarcely flags to the end, exhibits more and more of his seamy side. This is nowhere turned to the full light in Part I; but in Part II we see him as the heartless destroyer of Mrs Quickly, as a ruffian seriously defying the Chief Justice because his position as an officer on service gives him power to do wrong, as the pike preparing to snap up the poor old dace Shallow, and (this is the one scene where Henry and he meet) as the worn-out lecher, not laughing at his servitude to the flesh but sunk in it. Finally, immediately before the rejection, the world where he is king is exposed in all its sordid criminality when we find Mrs Quickly and Doll arrested for being concerned in the death of one man, if not more, beaten to death by their bullies; and the dangerousness of Falstaff is emphasised in his last words as he hurries from Shallow's house to London, words at first touched with humour but at bottom only too seriously meant: 'Let us take any man's horses; the laws of England are at my commandment. Happy are they which have been my friends, and woe unto my Lord Chief Justice.' His dismissal to the Fleet by the Chief Justice is the dramatic vengeance for that threat.

Yet all these excellent devices fail. They cause us momentary embarrassment at times when repellent traits in Falstaff's character are disclosed; but they fail to change our attitude of humour into one of seriousness, and our sympathy into repulsion. And they were bound to fail, because Shakespeare shrank from adding to them the one device which would have ensured success. If, as the Second Part of *Henry IV* advanced, he had clouded over Falstaff's humour so heavily that the man of genius turned into the Falstaff of the *Merry Wives*, we should have witnessed his rejection without a pang. This Shakespeare was too much of an artist to do – though even in this way he did something – and without this device he could not succeed. As I said, in the creation of Falstaff he overreached himself. He was caught up on the wind of his own genius, and carried so far that he could not descend to earth at the intended spot. It is not a misfortune that happens to many authors, nor is it one we can regret, for it costs us but a trifling inconvenience in one scene, while we owe to it perhaps the greatest comic character in literature. For it is in this character, and not in the judgment he brings upon Falstaff's head, that Shakespeare asserts his supremacy. To show that Falstaff's freedom of soul was in part illusory, and that the realities of life refused to be conjured away by his humour – this was what we might expect from Shakespeare's unfailing sanity, but it was surely no achievement beyond the power of lesser men. The achievement was Falstaff himself, and the conception of that freedom of soul, a freedom illusory only in part, and attainable only by a mind which had received from Shakespeare's own the

inexplicable touch of infinity which he bestowed on Hamlet and
Macbeth and Cleopatra, but denied to Henry the Fifth.

SOURCE: *Oxford Lectures on Poetry* (1909), first published in the
Fortnightly Review (1902).

NOTES

1. In this lecture I have mentioned the authors my obligations to
whom I was conscious of in writing or have discovered since; but other
debts must doubtless remain, which from forgetfulness I am unable
to acknowledge.

2. See on this and other points Swinburne, *A Study of Shakespeare*
(1879) pp. 106 ff.

3. Rötscher, *Shakespeare in seinen höchsten Charaktergebilden* (1864).

4. That from the beginning Shakespeare intended Henry's accession
to be Falstaff's catastrophe is clear from the fact that, when the two
characters first appear, Falstaff is made to betray at once the hopes with
which he looks forward to Henry's reign. See *Henry IV, Part I*,
Act I, scene ii.

5. Cf Hazlitt, *Characters of Shakespear's Plays* (1817).

6. It is to be regretted, however, that in carrying his guts away so
nimbly he 'roared for mercy'; for I fear we have no ground for rejecting Henry's statement to that effect, and I do not see my way to
adopt the suggestion (I forget whose it is) that Falstaff spoke the truth
when he swore that he knew Henry and Poins as well as he that made
them.

7. Panurge too was 'naturally subject to a kind of disease which at
that time they called lack of money'; it was a 'flux in his purse'
(Rabelais, Book II, chapters xvi, xvii).

8. I seem to remember that, according to Gervinus, Shakespeare
did disgrace Sir Toby – by marrying him to Maria!

PART TWO
Recent Studies

PART TWO

Recent Studies

H. B. Charlton

SHAKESPEARE, POLITICS, AND POLITICIANS (1929)

Is it possible in any of Shakespeare's plays to find anything which as an artist he had apprehended of the conditions governing the life political? His tragedies are glimpses of individual man as a nursling of immortality, his vision of the ways of God with man: his comedies are his imaginative experience of the same individual in his domestic and social relationship with other members of civilized society. But by pure chance there was in Shakespeare's day a type of theatrical entertainment which was neither tragedy nor comedy, neither focused mainly on the life eternal, nor on the life private, domestic, and social. There was the so-called History or Chronicle Play.

Perhaps no one but Shakespeare wrote the History Play proper. Others made plays on historical themes. Tragedy from its beginnings had demanded an historical warrant for its action and its heroes; invented tales from novelettes, like the story of *Romeo and Juliet*, were revolutionary novelties. But almost all serious plays on historical subjects are tragedies, not history-plays. In *Richard III*, it is the ruin of the man Richard which is the motive; and that his ruin is effected through his kingship merely indicates that history is the accidental form and tragedy the essential substance of the drama, So, too, in *Richard II*.

But to fob off the clamour for a history-play by providing an historical tragedy was to run away from an aesthetic problem. In its beginnings, the history-play was nothing but a chronicle panorama. A wave of exuberant national sentiment cried out for such stimulus as visible reminders of England's past could give it. The theatre, not as a temple of drama, but as a market-place for spectacle, was well enough qualified for this sort of cinematographic depiction. It could stage scenes from chronicles. But in so doing, it was catering primarily for a political, and not for an artistic, demand. It was exercising and fostering patriotism. Hence the pageantry of the chronicle play, and its undramatic structure, although, of course, by the accident of its environment, it took to itself freely incidental dramatic scenes, comic or tragic, as episodes in the spectacle. So, in the Cade incidents of *Henry VI*, or the Talbot episode, for a moment the quality of interest becomes in some sense mainly comic or tragic, and the audience is given something of the conventional appeal of comedy or of tragedy, by a playlet within a panorama. But the whole matter of *Henry VI* has no dramatic form. There is no dominant interest, recognizable as a dramatic interest, to hold the audience in continuous suspense.

It seemed as if the political emotion which gave birth to the chronicle play was to remain a manifestation of life, of which the dramatist as a dramatist could only take partial cognizance, either by diverting it to an occasion for comedy or for tragedy, or by giving it free stage play though with only one or two articles, and those the most mechanical, of the many and complex instruments which in full concert make up the art of drama.

The problem was too much for all the Elizabethans but Shakespeare. His *King John* stands at the parting of the ways. It is neither chronicle play nor tragedy: nor is it a history-play. It is a chronicle play leaning to tragedy for as much artistic discipline as will give it the semblance of dramatic shape; but it is unwilling to pay the price of such dramatic organization by sacrificing as much of chronicle-spectacle as *Richard III* had done. . . . Its insufficiency is plain to be seen in the technical career of its nominal hero, King John, and in the circumstances of his final catastrophe. As a conventional tragic hero he must finally die. But his death at the hands of a monk fulfils no dramatic expectancy and satisfies no awakened sense of inevitable doom. What it very clearly does excite and satisfy, however, is a contemporary political sentiment, the anti-papalism which was momentarily a form of English patriotism; and, of course, it adopts another equally un- or extra-artistic principle, that, namely, of conformity with recorded fact. John's death is thus determined by historical and political motives. No less within the play is his life ordained by the same powers. Substantially, he forfeits his place as a technical hero, and the first call on our theatrical interest is won from him by the Bastard.

At first glance, the Bastard's qualifications to offer himself as hero seem grotesque. . . . Boisterousness of animal spirits and a riotous disregard of proprieties may, of course, express themselves in a low and vigorous sort of humour sufficient to make their owner entertaining. But Falconbridge is more than entertaining in the play. His title is not merely honorary; he establishes his dramatic worth by determining the action of the play. He becomes in fact a pledge of victory for his side. Despicable as he may be as a private individual, he is a national asset. It is in virtue of this capacity that he looms so largely in the play. He is a rudimentary John Bull, a bulwark of England. His technical promotion to the middle stage, and the pushing of John into the wings, marks the transition from tragedy to the history play, a transition, however, which only makes tentative steps in *King John*. But what ultimately will distinguish the history-play from tragedy is beginning to appear. Comedy and tragedy are concerned with the eternal or ephemeral fate of individual man. The history-play is concerned with communities of men, and primarily with nations. The real hero of the English history-play is England.

But just as the author of tragedy, moving his hero from predicament to predicament and at last to his ruin, weaves into the design of his play his apprehension of the ultimate forces which sway the life of individual man in our universe, so in the history play. At its beginning England is presented in such and such a condition. As the action proceeds, there are changes in the protagonist's welfare; and at the end, if the author is a dramatist with a dramatist's genius and apprehension, the state of affairs ensues as the inevitable outcome of what has gone before. But to give such conviction to his ending the dramatist must have apprehended the fundamental principles conditioning the form of life he is displaying. In the history-play, it is the welfare of a nation as a nation; that is, it is a specifically political interest. The

ups and downs of England's national fortune in *King John* are
not presented as a succession of chances. They are visible effects
of operant causes shown in the action which is the play. Shakespeare's picture of Falconbridge is his first sketch of the forces
which sway to its advantage the destiny of a nation. He is
Shakespeare's first portrait of an unofficial statesman, a natural
politician, a realization in untrammelled circumstance of such a
figure as Bolingbroke would have been if he had not been called
upon to play a part in tragedy.

Falconbridge does not hide the grounds of his political worth.
More than once he himself expounds his own guiding principles;
and the actions he instigates in the play are direct expressions of
these principles. Expediency is his watchword: 'commodity the
bias of the world'. An eye for the main chance, and utter im-
munity from every moral or decent scruple which might trammel
one's freedom to perform the expedient act expeditiously: that is
the secret of policy. . . .

It is no doubt dangerous to attribute validity to opinions
deduced from an artist's apprehension in a play which is only
intermittently and dubiously artistic. The impression of Falconbridge's unscrupulousness as the main instrument of his political
efficiency may proceed not from Shakespeare's intuitive and
imaginative grasp of the life political: it may be no more than a
casual prejudice. Even so, there is no room for doubt that his
habitual view of the art of diplomacy was that it was an immoral
game. Kings break faith upon commodity. John's pseudo-
judicial determination of the Falconbridge heritage is a farcical
travesty of justice:

> My mother's son did get your father's heir;
> Your father's heir must have your father's land.

And when the Dauphin has a faintly moral reluctance to enter
into certain complicated political fetches, it is characteristically a
high ecclesiastic who reproaches him for being so green and
fresh in the ways of the world.

But if *King John*, by permitting a distinction between the craft
of policy and the art of government, allows no unassailable

ground for attributing to Shakespeare a distinctly contemptuous view of statesmen and statecraft, his two fully developed history-plays, *Henry IV* and *Henry V*, make such an escape impossible. They are perhaps the only perfect specimens of a dramatic type which, even in an age of creative dramatists, only Shakespeare's genius could invent. They are not chronicle-pageants: they are not tragedies, nor are they comedies, though they come closer to comedy than to other recognized types, and indeed curiously so, since the traditional affinities of the chronicle play had been with tragedy. They are history-plays. A better name would be political plays, for they are plays in which the prevailing dramatic interest is in the fate of a nation. Since that is their nature, there will be in them much of what Shakespeare's insight had apprehended of the forces which shape a nation's destiny.

The plot of both of them is specifically political, and the nominal hero of each is elected to the office in his capacity as a political agent, a wielder of government. To an Elizabethan, the welfare of England was in the hands of its sovereign. These two history-plays are representations of two kings, each contributing his particular service to the good of his country by virtue of his gifts, his principles, and his personality. At the end of them, England is what it has become in each, because this or that trait in its king has visibly produced these political consequences. They are, psychologically, studies in kings; but, dramatically, they are views of kingship.

It is plain to see what makes Henry IV an efficient governor. As a man, he is unattractive, cold, secretive. He can suppress or hide every tremor of personal sentiment and of natural instinct. Touches of nature are interspersed to diversify the portrait – the conflict, for instance, in Henry between the father and the king, and the elemental human torments such as sleeplessness, attacking the natural man through the strain imposed by the statesman. But these not only add lifelikeness to the picture; they emphasize the dramatic theme. It is Henry's political virtue that, up to the limit of all but simple physical necessity, he can always subdue the man to the official. He cloaks even the most natural impulses; on both occasions, for instance, when he talks as a father with his son, he has carefully secured privacy by dismissing all his attendants and counsellors. His life has been governed by policy. He has been eminently successful as a politician; he has led his country to larger prosperity. The public benefit ensuing from his achievement is clear in the sequence of events which make the play. Less obvious, but no less certain, is Henry's own single-mindedness in directing his policy to public good. When, unheard by the world, he is in intimate discourse with his offending son, his obsessing fear is that his son's dissipation will spell ruin for England:

> the fifth Harry from curb'd licence plucks
> The muzzle of restraint, and the wild dog
> Shall flesh his tooth on every innocent.
> O my poor kingdom, sick with civil blows!

The principles of policy by which Henry has conferred so much good on the nation are plain to be seen. Absolute expediency and resolute pragmatism. 'Are these things then necessities? Then let us meet them like necessities.' This, of course, means the suspension of all moral considerations except in so far as they may be tools of expediency. 'Nothing can seem foul to those that win.' The natural and the moral man must be overcome; all impulses of conscience and all promptings of humane instinct must be rigorously controlled, so that the perfect official, the ideal civil servant, may emerge. Such a victory has Henry won over himself.

The sources of his political worth are thrown into clearer light by dramatic comparison and contrast. He is set over against Hotspur, who, as a man, has the irresistible attractiveness of high-spirited nobility:

> no braver gentleman
> More active-valiant or more valiant-young,
> More daring or more bold, is now alive
> To grace this latter age with noble deeds.

But because he is so much at the mercy of his human and manly instincts, he is a complete political failure. He cannot govern, because he cannot control and organize even himself. Officially, he is a hare-brained Hotspur, governed by a spleen, or by a romantic sentiment. How complete is his failure to participate in corporate scheming is apparent even in his demeanour as a husband. Luckily for him, marriage is not entirely a political association, and may even yet be held fast by links of purely personal preference. Hotspur's shortcomings in regard to domestic strategy are insufficient to fracture a union welded so firmly by the devotion of a wife so strongly under the spell of his personality. But his heedlessness as she fondly and lengthily inquires for the cause of his distemperature; his indifference to her anxieties; his spasmodic awakening from brooding abstraction, but only to summon a servant for information about posts and horses; above all, the casual callousness of the notice he deigns in the end to give to her – 'What say'st thou, my lady?' – these are enough to indicate Hotspur's ineptitude even in the politics of domesticity. He is always so passionately himself, and so enthusiastically the man, that he can never conduct himself as the unfailing official.

Falstaff, at first a mere unhistorical intruder strangely allowed entry into a history play, quickly asserts his right to a main role in the play's dramatic idea. He is the marvellous offspring of Shakespeare's full perception of the artistic affinity between history play and comedy. Comedy approaches life as something to be lived, and the living of it is a practical art. Falstaff's problem as a comic character is to maintain the corporation of Sir John. His task is of an order similar to Henry's political occupation to maintain the community of England. Falstaff's principles are Henry's, applied to the domain of private life. He fights no longer than he sees reason; for a comic hero endangers his professional qualification as a comic hero whenever he risks his life and hazards an uncovenanted tragic ending. He is neither brave nor cowardly, neither truthful nor a liar; for such moral distinctions do not exist in his world. Virtue for him is merely the ability to survive and succeed by the exercise of his capacity for overcoming all obstacles and for extricating himself from all dangers. Wit is his instrument, as a closely allied form of intellectual ingenuity, craft, is Henry's. And Falstaff's banishment of honour from his scale of values is no less necessary to his efficiency than is Henry's oblivion of it to his. But of course Falstaff's task to be a man moving triumphantly amongst men does not require him to renounce his manhood. Indeed he must preserve in particular its primary elements, the qualities which pertain to the flesh. There are no more universal touches of nature; and they make Falstaff heartily welcome to all mankind. Henry has nothing but success in office to give him a hold on our regard. He remains outside our affection, a perfect politician.

In popular estimation Shakespeare's Henry V is probably a more perfect king than Henry IV. Admittedly he is a far more likeable fellow – once he has ceased to explain his wild oats. And what enterprises of kingship he undertakes he performs no less successfully than did his father. But Shakespeare can only allow him to purchase our personal affection by considerably reducing his duties as a king. His father had to exercise the whole art of government, maintaining peace at home and securing glory abroad. It was in the more exacting office of governing at home that his subtlest craft was needed. But Hal is largely relieved of these routine trials, and for the most part his kingship is circumscribed to military leadership. At the head of his army, in embarkation, in siege, and in battle, he treads the surest of traditional ways to popular acclamation. He is a great commander whose greatness as a king is tacitly and sentimentally assumed. In a field-command he can keep so much of the humanity he would perforce have to leave outside the door of civil office. Soldiers are much more obviously human than clerks of the Treasury.

But on the rare occasions when Hal is called upon for a definitely political decision, are the factors determining political wisdom different from what they were in his father's case? Hal's mode of leading his army to victory is his most obvious national asset. But it was, so to speak, a secondary achievement, and the good it did was entirely dependent on the prior decision to make war on France. The first scene of *Henry V* – a scene which critics curiously pass by – unmistakably deprives Hal of all personal credit for that decision. He is trapped into declaration of war by the machinations of a group of men whose sole and quite explicit motive is to preserve their own revenues; and the political implication is more flagrant in that these men are an ecclesiastical synod. Hal, in fact, owes his political achievement, not as did his father, to his own insight, but rather to something so near to intellectual dullness that it permits of his being jockeyed into his opportunities. He can be saved from such imputation only by the assumption that he saw through the bishops' subtlety and quietly used them as an excuse to embark on a foreign war with the idea of securing domestic peace, even as his father in his dying words had advised him to do. But such Machiavellian astuteness does not fit in with the indubitable traits of Hal's nature. On one occasion, and on one occasion only, there is a faint suspicion of political sophistication. In the preceding play, Hotspur contributed to his own political ruin by a noble gesture of bravado. Too eager to await reinforcements, he joined immediate battle with the vaunt that the reduction of his forces

> lends a lustre and more great opinion
> A larger dare to our great enterprise.

As a moral attitude its effect is magnificent; as a political decision it is disastrous. But on a similar occasion, Henry V displays a like temper. When, on the night before Agincourt, Westmoreland wishes that they had but one ten thousand more recruits from England, Henry will have none of it.

> The fewer men, the greater share of honour,
> ... wish not a man from England.
> God's peace, I would not lose so great an honour
> As one man more methinks would share from me.

He exceeds Hotspur in moral generosity and in thirst for glory: he would even reduce the army he has:

> Rather proclaim it, Westmoreland, through my host,
> That he which hath no stomach to this fight,
> Let him depart: his passport shall be made
> And crowns for convoy put into his purse –

and all because

> We would not die in that man's company
> That fears his fellowship to die with us.

But his gesture does not lead to defeat. It is not in fact a procla-
mation and a firm offer to the army. It is merely a remark to one of
his chiefs of staff. Nor would there have been much opportunity
for wholesale demobilization on the very eve of battle. The offer,
which was no offer, was either a piece of strategy or the natural
outcome of Henry's military enthusiasm. Either his guardian
spirit once more urges Henry to make what, in spite of first
appearances, proves in the end to be the politic move, or Henry
is sounder in the theory of military numbers than he appears in
this speech to be. There is more of the general's acumen in
another of his battle-prayers:

> O God of battles, steel my soldiers' hearts,
> Possess them not with fear; take from them now
> The sense of reckoning, if the opposed numbers
> Pluck their hearts from them.

Altogether, then, the play of *Henry V* does not really imply
substantial modifications in Shakespeare's apprehension of the
political life. There remains in it the sense that what is good in
the world of politics is entirely unrelated to and generally the
opposite of what makes for goodness in the moral life. It is the
distinction between Machiavelli's *virtù* and the moralist's virtue,
or, as Mr G. B. Shaw puts it, between virtue and goodness. But
more of that later. Henry IV achieves political greatness and
proves his political worth by the deliberate exercise of his
political acumen: whence our coldness to him as a man. To a
large extent, Henry V is thrust into political greatness by sheer
instinct. His genius leads him to take steps his moral nature would
have prohibited his taking; and his ingratiating commonplaceness
of mind hides from him their immoral implications or even glosses
them with conventional moral sanctions. He is secured in our
affections, because he is dispensed by Shakespeare from requiring
such intellectual greatness as his father had. He stands before us

always as the great plain man, and there is a sort of gratification felt by Shakespeare, as by most of us, in installing the plain man in high political office. Illogical, it probably is; a mere gamble with fate. We trust that a blind instinct will prompt the plain man to do those things the competent politician would clearly see to be necessary; and we are willing to take our chance, though at such very long odds against us, because, as human beings and unpolitical animals, we prefer to sacrifice the probability of good government to secure ourselves against the fear of exploitation by the expert. A pledge to do nothing at all is not without advantages as an electioneering cry. Henry V wins our hearts as the greatest of plain men. His common text is that the king is but a man; that all his senses have but human conditions, and that, his ceremonies laid by, in his nakedness he appears but a man. Note, however, how his guardian angel saw to it that he should preserve his incognito whilst preaching this sermon. Henry has all the admirable propensities of the average Englishman, his conventions, his manners, and his opportune lack of them, his prejudices, and even his faith. He would have welcomed Robinson Crusoe as a brother in God. In all except generalship, he is that most attractive and delightful being, the magnificent commonplace, and we needs must love the glorified image of ourselves.

Thus did Shakespeare sweeten the savour of the political life, without giving the lie to what he had apprehended of its sordid necessities. Though it may be largely hidden, the truth as Shakespeare grasped it, remains even in *Henry V*: the sense that not only is politics a nasty business, but that a repugnant unscrupulousness is an invaluable asset in the art of government. That is the burden of the English History Plays, jubilant as they are in pride of country and of race. . . .

SOURCE: *Shakespeare, Politics, and Politicians* (1929).

J. Dover Wilson

RIOT AND THE PRODIGAL
PRINCE (1943)

FALSTAFF may be the most conspicuous, he is certainly the most fascinating, character in *Henry IV*, but all critics are agreed, I believe, that the technical centre of the play is not the fat knight but the lean prince. Hal links the low life with the high life, the scenes at Eastcheap with those at Westminster, the tavern with the battlefield; his doings provide most of the material for both Parts, and with him too lies the future, since he is to become Henry V, the ideal king, in the play that bears his name; finally, the mainspring of the dramatic action is the choice I have already spoken of, the choice he is called upon to make between Vanity and Government, taking the latter in its accepted Tudor meaning, which includes Chivalry or prowess in the field, the theme of Part I, and Justice, which is the theme of Part II. Shakespeare, moreover, breathes life into these abstractions by embodying them, or aspects of them, in prominent characters, who stand, as it were, about the Prince, like attendant spirits: Falstaff typifying Vanity in every sense of the word, Hotspur Chivalry, of the old anarchic kind, and the Lord Chief Justice the Rule of Law or the new ideal of service to the state.[1]

Thus considered, Shakespeare's *Henry IV* is a Tudor version of a time-honoured theme, already familiar for decades, if not centuries, upon the English stage. Before its final secularization in the first half of the sixteenth century, our drama was concerned with one topic, and one only: human salvation. It was a topic that could be represented in either of two ways: (i) historically, by means of miracle plays, which in the Corpus Christi cycles unrolled before spectators' eyes the whole scheme of salvation from the Creation to the Last Judgement; or (ii) allegorically, by means of morality plays, which exhibited the process of salvation

in the individual soul on its road between birth and death, beset
with the snares of the World or the wiles of the Evil One. In
both kinds the forces of iniquity were allowed full play upon the
stage, including a good deal of horse-play, provided they were
brought to nought, or safely locked up in Hell, at the end.
Salvation remains the supreme interest, however many capers the
Devil and his Vice may cut on Everyman's way thither, and
always the powers of darkness are withstood, and finally overcome, by the agents of light. But as time went on the religious
drama tended to grow longer and more elaborate, after the
encyclopaedic fashion of the middle ages, and such development
invited its inevitable reaction. With the advent of humanism and
the early Tudor court, morality plays became tedious and gave
place to lighter and much shorter moral interludes dealing, not
with human life as a whole, but with youth and its besetting sins.

An early specimen, entitled *Youth*[2] and composed about 1520,
may be taken as typical of the rest. The plot, if plot it can be
called, is simplicity itself. The little play opens with a dialogue
between Youth and Charity. The young man, heir to his father's
land, gives insolent expression to his self-confidence, lustihood,
and contempt for spiritual things. Whereupon Charity leaves
him, and he is joined by Riot,[3] that is to say wantonness, who
presently introduces him to Pride and Lechery. The dialogue
then becomes boisterous, and continues in that vein for some
time, much no doubt to the enjoyment of the audience. Yet, in
the end, Charity reappears with Humility; Youth repents; and
the interlude terminates in the most seemly fashion imaginable.

No one, I think, reading this lively playlet, no one certainly
who has seen it performed, as I have seen it at the Malvern
Festival, can have missed the resemblance between Riot and
Falstaff. The words he utters, as he bounces on to the stage at his
first entry, give us the very note of Falstaff's gaiety:

> Huffa! huffa! who calleth after me?
> I am Riot full of jollity.
> My heart is as light as the wind,
> And all on riot is my mind,
> Wheresoever I go.

And the parallel is even more striking in other respects. Riot, like Falstaff, escapes from tight corners with a quick dexterity; like Falstaff, commits robbery on the highway; like Falstaff, jests immediately afterwards with his young friend on the subject of hanging; and like Falstaff, invites him to spend the stolen money at a tavern, where, he promises, 'We will drink diuers wine' and 'Thou shalt haue a wench to kysse Whansoeuer thou wilte'; allurements which prefigure the Boar's Head and Mistress Doll Tearsheet.

But Youth at the door of opportunity, with Age or Experience, Charity or Good Counsel, offering him the yoke of responsibility, while the World, the Flesh, and the Devil beckon him to follow them on the primrose way to the everlasting bonfire, is older than even the medieval religious play. It is a theme to which every generation gives fresh form, while retaining its eternal substance. Young men are the heroes of the Plautine and Terentian comedy which delighted the Roman world; and these young men, generally under the direction of a clever slave or parasite, disport themselves, and often hoodwink their old fathers, for most of the play, until they too settle down in the end. The same theme appears in a very different story, the parable of the Prodigal Son. And the similarity of the two struck humanist teachers of the early sixteenth century with such force that, finding Terence insufficiently edifying for their pupils to act, they developed a 'Christian Terence' by turning the parable into Latin plays, of which many examples by different authors have come down to us.[4] In these plot and structure are much the same. The opening scene shows us Acolastus, the prodigal, demanding his portion, receiving good counsel from his father, and going off into a far country. Then follow three or four acts of entertainment almost purely Terentian in atmosphere, in which he wastes his substance in riotous living and falls at length to feeding with the pigs. Finally, in the last act he returns home, penniless and repentant, to receive his pardon. This ingenious blend of classical comedy and humanistic morality preserves, it will be noted, the traditional ratio between edification and amusement, and distributes them in the traditional manner. So long as the serious note is duly emphasized at the beginning and end of the play, almost any quantity of fun, often of the most unseemly nature, was allowed and expected during the intervening scenes.

All this, and much more of a like character, gave the pattern for Shakespeare's *Henry IV*. Hal associates Falstaff in turn with the Devil of the miracle play, the Vice of the morality, and the Riot of the interlude, when he calls him 'that villainous abominable misleader of Youth, that old white-bearded Satan',[5] 'that reverend Vice, that grey Iniquity, that father Ruffian, that Vanity in years',[6] and 'the tutor and the feeder of my riots'.[7] 'Riot', again, is the word that comes most readily to King Henry's lips when speaking of his prodigal son's misconduct.[8] And, as heir to the Vice, Falstaff inherits by reversion the functions and attributes of the Lord of Misrule, the Fool, the Buffoon, and the Jester, antic figures the origins of which are lost in the dark backward and abysm of folk-custom.[9] We shall find that Falstaff possesses a strain, and more than a strain, of the classical *miles gloriosus* as well. In short, the Falstaff-Hal plot embodies a composite myth which had been centuries amaking, and was for the Elizabethans full of meaning that has largely disappeared since then: which is one reason why we have come so seriously to misunderstand the play.

Nor was Shakespeare the first to see Hal as the prodigal. The legend of Harry of Monmouth began to grow soon after his death in 1422; and practically all the chroniclers, even those writing in the fifteenth century, agree on his wildness in youth and on the sudden change that came upon him at his accession to the throne. The essence of Shakespeare's plot is, indeed, already to be found in the following passage about King Henry V taken from Fabyan's *Chronicle* of 1516:

This man, before the death of his fader, applyed him unto all vyce and insolency, and drewe unto hym all ryottours and wylde disposed persones; but after he was admytted to the rule of the lande, anone and suddenly he became a newe man, and tourned al that rage into sobernesse and wyse sadnesse, and the vyce into constant vertue. And for he wolde contynewe the vertue, and not to be reduced thereunto by the familiarytie of his old nyse company, he therefore, after rewardes to them gyuen, charged theym upon payne of theyr lyues, that none of theym were so hardy to come within x. myle of such place as he were lodgyd, after a day by him assigned.[10]

There appears to be no historical basis for any of this, and Kingsford has plausibly suggested that its origin may be 'contemporary scandal which attached to Henry through his youthful association with the unpopular Lollard leader' Sir John Oldcastle. 'It is noteworthy', he points out, 'that Henry's political opponents were Oldcastle's religious persecutors; and also that those writers who charge Henry with wildness as Prince find his peculiar merit as King in the maintaining of Holy Church and destroying of heretics. A supposed change in his attitude on questions of religion may possibly furnish a partial solution for his alleged "change suddenly into a new man".'[11] The theory is the more attractive that it would account not only for Hal's conversion but also for Oldcastle's degradation from a protestant martyr and distinguished soldier to what Ainger calls 'a broken-down Lollard, a fat old sensualist, retaining just sufficient recollection of the studies of his more serious days to be able to point his jokes with them.'

Yet when all is said, the main truth seems to be that the fifteenth and early sixteenth centuries, the age of allegory in poetry and morality in drama, needed a Prodigal Prince, whose miraculous conversion might be held up as an example by those concerned (as what contemporary political writer was not?) with the education of young noblemen and princes. And could any more alluring fruits of repentance be offered such pupils than the prowess and statesmanship of Henry V, the hero of Agincourt, the mirror of English kingship for a hundred years? In his miracle play, *Richard II*, Shakespeare had celebrated the traditional royal martyr;[12] in his morality play, *Henry IV*, he does the like with the traditional royal prodigal.

He made the myth his own, much as musicians adopt and absorb a folk-tune as the theme for a symphony. He glorified it, elaborated it, translated it into what were for the Elizabethans modern terms, and exalted it into a heaven of delirious fun and frolic; yet never, for a moment, did he twist it from its original purpose, which was serious, moral, didactic. Shakespeare plays no tricks with his public. He did not, like Euripides, dramatize the stories of his race and religion in order to subvert the traditional ideals those stories were first framed to set forth. Prince Hal is the prodigal, and his repentance is not only to be taken seriously, it is to be admired and commended. Moreover, the story of the prodigal, secularized and modernized as it might be, ran the same course as ever and contained the same three principal characters: the tempter, the younker, and the father with property to bequeath and counsel to give. It followed also the fashion set by miracle, morality and the Christian Terence by devoting much attention to the doings of the first-named. Shakespeare's audience enjoyed the fascination of Prince Hal's 'white-bearded Satan' for two whole plays, as perhaps no character on the world's stage had ever been enjoyed before. But they knew, from the beginning, that the reign of this marvellous Lord of Misrule must have an end, that Falstaff must be rejected by the Prodigal Prince, when the time for reformation came. And they no more thought of questioning or disapproving of that finale, than their ancestors would have thought of protesting against the Vice being carried off to Hell at the end of the interlude.

The main theme, therefore, of Shakespeare's morality play is the growing-up of a madcap prince into the ideal king, who was Henry V; and the play was made primarily – already made by some dramatist before Shakespeare took it over – in order to exhibit his conversion and to reveal his character unfolding towards that end, as he finds himself faced more and more directly by his responsibilities. It is that which determines its very shape. Even the 'fearful symmetry' of Falstaff's own person was welded upon the anvil of that purpose. It is probably because the historical Harry of Monmouth 'exceeded the meane stature of men', as his earliest chronicler tells us; 'his necke . . . longe, his body slender and leane, his boanes smale',[13] – because in Falstaff's words he actually was a starveling, an eel-skin, a tailor's yard, and all the rest of it – that the idea of Falstaff himself as 'a huge hill of flesh' first came to Shakespeare.[14] It was certainly, at any rate in part, in order to explain and palliate the Prince's love of rioting and wantonness that he set out to make Falstaff as enchanting as he could. [15] And he succeeded so well that the young man now lies under the stigma, not of having yielded to the tempter, but of disentangling himself, in the end, from his toils. After all, Falstaff *is* 'a devil . . . in the likeness of an old fat man', and the Devil has generally been supposed to exercise limitless attraction in his dealings with the sons of men. A very different kind of poet, who imagined a very different kind of Satan, has been equally and similarly misunderstood by modern critics, who no longer believing in the Prince of Darkness have ceased to understand him. For, as Professor R. W. Chambers reminded us in his last public utterance, [16] when Blake declared that Milton was 'of the Devil's party without knowing it', he overlooked the fact, and his many successors have likewise overlooked the fact, that, if the fight in Heaven, the struggle in Eden, the defeat of Adam and Eve, and the victory of the Second Adam in *Paradise Regained*, are to appear in their true proportions, we must be made to realize how immeasurable, how indomitable, is the spirit of the Great Enemy. It may also be noted that Milton's Son of God has in modern times been charged with priggishness no less freely than Shakespeare's son of Bolingbroke.

Shakespeare, I say, translated his myth into a language and endued it with an atmosphere that his contemporaries would best appreciate. First, Hal is not only youth or the prodigal, he is the young prodigal *prince*, the youthful heir to the throne. The translation, then, already made by the chroniclers, if Kingsford be right, from sectarian terms into those more broadly religious or moral, now takes us out of the theological into the political sphere. This is seen most clearly in the discussion of the young king's remarkable conversion by the two bishops at the beginning of *Henry V*. King Henry, as Bradley notes, 'is much more obviously religious than most of Shakespeare's heroes', [17] so that one would expect the bishops to interpret his change of life as a religious conversion. Yet they say nothing about religion except that he is 'a true lover of the holy church' and can 'reason in divinity'; the rest of their talk, some seventy lines, is concerned with learning and statecraft. In fact, the conversation of these worldly prelates demonstrates that the conversion is not the old repentance for sin and amendment of life, which is the burden, as we have seen, of Fabyan and other chroniclers, but a repentance of the renaissance type, which transforms an idle and wayward prince into an excellent soldier and governor. Even King Henry IV, at the bitterest moments of the scenes with his son, never taxes him with sin, and his only use of the word refers to sins that would multiply in the country, when

> the fifth Harry from curbed licence plucks
> The muzzle of restraint.[18]

If Hal had sinned, it was not against God, but against Chivalry, against Justice, against his father, against the interests of the crown, which was the keystone of England's political and social stability. Instead of educating himself for the burden of kingship, he had been frittering away his time, and making himself cheap, with low companions

> that daff the world aside
> And bid it pass.

In a word, a word that Shakespeare applies no less than six times to his conduct, he is guilty of Vanity. And Vanity, though not in the theological category of the Seven Deadly Sins, was a cardinal iniquity in a young prince or nobleman of the sixteenth and seventeenth centuries; almost as heinous, in fact, as Idleness in an apprentice.

I am not suggesting that this represents Shakespeare's own view. Of Shakespeare's views upon the problems of conduct, whether in prince or commoner, we are in general ignorant, though he seems to hint in both *Henry IV* and *Henry V* that the Prince of Wales learnt some lessons at least from Falstaff and his crew, Francis and his fellow-drawers, which stood him in good stead when he came to rule the country and command troops in the field. But it is the view that his father and his own conscience take of his misreadings; and, as the spectators would take it as well, we must regard it as the thesis to which Shakespeare addressed himself.

When, however, he took audiences by storm in 1597 and 1598 with his double *Henry IV* he gave them something much more than a couple of semi-mythical figures from the early fifteenth century, brought up to date politically. He presented persons and situations at once fresh and actual. Both Hal and Falstaff are denizens of Elizabethan London. Hal thinks, acts, comports himself as an heir to the Queen might have done, had she delighted her people by taking a consort and giving them a Prince of Wales; while Falstaff symbolizes, on the one hand, all the feasting and good cheer for which Eastcheap stood, and reflects, on the other, the shifts, subterfuges, and shady tricks that decayed gentlemen and soldiers were put to if they wished to keep afloat and gratify their appetites in the London underworld of the late sixteenth century. It is the former aspects of the old scoundrel that probably gave most pleasure to those who first saw him on the stage; and they are also those that we moderns are most likely to miss.

SOURCE: *The Fortunes of Falstaff* (1943).

NOTES

1. In what follows I develop a hint in Sir Arthur Quiller-Couch's *Shakespeare's Workmanship* (1918) p. 148: 'The whole of the business [in *Henry IV*] is built on the old Morality structure, imported through the Interlude. Why, it might almost be labelled, after the style of a Morality title, *Contentio inter Virtutem et Vitium de anima Principis.*'

2. *The enterlude of youth*, ed. W. Bang and R. B. McKerrow (Louvain, 1905).

3. riot = 'wanton, loose, or wasteful living; debauchery, dissipation, extravagance' (*OED*). Cf the Prodigal Son, who 'wasted his substance with riotous living' (Luke, 15: 13).

4. See C. H. Herford, *The Literary Relations between England and Germany in the Sixteenth Century* (1886) ch. III, pp. 84–95.

5. Part I, II iv 450 (508); cf l. 435 (491): 'Thou art violently carried away from grace, there is a devil haunts thee in the likeness of an old fat man.'

6. Ibid. II iv 442 (500).

7. Part II, v v 63 (66).

8. Cf Part I, I i 85: 'Riot and dishonour stain the brow / Of my young Harry'; Part II, IV iv 62: 'His headstrong riot hath no curb', IV v 135: 'When that my care could not withhold thy riots, / What wilt thou do when riot is thy care?'

9. In particular, the exact significance of the Vice is exasperatingly obscure. Cf the discussion by Sir E. K. Chambers (*Medieval Stage* (1903) II 203–5), who concludes 'that whatever the name may mean ... the character of the vice is derived from that of the domestic fool or jester'. I hazard the suggestion that it was originally the title or name of the Fool who attended upon the Lord of Misrule. See Feuillerat, *Revels of the time of Edward VI*, p. 73: 'One vyces dagger & a ladle with a bable pendante ... deliuerid to the Lorde of Mysrules foole.'

10. Fabyan's *Chronicle* (1516) p. 577.

11. C. L. Kingsford, *The First English Life of King Henry the Fifth*, (1911) pp. xlii, xliii.

12. See pp. xvi–xix, lviii–lix of my Introd. to *Richard II*, 1939 ('The New Shakespeare').

13. Kingsford, *op. cit.* p. 16.

14. Ainger tries to persuade himself that there was a tradition associating the Lollard, Oldcastle, with extreme fatness; but his editor, Beeching, is obliged to admit in a footnote that he is not aware of any references to this fatness before Shakespeare; see Alfred Ainger, *Lectures and Essays* (1905) I 126–30.

15. Cf H. N. Hudson, *Shakespeare: his Life, Art and Characters* (ed. 1888) II 83: 'It must be no ordinary companionship that yields entertainment to such a spirit [as Prince Hal's] even in his loosest moments. Whatever bad or questionable elements may mingle with his mirth, it must have some fresh and rich ingredients, some sparkling and generous flavour, to make him relish it. Anything like vulgar rowdyism cannot fail of disgusting him. His ears were never organised to that sort of music. Here then we have a sort of dramatic necessity for the character of Falstaff. To answer the purpose it was imperative that he should be just such a marvellous congregation of charms and vices as he is.' See also A. H. Tolman, *Falstaff and other Shakespearian Topics* (1925) and W. W. Lawrence, *Shakespeare's Problem Comedies* (1931) p. 64 (an interesting contrast between Hal and Falstaff, Bertram and Parolles).

16. *Poets and their Critics: Langland and Milton*, British Academy Warton Lecture (1941) pp. 29–30.

17. *Oxford Lectures* (1909) p. 256.

18. Part II, IV v 131.

E. M. W. Tillyard

HENRY IV AND THE
TUDOR EPIC (1944)

TEN plays of the First Folio have English history as their theme. They are distributed in a curious regularity. First there is a sequence of four closely linked plays: the three parts of *Henry VI* and *Richard III*. There follows an isolated play, *King John*. Then comes a second sequence of four: *Richard II*, the two parts of *Henry IV*, and *Henry V*. And there is a second isolated play, *Henry VIII*. Disregarding the two isolated plays, we can say further that the two tetralogies make a single unit. Throughout the *Henry VI*s and *Richard III* Shakespeare links the present happenings with the past. We are never allowed to forget that, as Hall said in his preface, 'King Henry the Fourth was the beginning and root of the great discord and division.' For instance, in *Henry VI, Part I*, the dying Mortimer says to his nephew, the future Duke of York:

> Henry the Fourth, grandfather to this king,
> Depos'd his nephew Richard, Edward's son,
> The first-begotten and the lawful heir
> Of Edward King, the third of that descent;
> During whose reign the Percies of the north,
> Finding his usurpation most unjust,
> Endeavour'd my advancement to the throne.

In *Henry VI, Part II*, York, explaining his titles to Salisbury and Warwick, goes back to Edward III and his sons to the lucky number of seven, whom he solemnly enumerates, and fixes the mainspring of subsequent English history in the murder of Richard II:

> Edward the Black Prince died before his father
> And left behind him Richard, his only son:

Who after Edward the Third's death reign'd as king,
Till Henry Bolingbroke, Duke of Lancaster,
The eldest son and heir of John of Gaunt,
Crown'd by the name of Henry the Fourth,
Seiz'd on the realm, depos'd the rightful king,
Sent his poor queen to France, from whence she came,
And him to Pomfret; where, as all you know,
Harmless Richard was murder'd traitorously.

In *Richard III* Earl Rivers, awaiting execution in Pomfret Castle,
links present with past by recalling the murder of Richard II:

O Pomfret, Pomfret, O thou bloody prison,
Fatal and ominous to noble peers!
Within the guilty closure of thy walls
Richard the Second here was hack'd to death
And for more slander to thy dismal seat
We give thee up our guiltless blood to drink.

These are precisely the themes which Shakespeare repeated when
he makes Henry V before Agincourt pray to God,

Not to-day, O Lord,
O not to-day, think not upon the fault
My father made in compassing the crown.
I Richard's body have interred new,
And on it have bestow'd more contrite tears
Than from it issued forced drops of blood.

Further, Shakespeare seems himself to declare the continuity of
the two tetralogies when the Chorus at the end of *Henry V*
makes a link with the next reign and refers back to the earlier
written sequence:

Henry the Sixth, in infant bands crown'd king
Of France and England, did this king succeed;
Whose state so many had the managing,
That they lost France and made his England bleed:
Which oft our stage hath shown; and for their sake
In your fair minds let this acceptance take.

The last line and a half mean: let the good success of my plays
about *Henry VI* influence you in favour of the play you have just

witnessed, *Henry V*. Shakespeare not only implies the continuity of the two tetralogies but expresses satisfaction with the one he had written in his youth. That he should, as it were, accept responsibility for all eight plays at the end of the last written one is important because it helps to confirm what even without this confirmation should be evident: that Shakespeare had in his early years disposed what for the Elizabethans was the most exciting and significant stretch of English history into a pattern; a pattern of such magnitude that it needed the space of eight plays and about ten years in the execution. The outlines of the pattern he derived from Hall, but the sustained energy of mind needed to develop them he got from his own ambitions and the example of other works, particularly of the *Mirror for Magistrates*. . . .

When he wrote his first tetralogy, Shakespeare went for intellectual support to past literature: to Hall, the Homilies, *Gorboduc*, and the *Mirror for Magistrates*. The literature of his own age was not so immediately useful; for the writers of the Chronicle Plays were his intellectual inferiors, while Spenser and Sidney and Lyly, though fully aware of the same intellectual concerns, expressed them through other means, remote from the Chronicle Play. But there are works belonging to the period of his second tetralogy which, quite apart from any influences one way or the other, have the closest intellectual kinship with Shakespeare. It is worth saying a little about these in order to show how sensitive Shakespeare was to the intellectual climate of his time, how truly he was the voice of his own age first and only through being that, the voice of humanity. Further, he may have been encouraged to a very great effort by the thought that others were trying to say the same sort of thing. The writers I refer to are Daniel and Sir John Hayward.

Before dealing with these I must point out that their historical writings, so similar to Shakespeare's History Plays, are not mere isolated works but express powerful, serious, and widely held opinions on how English history evolved: opinions which continued many years after the age of Elizabeth. A single example will make my point. Christopher Goodman in his epistle dedicatory to the *Fall of Man*, a theological work published in 1616,

has a long account of the glories of Henry VII and their relation
to the present happy state of the British monarchy. He re-
counts how God raised him up to end the tyranny of Richard III;
how he united the virtues of Henry IV, Henry V, and Henry VI
(of fox, lion, and pelican); how he made loyal the unjustly op-
pressed Cambro-Britons, from whom he was descended; how
he called his eldest son Arthur in token of his descent; how he
healed the kingdom's divisions by his marriage with the York
heiress; how wise he was in marrying his eldest daughter to a
Scottish and not to a French prince, thereby providing the
ultimate means of uniting the two kingdoms of England and
Scotland. In fact, here in 1616 we find the Tudor myth of
Polydore Vergil and Hall in full vigour; only given a new turn
by the Stuarts being included within its scope. . . .

Shakespeare's History Plays become fuller and more authoritative, more truly the national voice when we bear Daniel's
respected and careful poem in mind.[1] For his service to Shakespeare we must take into account two matters: current ideas of
the epic and contemporary attempts to give them embodiment.
First, the superiority of the epic over every other literary form
was axiomatic in the Renaissance in spite of Aristotle's opinion;
and Shakespeare could no more have escaped the doctrine than
he could have escaped the correspondence of the sun in heaven
with the king on earth. Secondly, the idea of the epic was connected with the idea of patriotism. It was correct to make your
country's history the theme of your epic; and by achieving an
epic in your own tongue you glorified that tongue and hence the
land where it was spoken. Ronsard's *Franciade* and Camoens'
Lusiads combined both functions. Granted that Shakespeare
was not a freak but like other great poets, he must have been
normally ambitious, and, if ambitious, he would wish to excel
in the epic. During the years just before he wrote his second
tetralogy and while he was writing, the Elizabethan epic was at
its height. In 1590 Sidney's *Arcadia* in its revised form was published: posthumous and incomplete. It was modelled on Helio-
dorus' *Aethiopica*, which passed in the Renaissance for an important book, an authentic prose epic. In the same year appeared

the first three books of Spenser's *Fairy Queen*, while the first
six books appeared in 1596. Spenser openly professed himself
the Elizabethan Virgil. And lastly there was Daniel's *Civil Wars*,
published in part in 1595 and added to, presumably, during the
years when Shakespeare was writing his second tetralogy. Now
these were the men whose ideas Shakespeare shared, though he
worked in a different medium. He must have wanted to be one
of them, to compete with them. They would jointly have invited
competition, but Daniel's poem, using Shakespeare's most
essential source, Hall, and treating of identical material, must
surely have put it into Shakespeare's mind to achieve in his own
medium the epic intentions translated into the above three great
fragments. Further, Daniel's failure to animate his material
thoroughly may have encouraged Shakespeare to do better.

In the first tetralogy the Tudor myth and the Morality idea
of Respublica had been the great unifying motives. In the second
the epic idea is added to them. With so grandiose an expansion
of aim we should seek great things in it and we shall find them. . . .

In an article on 'Structural Unity in the two Parts of *Henry IV*'
R. A. Law maintains that Part II is a new structure, an unpremeditated addition. I think so decidedly the other way that I
shall treat the two parts as a single play (as Dover Wilson does
in *The Fortunes of Falstaff*). Indeed Shakespeare almost goes out
of his way to advertise the continuity by keeping the action
patently incomplete at the end of the first part. In iv iv the
Archbishop of York is shown preparing for the rebellious action
which is the main political theme of Part II but which is almost
irrelevant to Part I. In v ii there is a probable reference forward
to the second part. Here Worcester refuses to inform Hotspur
of the king's generous consent to confine the battle to a duel
between Hotspur and the Prince and of his generous offer of a
pardon to all the rebels. Worcester distrusts Henry and probably
without reason. Shakespeare was thinking ironically of John of
Lancaster's offer of pardon made to the other rebels in the second
part, which, though insincere, was trusted. And the first part
ends with Henry's sending Prince John and Westmoreland to

deal with Northumberland and the Archbishop; an action which is taken up immediately in the second part. . . .

The reason why Law wishes to separate the two parts is that he thinks their motives are different. According to him Part I shows the struggle of the Prince and Hotspur culminating in the Battle of Shrewsbury, while Part II, in strong contrast, shows the Prince in the background not fighting but fought over, as in the Moralities, by the royal household and the Lord Chief Justice on the one hand and by Falstaff, the epitome of the Seven Deadly Sins, on the other. Law was right in seeing the Morality pattern in Part II, but wrong in not seeing it in Part I likewise. The struggle between the Prince and Hotspur is subordinate to a larger plan.

The structure of the two parts is indeed very similar. In the first part the Prince (who, one knows, will soon be king) is tested in the military or chivalric virtues. He has to choose, Morality-fashion, between Sloth or Vanity, to which he is drawn by his bad companions, and Chivalry, to which he is drawn by his father and his brothers. And he chooses Chivalry. The action is complicated by Hotspur and Falstaff, who stand for the excess and the defect of the military spirit, for honour exaggerated and dishonour. Thus the Prince, as well as being Magnificence in a Morality Play, is Aristotle's middle quality between two extremes. Such a combination would have been entirely natural to the Elizabethans, especially since it occurred in the second book of the *Fairy Queen*. Guyon is at once the Morality figure fought over by the Palmer and Mammon and the man who is shown the Aristotelian allegory of Excess Balance and Defect in Perissa Medina and Elissa. Near the end of the play the Prince ironically surrenders to Falstaff the credit of having killed Hotspur, thus leaving the world of arms and preparing for the motive of the second part. Here again he is tested, but in the civil virtues. He has to choose, Morality-fashion, between disorder or misrule, to which he is drawn by his bad companions, and Order or Justice (the supreme kingly virtue) to which he is drawn by his father and by his father's deputy the Lord Chief Justice. And he chooses Justice. As in the first part the Aristotelian motive occurs, but it is only touched on. After Falstaff has exchanged words with John of Lancaster about his captive Sir John Colevile, he remains on the stage to soliloquise. He calls John a 'sober-blooded boy' and blames him for not drinking sack. John is thus cold-blooded and addicted to thin potations; Falstaff himself is warm-blooded and addicted to strong drink. The Prince is the mean, cold-blooded by inheritance but warmed 'with excellent endeavour of drinking good and good store of fertile sherris'. Temperamentally he strikes the balance between the parsimony of John and the extravagance of Falstaff. He does the same too in his practice of justice. The justice of John of Lancaster in his cold-blooded treatment of the rebels verges on rigour; Falstaff has no general standard of justice at all; Henry V uses his justice moderately in the way he treats his old companions – at least by Elizabethan standards.

I will develop the structure of *Henry IV* in rather fuller detail. The action of the first part opens with high themes of crusades, chivalry, and civil war. But the Prince is not there, and his father laments that he has not got Hotspur for his son. Soon after his words we see the Prince in Falstaff's company, showing, at least superficially, his inclination to idleness and vanity. When they arrange a robbery, his inclination seems confirmed; yet he will join in with a difference, planning with Poins a joke at the expense of Falstaff. Next there is the quarrel between the Percies and the king; and yet another action is planned, this time rebellion. Hotspur is in the very centre of the plot, unlike the Prince, who is only on the edge of his; he also discloses the exaggeration of his passions. From then on the two actions take their course, with various cross-references; the Prince maintaining his negligent aloofness, Hotspur growing more exclusively absorbed. As the action of the Gadshill robbery closes, the Prince hears of the rebellion and decides to join in it, but with how serious intent we cannot say; his resolve to gain amusement by giving Falstaff a charge of foot shows that at any rate he is not exclusively serious. Vanity having had a long turn, Chivalry must now be allowed to work on the Prince. His father rebukes him, and he promises amendment and his resolution to rob Hotspur of his rebellious honours. But what is his resolution worth when soon after at the tavern in Eastcheap he enters with Peto 'marching, and Falstaff meets them playing on his truncheon like a fife'? The business of the rebellion proceeds, the rebels raising their forces and Falstaff his ragged company, till the two armies are encamped against each other at Shrewsbury. The crisis occurs in the first scene of the fifth act, where Worcester comes to the king's camp as emissary of the rebels. It is important that Falstaff should be there and that in his presence the Prince should make his choice for chivalry (to which he actually says he has been a truant) by offering to settle the whole matter personally in single fight with Hotspur. Falstaff's speech on honour, which closes the scene, rounds off the main action of the play, for among other things it is really the epitaph of his own defeat. There is no excitement about the Battle of Shrewsbury, for the result has really been settled by the Prince's decision; but it allows Falstaff to come to life again and to acquire a bogus military reputation, which will be an important motive of the second part. In spite of his choice the Prince still finds Falstaff entertaining and backs up his lying claim to have killed Hotspur. He would have perceived, as the spectator should, how the Battle of Shrewsbury reversed the episode of Gadshill. At Gadshill the Prince deprived Falstaff of the money he had stolen from the travellers; at Shrewsbury Falstaff deprived the Prince of the honour of which he had spoiled Hotspur.

In the second part the military theme of rebellion is continued, but the Prince resigns his share in it to his brother John. He has proved his worth in chivalry; he must now prove it in civil life. As in the first part he begins with appearances against him. He has indulged his inclination to vanity by providing Falstaff with a page, and he has applied military methods to civil life (as well as indulging his passions) by striking the Lord Chief Justice. But we learn this by hearsay only: as he draws nearer to the throne the Prince must be less openly given to mischief. In compensation, the opposing principles between which he has to choose are brought face to face, as they never were in the first part. Thus there are two scenes of sparring between Falstaff and the Lord

Chief Justice. During the first of these we learn that the Justice has scored a point by having advised the king to post Falstaff to John of Lancaster's army, thus separating him from the Prince. In the middle portion of the play the Morality theme is kept in suspense, while other important business is transacted. The action broadens to include many phases of English life; Falstaff indulges in adventures that have nothing to do with the Prince; the political theme of Henry IV's many troubles draws to a close. Shakespeare naturally reassures us that the main action is only in suspense: for instance in the tavern scene with Falstaff and Doll Tearsheet the Prince recollects his duties when Peto enters with the news that the king is back at Westminster awaiting news of the Yorkshire rebels. The crisis comes just before the king's death, when the Prince persuades his father that he took the crown from his father's bedside in error, not out of indecent haste to begin a riotous reign. *We* are persuaded too and know that he will accept the rule of the Lord Chief Justice, who committed him to prison, and reject his old companions. Shakespeare knits the end closely not only to the beginning of Part II but to the whole play. For instance, Falstaff recalls his opposition to his chief enemy and hence the Morality pattern by his last words as he leaves Gloucestershire to salute the new king: 'Woe to my Lord Chief Justice.' But it is Henry V's words, as he rejects Falstaff, that have the function of gathering the themes together. Henry does not merely preach at Falstaff: every unkind thing he says and every piece of moral advice he gives echo words spoken to or by Falstaff. 'Fall to thy prayers' says Henry; and we should think of his earlier words to Falstaff: 'I see a good amendment of life in thee, from praying to purse-taking' spoken in the second scene of Part I, and 'Say thy prayers and farewell' spoken in a very different tone before the Battle of Shrewsbury. When Henry says

How ill white hairs become a fool and jester,

we should remember (as Falstaff must have remembered) the Chief Justice's words, 'There is not a white hair on your face but should have his effect of gravity.' And when Henry speaks

of the grave gaping for him, we should remember Doll's remark
to Falstaff about 'patching up thine old body for heaven' and
Falstaff's reply of 'Peace, good Doll! do not speak like a death's-
head; do not bid me remember mine end.' These echoes do not
make Henry V's speech any kinder but they give it a great deal
of point.

The final ratification, through justice administered and chivalric action, of the Prince's two choices is the theme of the next
play.

But though *Henry IV* is built on the Morality pattern it is
quite without the mental conflict that often marks that pattern,
as in *Doctor Faustus*. The action begins at its very latest phase as
in *Samson Agonistes* or the *Tempest*. The Prince, though the
constant victim of psychological strain, has made up his mind
from the start, and any twinges of conscience he feels at his
delay in putting his resolutions into action are minor affairs.
And unlike Samson he is fully aware that he has made up his
mind and is quite spared Samson's pangs of doubt concerning
the final issue. In other words there is not the smallest element of
tragedy in the main action. When we recollect how powerfully
Shakespeare had pictured mental conflict in the Bastard Falconbridge we must conclude that he kept off the tragic because he
wished to do so, not because he was incapable of dealing with it
at this stage of his development. The above analogy with so
superficially different a play as the *Tempest* is strange. Yet it can
be extended. Prospero is like the Prince in having already chosen:
between reason and passion, forgiveness and revenge. And both
plays gain their effect by an unanalysable unity obtained through
the subtlest blending of different strains.

Now the Morality pattern of *Henry IV* will have mainly a
formal or historical interest, if its hero is an insignificant figure.
Of what use thrusting the Prince into the centre, if all the time
we look to left and right at Falstaff and Hotspur? The Prince as a
character has failed to please greatly, because he appeals less to
softer sentiment than Hotspur or Antony, while his imputed
Machiavellianism is quite without the glamour of the same
quality in an out-and-out villain like Richard III. Yet I believe

that current opinion is wrong and that he can hold his own with any character in *Henry IV*. Dover Wilson in his *Fortunes of Falstaff* deserves gratitude for having helped to redress the balance between the Prince and Falstaff; but as I do not see the Prince altogether as he does, I will give my version of him.

The Prince as depicted in *Henry IV* (and what follows has no reference whatever to Henry V in the play which goes by that name) is a man of large powers, Olympian loftiness, and high sophistication, who has acquired a thorough knowledge of human nature both in himself and in others. He is Shakespeare's studied picture of the kingly type: a picture to which his many previous versions of the imperfect kingly type lead up: the fulfilment of years of thought and of experiment. Shakespeare sets forth his character with great elaboration, using both direct description and self-revelation through act and word. Though all the subtlety is confined to the second, there is no important discrepancy between the two versions. And first for the Prince's character as described from without.

At the end of the first scene in which he appears the Prince assumes the function of chorus to comment on himself: in the soliloquy beginning 'I know you all'. Here he pronounces his knowledge of his present companions and of what they are worth and the studied deliberateness of his present conduct. For his kingly style there is Vernon's description of him to Hotspur,

> As full of spirit as the month of May,
> And gorgeous as the sun at midsummer,

and of the godlike ease 'like feather'd Mercury' with which he vaults fully armed onto his horse. His father recognises the comprehensiveness of his mind and passions, when, late in the second part of the play (IV iv), he exhorts his son Thomas of Clarence to cherish his place in the Prince's affections so that he may 'effect offices of mediation' between the Prince's 'greatness' and his other brothers:

> For he is gracious, if he be observ'd.
> He hath a tear for pity, and a hand
> Open as day for melting charity.

> Yet notwithstanding, being incens'd, he's flint,
> As humorous as winter and as sudden
> As flaws congealed in the spring of day.
> His temper, therefore, must be well observ'd.
> Chide him for faults and do it reverently,
> When you perceive his blood inclin'd to mirth;
> But, being moody, give him line and scope,
> Till that his passions, like a whale on ground,
> Confound themselves with working.

But the king is pessimistic. Through the very abundance of his nature the Prince is as subject to excessive evil as to excessive good –

> Most subject is the fattest soil to weeds –

and he thinks the signs are that evil will prevail. But Warwick disagrees, arguing for the power of the Prince's deliberate and sophisticated nature and his appetite for knowledge:

> The prince but studies his companions
> Like a strange tongue, wherein, to gain the language,
> 'Tis needful that the most immodest word
> Be look'd upon and learn'd; which once attain'd,
> Your highness knows, comes to no further use
> But to be known and hated. So, like gross terms,
> The prince will in the perfectness of time
> Cast off his followers; and their memory
> Shall as a pattern or a measure live,
> By which his grace must mete the lives of others,
> Turning past evils to advantages.

Something indeed has to be allowed for in all these testimonies. The Prince in his choric self-comment is concerned first of all with justifying to an Elizabethan audience this apparent degradation of royalty: hence the powerful emphasis on the rich compensation for such degradation –

> My reformation, glittering o'er my fault,
> Shall show more goodly and attract more eyes
> Than that which hath no foil to set it off.

Henry not only describes his son but gives the general version
of the princely nature, as can be seen by comparing his words
with Belarius's description of the two princes in *Cymbeline:*

> Thou divine Nature, how thyself thou blazon'st
> In these two princely boys. They are as gentle
> As zephyrs, blowing below the violet
> Not wagging his sweet head; and yet as rough,
> Their royal blood enchaf'd, as the rud'st wind
> That by the top doth take the mountain pine
> And make him stoop to the vale.

Warwick is preparing for the rejection of Falstaff as well as
describing the Prince's character. But, for all these reservations,
the speakers do combine to testify to the comprehensiveness of
the Prince's mind and the deliberateness of his actions.

External testimony, however, is of small account compared
with what is revealed by action and speech; and we must now
consider what sort of person the Prince shows himself. This
means speaking of his relations to some of the other characters,
principally Falstaff. Those who cannot stomach the rejection
of Falstaff assume that in some ways the Prince acted dishonestly,
that he made a friend of Falstaff, thus deceiving him, that he
got all he could out of him and then repudiated the debt. They
are wrong. The Prince is aloof and Olympian from the start and
never treats Falstaff any better than his dog, with whom he
condescends once in a way to have a game. It is not the Prince
who deceives, it is Falstaff who deceives himself by wishful
thinking. The most the Prince does is not to take drastic measures
to disabuse Falstaff; doing no more than repeat the unkind truths
he has never spared telling. His first speech to Falstaff ('Thou art
so fat-witted . . .') is, as well as much else, a cool statement of
what he thinks of him. And the epithet 'fat-witted', so plainly the
very opposite of the truth in most of its application, is brutally
true of Falstaff's capacity for self-deceit. The Prince has a mind
far too capacious not to see Falstaff's limitations. In the same
scene he plays with him (and with a coolness in full accord with
the rejection), when he refers to the gallows. Falstaff dislikes the

subject, but the Prince will not let him off. And when later
Falstaff tries to attach the Prince to him with 'I would to God
thou and I knew where a commodity of good names were to be
bought', he gets not the slightest encouragement. The Prince
just watches and tells the truth. And not in this place alone: it is
his habit. He also relishes the ironic act of telling the truth in the
assurance that he will thereby deceive: indeed, to such an extent
that he once takes big risks and says things which if believed he
would have been far too proud to utter. I refer to the episode in
the second part (ii ii, at the beginning). This tells us so much of
the Prince that it requires close comment.

To understand this scene, we must remember that the Prince
has not appeared since the Battle of Shrewsbury, but that he has
since been reported to have struck the Lord Chief Justice: the
burden of continued chivalrous behaviour at the court has been
too great. Thus when he begins 'Before God, I am exceeding
weary', we naturally conclude that it is of court affairs that he is
tired. Poins, with characteristic simplicity, thinks that the
Prince's tiredness is but physical and answers with (for him)
considerable brightness,

Is't come to that? I had thought weariness durst not have attached
one of so high blood.

The Prince at once begins telling the truth about himself which
he knows Poins will fail to understand or believe:

Faith, it does me; though it discolours the complexion of my
greatness to acknowledge it.

In other words, he does find court affairs exhausting; but he is
genuinely ashamed to have to admit it. Then he adds,

Doth it not show vilely in me to desire small beer?

meaning by 'small beer' such unexacting company as Poins.
Poins misunderstands again, thinking the Prince is talking of the
actual liquor, and answers again with (for him) considerable
brightness,

Why, a prince should not be so loosely studied as to remember
so weak a composition.

Misunderstood, the Prince is encouraged to be both more confidential about himself and to tell Poins just what he thinks of him.

> Belike then my appetite was not princely got: for, by my troth, I do now remember the poor creature, small beer. But indeed these humble considerations make me out of love with my greatness. What a disgrace is it to me to remember thy name! or to know thy face to-morrow! or to take note how many pair of silk stockings thou hast, viz. these, and those that were thy peach-coloured ones! or to bear the inventory of thy shirts, as, one for superfluity and another for use!

By which the Prince means that he does indeed lack the taste for royal duties and that it is much more diverting to study human nature in the shape of that small beer, Poins. And he goes on to Poins's habits of life, and his illegitimate children. Poins, simple-mindedly supposing that the Prince's weariness with his duties has no more depth than his own easy life, asks how many good young princes would talk so idly when their fathers were 'so sick as yours at this time is'. This is a new turn to the conversation and it gives the Prince an opportunity for confidences he can count on Poins not to believe or understand:

> *Prince.* Shall I tell thee one thing, Poins?
> *Poins.* Yes, faith; and let it be an excellent good thing.
> *Prince.* It shall serve among wits of no higher breeding than
> thine.

By this the Prince means that he is willing to say what he is about to say to people as thick-witted as Poins. Poins, nettled at the accusation, protests and claims that he can cope with whatever the Prince has to tell him. Whereupon the Prince unfolds to him without reserve what he feels about his father. He *is* grieved for him, but, having acquired a bad reputation, any show of grief would be interpreted by the ordinary person as sheer hypocrisy. And so saying he turns on Poins and asks if he is not right on this point of public opinion.

> *Prince.* What wouldst thou think of me, if I should weep?
> *Poins.* I would think thee a most princely hypocrite.

Delighted that Poins has not believed his confession of grief, the Prince continues:

It would be every man's thought; and thou art a blessed fellow to think as every man thinks. Never a man's thought in the world keeps the road-way better than thine. Every man would think me an hypocrite indeed.

He is at once contemptuous of Poins's perception – Poins who had enjoyed his company and who had not the excuse of the general public for knowing nothing of his mind – fascinated at the display of human nature, and relieved at having opened his mind even to some one whom in so doing he completely bewildered.

So much for the Prince's ironic detachment: the characteristic and most attractive side of his deliberate way of acting. His comprehensive nature comes out most brilliantly in an episode that is usually taken as trivial if not positively offensive: the foolery of the Prince and Poins with Francis and the other drawers in the Eastcheap tavern, before Falstaff arrives from the Gadshill robbery. It is a difficult scene, for the editors have not been able to find any meaning in it that at all enriches the play, and the sense of one or two sentences remains obscure. But the general drift should be clear from the Prince's satirical account of Hotspur killing 'six or seven dozen of Scots at a breakfast' at the end of the incident and from his own reference to 'honour' at the beginning. After what Hotspur has said already of honour earlier in the play it is impossible that there should not be a connection between Hotspur and honour here. The Prince has been drinking and making friends with the drawers of the tavern. He has won their hearts and learnt their ways:

To conclude, I am so good a proficient in one quarter of an hour that I can drink with any tinker in his own language during my life. I tell thee, Ned, thou hast lost much honour that thou wert not with me in this action.

In other words the Prince has won a signal victory and great honour in having mastered this lesson so quickly. It was Johnson who perceived that the Prince's satire on Hotspur is logically connected with what goes before and not a mere unmotivated outburst. But later critics have not given due weight to that perception. Poins and the Prince have just had their game with Francis, Poins being as ignorant of the Prince's true meaning as he was in the scene from the second part just examined.

> *Poins.* But hark ye; what cunning match have you made with this jest of the drawer? Come, what's the issue?
>
> *Prince.* I am now of all humours that have showed themselves since the old days of goodman Adam to the pupil age of this present twelve o'clock at midnight.
>
> > *Re-enter* Francis.
>
> What's o'clock, Francis?
>
> *Fran.* Anon, anon, sir. *Exit.*
>
> *Prince.* That ever this fellow should have fewer words than a parrot, and yet the son of a woman! His industry is upstairs and downstairs; his eloquence the parcel of a reckoning. I am not yet of Percy's mind, the Hotspur of the north . . .

Johnson saw that the reference to Hotspur connects with the Prince's declaration that he is 'now of all humours', the entry and exit of Francis with the Prince's comment being a mere interruption. The Prince's wealth of humours is contrasted with the single humour of Hotspur. Once again the Prince says just what he means but in words that will bear another meaning. On the face of it his words mean that he is greatly excited, being ruled simultaneously by every human motive that exists; but he also means that having learnt to understand the drawers he has mastered all the springs of human conduct, he has even then completed his education in the knowledge of men. We can now understand his earlier talk of honour he has won a more difficult action than any of Hotspur's crudely repetitive slaughters of Scotsmen. Bearing this in mind, we may perceive things at the beginning of the episode which can easily be passed over. To Poins's question where he has been the Prince answers:

With three or four loggerheads among three or four score hogsheads. I have sounded the very base string of humility. Sirrah,

I am sworn brother to a leash of drawers and can call them all by their christen names, as Tom Dick and Francis. They take it already upon their salvation that though I be but Prince of Wales yet I am the king of courtesy.

When the Prince speaks of sounding the base string of humility he uses a musical metaphor. He means in one sense that he has touched the bottom limit of condescension. But he means something more: he is the bow that has got a response from the lowest string of the instrument, namely the drawers. We are to think that he has sounded all the other human strings already: he has now completed the range of the human gamut; he is of all humours since Adam. Now the idea of the world as a complicated musical harmony was a cosmic commonplace, which would evoke all the other such commonplaces. The drawers are not only the base or lowest string of the instrument; they are the lowest link in the human portion of the chain of being and as such nearest the beasts. And that is why the Prince directly after compares them to dogs by calling them 'a leash of drawers'. At the risk of being accused of being over ingenious I will add that 'sounding' and 'base' suggest plumbing the depths of the sea as well as playing on a stringed instrument and that there is a reference to Hotspur's boast earlier in the play that he will

> dive into the bottom of the deep,
> Where fathom-line could never touch the ground,
> And pluck up drowned honour by the locks.

It is not for nothing too that the Prince says the drawers think him the king of courtesy. As I shall point out later this is precisely what Shakespeare makes him, the *cortegiano*, the fully developed man, contrasted with Hotspur, the provincial, engaging in some ways, but with a one-track mind.

There remains a puzzle. Why should the Prince, after Francis has given him his heart, and, symbol of it, his pennyworth of sugar (which he wished he could make two) join with Poins to put him through a brutal piece of horseplay? Is not Masefield justified in his bitter attack on the Prince for such brutality? The answer is first that the Prince wanted to see just how little brain

Francis had and puts him to the test, and secondly that in matters
of humanity we must not judge Shakespeare by standards of
twentieth-century humanitarianism. In an age when men watched
the antics of the mad and the sufferings of animals for sport we
must not look for too much. Further we must remember the
principle of degree. At the siege of La Rochelle costly dishes were
carried into the town under a flag of truce to a Catholic hostage
of noble birth, through a population dying of starvation; and
such discrimination between classes was taken for granted. It may
look strange when Shakespeare in one play represents the beautiful tact of Theseus in dealing with Bottom and his fellows, and
in another allows his king of courtesy to be ungrateful and brutal
to Francis. But Francis was a base string; Bottom a tenor string,
a man in his way of intelligence and substance. Francis could
not expect the same treatment. The subhuman element in the
population must have been considerable in Shakespeare's day;
that it should be treated almost like beasts was taken for granted.

From what I have said so far about the Prince it turns out that
far from being a mere dissolute lout awaiting a miraculous transformation he is from the very first a commanding character,
deliberate in act and in judgement, versed in every phase of
human nature. But he is more than that. When the drawers think
him the 'king of courtesy' they know him better than his enemy
Hotspur and even his own father do. And when Shakespeare
put the phrase in their mouths he had in mind the abstract Renaissance conception of the perfect ruler. I will discuss how this
conception enters and affects the play.

First, it is not for nothing that Elyot's *Governor* provided
Shakespeare with the episode of the Prince being committed by
the Lord Chief Justice. True, Shakespeare modified the episode
to suit his special dramatic ends; but he must have known that
Elyot held up Prince Hal, even during his father's lifetime, as
one who was able to subordinate his violent passions to the sway
of his reason. If Shakespeare got an episode from the *Governor*
concerning his hero, it is likely that in shaping him he would have
heeded the class of courtly manual to which the *Governor* belongs
and of which Castiglione's *Cortegiano* was the most famous

example. Then, there are passages in *Euphues* which are apt
enough to the Prince's case. I do not mean that Shakespeare used
them directly, but that, occurring in a conventional didactic
book on the education of a typical gentleman, they exemplify
the assumptions Shakespeare would have been forced to go on
if he meant to picture his perfect prince in accord with contemporary expectation. Here is Euphues's picture of himself
uncorrupted by the vices of Naples, as the Prince was uncorrupted
by the vices of London:

Suppose that Naples is a cankered storehouse of all strife, a
common stews for all strumpets, the sink of shame, and the very
nurse of all sin: shall it therefore follow of necessity that all that
are wooed of love should be wedded to lust; will you conclude as
it were *ex consequenti* that whosoever arriveth here shall be enticed to folly and, being enticed, of force shall be entangled? No,
no, it is the disposition of the thought that altereth the nature of
the thing. The sun shineth upon the dunghill and is not corrupted;
the diamond lieth in the fire and is not consumed; the crystal
toucheth the toad and is not poisoned; the bird Trochilus liveth
by the mouth of the crocodile and is not spoiled; a perfect wit is
never bewitched with lewdness neither enticed by lasciviousness.

And here is Lyly's version, put into the mouth of old Fidus, of
the central Renaissance doctrine of the all-round man:

And I am not so precise but that I esteem it expedient in feats of
arms and activity to employ the body as in study to waste the
mind: yet so should the one be tempered with the other as it
might seem as great a shame to be valiant and courtly without
learning as to be studious and bookish without valour.

Now the Prince in addition to skill in arms has a brilliant and
well-trained intellect, which shows itself in his talk with Falstaff,
of whose extraordinary character the recollection of a good
education is an important part. But the Prince makes not the
slightest parade of his intelligence, being apparently negligent of
it. And this leads to another mark of the courtier. This is the
quality of *sprezzatura* (which Hoby translates by *disgracing* or
recklessness and to which *nonchalance* may be a modern approxi-

mation) considered by Castiglione to be the crown of courtliness, and the opposite of the vice of *affettazione* (translated by Hoby *curiousness*):

Trovo una regula universalissima la qual mi par valer circa questo in tutte le cose umane che si facciano o dicano più che alcuna altra: e ciò é fuggir quanto più si po, e come un asperissimo e periculoso scoglio, la affettazione; e, per dir forse una nova parola, usar in ogni cosa una certa sprezzatura, che nasconda l'arte e dimonstri, ciò che si fa e dice venir fatto senza fatica e quasi senza pensarvi.*

Sprezzatura is a genuine ethical quality of the Aristotelian type: the mean between a heavy and affected carefulness and positive neglect. It is in the gift of this crowning courtly quality that the Prince so greatly excels Hotspur. He takes the Percies' rebellion with apparent lightness yet he is actually the hero in it. He gets news of it through Falstaff in the tavern scene after the Gadshill robbery. 'There's villainous news abroad' says Falstaff, and goes on to name the different rebels. The Prince, quite unmoved apparently, makes a few idle remarks about Douglas and then goes on to the game of letting Falstaff act his father. Yet at the very end of the scene he lets out his true sentiments with the casual remark, 'I'll to the court in the morning.' Alone with his father at the court, he is forced by his father's reproaches out of his nonchalance into declaring the full seriousness of his intentions. But this does not stop him in the next scene from relapsing into his apparent frivolity:

Enter the Prince *and* Peto *marching, and* Falstaff *meets them playing on his truncheon like a fife.*

This may be too frivolous for the Italianate courtliness of Castiglione, but Vernon's description of the Prince vaulting with

* I find one rule that is most general, which in this part, me think, taketh place in all things belonging to a man in word or deed, above all other. And that is to eschew as much as a man may, and as a sharp and dangerous rock, too much curiousness and (to speak a new word) to use in everything a certain disgracing to cover art withal and seem whatsoever he doth and saith to do it without pain and, as it were, not minding it. (Hoby's translation.)

effortless ease onto his horse is the perfect rendering of it. Finally there is the Prince's nonchalant surrender to Falstaff of his claim to have killed Hotspur and his good-humoured but sarcastic willingness to back up Falstaff's lie:

> For my part, if a lie may do thee grace,
> I'll gild it with the happiest terms I have.

Hotspur both offends against the principle of *sprezzatura* in his blatant acclamation of honour, and is satirised by the Prince for the extreme clumsiness of his would-be nonchalance in the very scene where the Prince takes the news of the rebellion so coolly.

> *Prince.* I am not yet of Percy's mind, the Hotspur of the north;
> he that kills me some six or seven dozen of Scots at a
> breakfast, washes his hands, and says to his wife 'Fie
> upon this quiet life! I want work.' 'O my sweet Harry,'
> says she, 'how many hast thou killed to-day?' 'Give
> my roan horse a drench,' says he; and answers 'Some
> fourteen,' an hour after; 'a trifle, a trifle.'

The Prince here is the complete, sophisticated, internationally educated courtier ridiculing the provincial boorishness of Percy, the Hotspur of the north, much like a character in Restoration Comedy ridiculing the country bumpkin.

This is not to say that Hotspur is not a most engaging barbarian; adorable in the openness and simplicity of his excesses, infectious in his vitality, and well-flavoured by his country humour. The child in him goes straight to the female heart; and when his wife loves him to distraction for all his waywardness, we are completely convinced.

To return to the Prince, as well as fashioning him on the theoretical principles of the kingly character expected by his age, Shakespeare introduces a subtlety of motivation into his mind which if it were legitimate to isolate could quite reconcile one to the habits of the motive-hunting critics of the nineteenth century.

And here let me digress on a danger to modern criticism of Shakespeare. Scholars, having learnt how well versed Shakespeare was in contemporary psychological theory, have been tempted to put the natures of his characters in terms of it rather than in terms of human probability as understood to-day. Miss Lily Campbell, for instance, sees Lear as an embodiment of wrath in old age. He may be; but, once you have thus described him, it is much too easy to assume that this new truth has quite supplanted an old error, when all it has done is to modify an existing accumulation of false and true. That the Elizabethans constructed their characters on rigid, academic, *a priori* suppositions does not mean that they were incapable of first-hand observation. Where they are strange is in the way they combine both methods, or jump from one to another. Something of this kind occurs in Spenser. He can in the same poem present the most inhuman allegorical abstractions and the terrifying and realistic and truthful picture of the jealous Britomart riding to rescue Artegal from his Amazon captor with looks bent to the ground to hide the 'fellness of her heart'. When we consider the psychological truth and complexity of the Bastard Falconbridge in *King John* and the inhumanity of the head gardener in *Richard II* we must not be surprised at any extreme of realism or the reverse or of any blending of them in the same character.

The psychological interest of the Prince's character centres in his relations with his father and his youthful apprehension of what it means to be a king. As well as making Hal all that was expected of him as a prince in the days of Elizabeth, Shakespeare entered imaginatively into the predicament in which he found himself as the destined successor of a man who had usurped the crown and thereafter worn himself out in upholding the usurpation. Shakespeare knew the legends of the Prince's wildness and he adopts them; but in so doing he justifies them psychologically by relating them to the conditions in which the Prince was brought up. Having a lively apprehension as well as a powerful nature the Prince would understand his father's troubles and face the terrible fact of the burden of kingship. Added to that was the burden of what his father expected of him. For a youth of his insight the burden was temporarily too great and he had to escape it as best he could: by evasion and revolt. But though he evades the intolerable solemnity of the court, he does no more than postpone a responsibility which fundamentally he knows and accepts. Unable under his father's eye to face being the impeccable prince, he compensates by practising the regal touch among his inferiors and proving himself the king of courtesy. His irony, though practised on so humble an object as Poins, springs from his recognition that the conscientious ruler must always be detached and isolated. His life with Falstaff is at once an escape from a present he cannot face and the incubation of a future which he will surely command. The king's relations with his son come out from his references to Hotspur and from his regrets that the two could not change places. Henry does not understand his son's richer character and mistakenly thinks Hotspur the better man. Nothing could be truer to the working of the human mind than Henry's bewilderment at his son's behaviour and his consequent attempt to explain it as heaven's punishment of his own sins.

> I know not whether God will have it so
> For some displeasing service I have done,
> That, in his secret doom, out of my blood
> He'll breed revengement and a scourge for me;
> But thou dost in thy passages of life
> Make me believe that thou art only mark'd
> For the hot vengeance and the rod of heaven
> To punish my mistreadings. Tell me else,
> Could such inordinate and low desires,
> Such poor, such bare, such lewd, such mean attempts,
> Such barren pleasures, rude society,
> As thou art match'd withal and grafted to,
> Accompany the greatness of thy blood
> And hold their level with thy princely heart?

Tell me else, says Henry; and, without pausing to ponder what the obvious and human reason might be, he issues into bitter censure of the surface facts of his son's behaviour. And he goes on to rub in Hotspur's perfections, calling him 'Mars in swaddling clothes' and enlarging picturesquely on his exploits against Douglas. The Prince, while admiring his father and sympathising with his difficulties, hates him for holding up Hotspur as a model.

This is why he speaks so satirically of Hotspur; until, having
overcome him, he can afford to let his natural generosity have
scope. When we consider how wonderfully Shakespeare pictured
the relations between mother and son in *Coriolanus*, we need not
hesitate to trace the above motives in the relations between
Henry IV and Prince Hal.

SOURCE: *Shakespeare's History Plays* (1944).

NOTE

1. *History of the Civil Wars between the Houses of York and Lancaster* (1595).

J. I. M. Stewart

THE BIRTH AND DEATH
OF FALSTAFF (1949)

CAN we find some light in which the rejection of Falstaff commends itself to our sympathies while operating wholly within the sphere of psychological realism? I must say in advance that I think the answer to be 'No'. All through the trilogy there are penetrations enough into a deeper Harry Monmouth, and the rejection can be analysed in terms of these. But, by and large, I think something profounder is operating here than Shakespeare's understanding of the son of Henry Bolingbroke. There are times in all drama when immemorial forces come into play, and with the end of Falstaff we touch once more what Professor Schücking is fond of calling the limits of Shakespearian realism. . . .

In *The Merry Wives of Windsor* Shakespeare, as it were, re-conventionalises Falstaff; turns him so decidedly into a gull and a buffoon that the thing is like a rejection in itself, or a manifesto of complete eventual disinterest in the character. Why does Shakespeare, even more cruelly than Henry, thus trample Falstaff into extinction? Because, Charlton says, Falstaff had let Shakespeare down. Falstaff revealed himself as being not what Shakespeare sought: an adequate comic hero, equipped for the true freedom of the world of comedy. And this letting Shakespeare down seems to have provoked a positive animus in the poet against his creation. Not only did it produce the 'ruthless exposure, [the] almost malicious laceration' of the *Merry Wives*; it is the reason why Falstaff was not gently dismissed on some pre-coronation deathbed, but brutally in 'a scene which has aroused more repugnance than any other in Shakespeare', and as a result of actions in Henry which are 'an offence against humanity, and an offence which dramatically never becomes a skill.' . . .

If there is anything in the argument that the major creations of a dramatist represent so many possible blendings or equilibriums of the abundant raw materials of personality which are his in virtue of his artist's nature – we must regard Charlton's argument as of considerable interest. But whatever be the dynamics of dramatic creation it would surely be extravagant to suggest that the artist's various progeny represent so many tentative essays in self-improvement – the bad shots among which he will then be prompted to 'trample into extinction'. For the dramatist is quite plainly not seeking about for an exemplar; rather he is like a pagan constructing a pantheon in which there shall be variously reflected the many sides of his own nature; and his satisfaction is simply in creation and in abundance. Thus such a psychological theory as I have hinted at affords no reason to suppose that Shakespeare would be particularly prone to turn upon Falstaff and disown or destroy him. If, on the other hand, we eschew psychology and stick to aesthetics, and with Charlton view Shakespeare's problem simply as one within the theory of comedy, we may believe indeed that Shakespeare might lose interest in Falstaff, but not that he would harry him. And it is just our sense of a persecution that has to be explained. Bradley's is still, perhaps, the best explanation: our having this sense results from Shakespeare's failing of his intention to manœuvre Falstaff into an unsympathetic light. But is there anything more to be said?

Obviously, one possibility remains. Shakespeare *succeeded* in manœuvring Falstaff into an unsympathetic light. If, with Bradley, we feel otherwise, we are being sentimental, un-Elizabethan, and disregardful of the fortunes of Falstaff as the drama develops. This is the contention of Professor Dover Wilson. . . .

What Dover Wilson is really providing here, it might be maintained, is a sort of second line of defence. As a person, or character in a drama realistically conceived, Falstaff is gradually so developed that we are not disturbed at seeing him turned off by another character carefully developed in terms of the same sort of realistic drama. But if we *are* disturbed we are to recall that this representation has a sort of abstract or allegorical quality as well, and fortify ourselves by considering 'what would have followed had the Prince chosen Vanity instead of Government, Falstaff and not the Lord Chief Justice'. Is this an illogical way of tackling the problem, arguing both. for the psychological integrity of the drama and for an overriding myth which the characters must obey? It seems to me an explanation not much contrary to the logic of the theatre, where actions and situations have frequently more than one significance, and where these significances are often at an obscure interplay. Shakespeare's characters, I think, are nearly always real human beings before they are anything else; but undeniably they *are* at times something else: they take on the simpler rôles of archetypal drama; and then there will be 'edges' (as the painters say) between generic charac-ter and psychological portraiture which the dramatist must cope with, using what finesse he can. It seems to me, therefore, that Dover Wilson gets furthest with the problem; and I am only concerned to wonder whether a further stone or two may yet be added to the edifice he has raised.

Two points would seem to be significant. If Shakespeare does indeed succeed in making the rejection palatable to persons adequately aware of traditional matters lying behind the play, it is yet in the theatre that he does so, for that the thing continues to *read* uncomfortably after all that Dover Wilson has to say I believe there will be few to deny. What does this mean? It means that although Shakespeare doubtless relied on certain con-temporary attitudes to Riot and the like, he relied even more on something perennially generated in the consciousness or dis-position of an audience in a theatre – whether they belong to Elizabethan times or to our own. And it is here that I would knit the debate on Falstaff to the theme of the present book. For what I have tried to urge is simply this: that in the interpretation of Shakespeare a study of the psychology of poetic drama (which leads us to understand his *medium*) is at least as important as a study of the contemporary climate of opinion (which gives simply *conditions* under which he worked).

The second point concerns the emphatic and wonderful account in *Henry V* of the death of Falstaff. It is all very well for Dover Wilson to point to the promise of more Falstaff made in the Epilogue to *Henry IV*, *Part II* and infer that the subsequent death was a matter of mere theatrical convenience. But surely the Epilogue to *Henry IV* is dramatically altogether less authoritative than the account of Falstaff's passing in the later play; and what Shakespeare there wrote appears to me (because it is so wonderful) much less like an expedient dictated by changes in personnel in his company than the issue of his reflections on the inner significance of what had happened at the close of the earlier drama. 'The King has kild his heart,' says Mistress Quickly as Falstaff lies dying. 'The King hath run bad humors on the Knight,' says Nym, and Pistol at once responds: '*Nym*, thou hast spoke the right, his heart is fracted and corroborate.' None of these worthies would cut much of a figure in a witness-box; nevertheless there is no mistaking the dramatic function of the three consenting voices. The truth of the matter is summed here; there follows the new king's dexterous, necessary but none too pleasant entrapping of Cambridge, Scroope and Gray; then comes the tremendous account of Falstaff's end – and after that we are set for Agincourt and the regeneration and triumph of England. It is of set purpose, then, that the rejection of Falstaff is so resounding, so like a killing. And the reverberation of that purpose sounds here in *Henry V*. What is it? There is an allegorical purpose, Dover Wilson says, and with this I agree. But I think, too, that among the 'notions and associations . . . gone out of mind' embodied in this 'composite myth which had been centuries amaking' there conceivably lies something deeper, something which belongs equally with drama and with magic.

When Shakespeare makes Falstaff die 'ev'n just betweene Twelve and One, ev'n at the turning o' th' Tyde', he is touching a superstition, immemorial not only along the east coast of England from Northumberland to Kent but in many other parts of the world too – one shared by Dickens's Mr Peggotty (who speaks of it expressly) and the Haidas on the Pacific coast of North America.[1] But there is more of magic about Falstaff than this; and Dover Wilson, whom the editing of Shakespeare has schooled in a fine awareness of the reverberations of English words, is more than once well on the scent. 'How doth the Martlemas, your Master?' Poins asks Bardolph. And Dover Wilson comments:

Martlemas, or the feast of St Martin, on 11 November, was in those days of scarce fodder the season at which most of the beasts had to be killed off and salted for the winter, and therefore the season for great banquets of fresh meat. Thus it had been for centuries, long before the coming of Christianity. In calling him a 'Martlemas' Poins is at once likening Falstaff's enormous proportions to the prodigality of fresh-killed meat which the feast brought, and acclaiming his identity with Riot and Festivity in general.

Falstaff, in fact, is the 'sweet beef', 'the roasted Manning-tree ox with the pudding in his belly', who reigns supreme on the board of the Boar's Head in Eastcheap – 'a London tavern . . . almost certainly even better known for good food than for good drink'. There is thus from the first a symbolical side to his vast and genuine individuality; and again and again the imagery in which he is described likens him to a whole larder of 'fat meat':

'Call in Ribs, call in Tallow' is Hal's cue for Falstaff's entry in the first great Boar's Head scene; and what summons to the choicest feast in comedy could be more apt? For there is the noblest of English dishes straightaway: Sir John as roast Sir Loin-of-Beef, gravy and all.

Is it not – I find myself asking – as if the 'brawn', Sir John, 'the sow that hath overwhelmed all her litter but one', were some vast creature singled out from the herd and dedicated to a high festival indeed? But such festivals commemorate more than the need to reduce stock against a winter season. They commemorate a whole mythology of the cycle of the year, and of sacrifices offered to secure a new fertility in the earth.

Now, anthropologists are always telling us of countries gone waste and barren under the rule of an old, impotent and guilty king, who must be ritually slain and supplanted by his son or another before the saving rains can come bringing purification and regeneration to the land.[2] Is not Henry IV in precisely the situation of this king? Dover Wilson avers that it is so, without any thought of magical implication:

> ... his reign and all his actions are overhung with the conscious-ness ... of personal guilt ... a fact that Shakespeare never misses an opportunity of underlining. ... We see him first at the begin-ning of act 3 crushed beneath the disease that afflicts his body and the no less grievous diseases that make foul the body of his kingdom.

Perhaps, then, we glimpse here a further reason why the rejection of Falstaff is inevitable – not merely traditionally and moralistically inevitable but symbolically inevitable as well. And this may be why, when in the theatre, we do not really rebel against the rejection; why we find a fitness too in its being sudden and catastrophic. As long as we are in the grip of drama it is profoundly fit that Hal, turning king and clergyman at once, should run bad humours on the knight, should kill his heart. For the killing carries something of the ritual suggestion, the obscure *pathos*, of death in tragedy.

I suggest that Hal, by a displacement common enough in the evolution of ritual, kills Falstaff instead of killing the king, his father. In a sense Falstaff *is* his father; certainly he is a 'father-substitute' in the psychologist's word; and this makes the theory of a vicarious sacrifice the more colourable. All through the play there is a strong implicit parallelism between Henry Bolingbroke and his policies and Falstaff and *his* policies; and at one point in the play the two fathers actually, as it were, fuse (like Leonardo's two mothers in his paintings of the Virgin and St Anne), and in the Boar's Head tavern King Falstaff sits on his throne while his son Prince Henry kneels before him. And Falstaff, in standing for the old king, symbolises all the accumulated sin of the reign, all the consequent sterility of the land. But the young king draws his knife at the altar – and the heart of that grey iniquity, that father ruffian, is as fracted and corroborate as Pistol avers. Falstaff's rejection and death are very sad, but Sir James Frazer would have classed them with the Periodic Expulsion of Evils in a Material Vehicle, and discerned beneath the skin of Shakespeare's audience true brothers of the people of Leti, Moa and Lakor.[3]

If this addition of another buried significance to the composite myth of Hal and Falstaff should seem extravagant, or an injudicious striving after Morgann's 'lightness of air', let it be remembered that drama, like religious ritual, plays upon atavic impulses of the mind. All true drama penetrates through representative fiction to the condition of myth. And Falstaff is in the end the dethroned and sacrificed king, the scapegoat as well as the sweet beef. For Falstaff, so Bacchic, so splendidly with the Maenads Doll and Mistress Quickly a creature of the wine-cart and the cymbal, so fit a sacrifice (as Hal early discerns) to lard the lean, the barren earth, is of that primitive and magical world upon which all art, even if with a profound unconsciousness, draws.

SOURCE: *Character and Motive in Shakespeare* (1949).

NOTES

1. The superstition is noticed by Sir J. G. Frazer, *The Golden Bough* (abridged ed., 1922) p. 35.
2. See F. M. Cornford, *The Origin of Attic Comedy* (1914) chap. iv, 'Some Types of Dramatic Fertility Ritual', sec. 28, 'The Young Man and the Old King'.
3. For Leti, Moa and Lakor see Frazer, op. cit. p. 566. I hope it will be clear that what I am here concerned with is the *multiple* significance of the Falstaff story. To assert that Falstaff 'is' the sacrificial object in a fertility ritual is not in the least to deny that he 'is' (a good deal less remotely indeed) the Riot of a Morality; nor, again, that he 'is' a latent personality of Shakespeare's; nor, yet again, that he 'is' an aspect of the human psyche in general. For notice of one interpretation in terms

of this last idea I am indebted to Mr Lionel Trilling's *Freud and Litera-ture*, which cites an essay by Dr Franz Alexander not available to me as these sheets are passing through the press.

Dr Alexander undertakes nothing more than to say that in the development of Prince Hal we see the classic struggle of the ego to come to normal adjustment, beginning with the rebellion against the father, going on to the conquest of the super-ego (Hotspur, with his rigid notions of honour and glory), then to the conquest of the *id* (Falstaff, with his anarchic self-indulgence), then to the identification with the father (the crown scene) and the assumption of mature responsibility. An analysis of this sort is not momentous and not exclusive of other meanings.

The last sentence assuredly applies to the various significances that I have endeavoured to educe in the present book. Mr Trilling's essay (*Horizon* (Sept 1947) XVI 92) is a most valuable treatment of its subject and may usefully be compared with Mr C. S. Lewis's *Psycho-Analysis and Literary Criticism* (*Essays and Studies*, XXVII (1941)).

William Empson

FALSTAFF AND
MR DOVER WILSON (1953)

I THINK that the whole Falstaff series needs to be looked at in terms of Dramatic Ambiguity, before one can understand what was happening in the contemporary audience; and I think that if this is done the various problems about Falstaff and Prince Hal, so long discussed, are in essence solved. Nor would this approach seem strange to Mr Dover Wilson, who has done much the most interesting recent work on the subject. Most of this essay has the air of an attack on him, but my complaints are supposed to show cases where he has slipped back into taking sides between two viewpoints instead of letting both be real. Slipped back, because on at least one occasion he uses explicitly and firmly the principle I want to recommend; and perhaps I will look more plausible if I begin with that illustration of it.

The question whether Falstaff is a coward may be said to have started the whole snowball of modern Shakespearean criticism; it was the chief topic of Morgann's essay nearly two hundred years ago, the first time a psychological paradox was dug out of a Shakespeare text. Mr Dover Wilson, discussing the plot about the robbery in the first three scenes where we meet Falstaff, says that the question whether Falstaff sees through the plot against him, and if so at what point he sees through it – for instance, whether he runs away from the Prince on purpose or only tells increasingly grotesque lies to him afterwards on purpose – is *meant* to be a puzzle, one that the audience are challenged to exercise their wits over; and that this had an important practical effect (it is not a matter of deep intellectual subtlety of course) because you would pay to see the play again with your curiosity undiminished. The whole joke of the great rogue is that *you* can't see through him, any more than the Prince could. I think that Mr Dover Wilson's analysis of the text here is the final word about the question, because he shows that you aren't meant to find anything more; the dramatic effect simply *is* the doubt, and very satisfying too. Mr Dover Wilson is a rich mine of interesting points, and it seems rather parasitic of me to keep on repeating them as weapons against him; but it seems important to urge that the method he has established here should be tried out on adjoining cases.

However, I recognize that this approach is liable to become tiresomely intellectualistic; a man who takes it into his head that he is too smart to look for the answer, on one of these points, because he knows the author means to cheat him, is liable to miss getting any real experience from the play. Besides, the actor and producer have to work out their own 'conception' of Falstaff, in each case, and are sometimes felt to have produced an interesting or 'original' one; it would be fatuous for the theoretical critic to say that they are merely deluding themselves, because there isn't any such thing. I do not mean that; the dramatic ambiguity is the source of these new interpretations, the reason why you can go on finding new ones, the reason why the effect is so rich. And of course there must be a basic theme which the contradictions of the play are dramatizing, which some interpretations handle better than others; after planting my citadel on the high ground of the Absolute Void, I still feel at liberty to fight in the plains against Mr Dover Wilson at various points of his detailed interpretation. But this way of putting it is still too glib. The basic argument of Mr Dover Wilson is that the plays ought to be taken to mean what the first audiences made of them (and they took not merely a moral but a very practical view of the importance of social order and a good king). I agree with all of that, and merely answer that the reaction of an audience is not such a simple object as he presumed. No doubt he succeeds in isolating what the first audiences would find obvious; but we may still believe that other forces had to be at work behind Falstaff, both in the author and the audiences which he understood, to make this figure as Titanic as we agree to find him;

nor need we plunge for them deep into the Unconsciousness. The plays were an enormous hit, appealing to a great variety of people, not all of them very high-minded, one would think. Obviously a certain amount of 'tact' was needed, of a straightforward kind, to swing the whole of this audience into accepting the different stages of the plot. To bring out examples of this tact as evidence of the author's single intention, or of a single judgment which he wanted to impose on the audience, seems to me naïve. So far from that, I think that on several occasions he was riding remarkably near the edge; a bit breathtaking it may have been, to certain members of the first audiences.

One cannot help feeling some doubt when Mr Dover Wilson insists that Hal was never a 'sinner', only a bit wild; especially when it becomes rather doubtful, as he goes on, what even the wildness may have consisted in. Not sex, we gather; it seems only old men like Falstaff go wrong like that. The same applies to drunkenness. Even the bishops in *Henry V*, Mr Dover Wilson maintains, do not say that he has been converted, only that he has begun working hard (actually they say more); and even his father in reproaching him only speaks of sins in others which his wildness might encourage. Robbery, the reader is now to decide, he could not possibly have committed; to suppose that he even envisaged such a thing is to misread the whole play.

It is true that the early scenes of *Henry IV*, *Part I* can be read as Mr Dover Wilson does. I ought to admit this the more prominently because I said in my book *Pastoral* that 'we hear no more' about the Prince's claim that he will repay the stolen money, which we do (III iv 177). But after admitting this mistake I claim all the more that the dramatic effect is inherently ambiguous. Mr Dover Wilson points out that we ought to consider the order of events on the stage, how the thing is planned to impress you; I warmly agree, but he only uses this rule for his own purpose. It is plain, surely, that we are put in doubt whether the Prince is a thief or not, at any rate in the early scenes; if you got a strong enough impression from those scenes that he was one, you would only regard the later return of the money as a last-minute escape from a major scandal. No doubt, if you felt sure from the start that he couldn't really be one, the return of the money would act as laughing the whole thing off; but even so, the dramatist has put you through a bit of uncertainty about what he will ask you to believe. So to speak, an escape from a scandal is what happens to the audience, whether it happened to the Prince or not; and a dramatic structure of this kind assumes that at least some of the audience do not know the answer beforehand. It is therefore ridiculous, I submit, for a critic to argue heatedly that he has discovered the answer by a subtle analysis of the text. Such a critic, however, could of course, turn round on me and say I am wrong to suppose it is 'this kind of dramatic structure'; so far from that, he would say, he has shown the modern actor and producer how to make the play intelligible and coherent even to a fresh audience from the beginning. I therefore need to join in his labors, instead of calling them ridiculous; I need to show that the text is so arranged that the uncertainty can still not be dispelled even after the most careful study.

Among the first words of Falstaff, who is then alone with the Prince, he says 'when thou art King, let not us that are squires of the night's body be called thieves of the day's beauty' and so on, and *us* is quite positively accepted by the Prince in his reply (whether for a joke or not) as including himself: 'the fortune of us that are the moon's men doth ebb and flow like the sea' and so on. Of course I am not pretending that this proves he is a thief; I give it as an example of the way the dramatist starts by making us think he *may* be a thief. The next point, as the jokes turn over, is a grave appeal from Falstaff: 'Do not thou, when thou art King, hang a thief.' Falstaff gets much of his fun out of a parody of moral advice, especially in these earlier scenes, and the point here must be that the Prince has no right to hang a thief because he is one himself. His reply (a very sufficient one) is that Falstaff will do it. Falstaff then inverts the obvious by upbraiding the Prince for leading him astray; he threatens to reform, and the Prince's answer is, 'Where shall we take a purse tomorrow, Jack?' Falstaff accepts this as if they are old partners in robbery, and is only concerned to defend his courage – 'Zounds, where thou wilt, lad, I'll make one, an I do not, call me villain and baffle me.' Poins now enters and announces a scheme for robbery, and when the Prince is asked if he will join he speaks as if the idea was absurdly outside his way of life – 'Who, I? rob? I a thief? Not I, by my faith.' Falstaff has already assumed that the Prince knows this plan is being prepared ('Poins! Now we shall know if Gadshill hath set a match'), and Poins is the Prince's own gentleman-in-waiting; however, Mr Dover Wilson naturally makes the most of this brief retort:

> The proposal that the Prince is to take part in the highway robbery is received at first with something like indignation, even with a touch of haughtiness, and only consented to when Poins intimates, by nods and winks behind Falstaff's back, that he is planning to make a practical joke of it.

The nods and winks are invented by the critic, of course (and printed in his text of the play), but they seem plausible enough; indeed the line, 'Well, then, once in my days I'll be a madcap,' reads like a rather coarse attempt to keep the respectable part of the audience from being too shocked. They are welcome to decide that the Prince is not really a thief after all. The point I want to make is that another part of the audience is still quite free to think he is one; indeed, this pretence of innocence followed immediately by acceptance (followed by further riddles) is just the way Falstaff talks himself. Poins then arranges the plot against Falstaff with the Prince, and finally the Prince makes his famous soliloquy, claiming that his present behavior is the best way to get himself admired later on. I do not think that the words suggest he is doing nothing worse than play practical jokes on low characters. To be sure, the 'base contagious clouds', the 'foul and ugly mists', only *seem* to strangle the sun; you can still think the Prince innocent here; and he only describes his own behavior as 'loose'. But then we hear about a reformation of a fault, and about an offence which must apparently be redeemed (though literally it is only time which must be redeemed). It seems to me that the balance is still being kept; you can decide with relief that surely after this he can't be a thief, or you can feel, if you prefer, he has practically admitted that for the present he is one.

The more usual question about this soliloquy is whether it shows the Prince as 'callous and hypocritical', determined to betray his friends. Naturally Mr Dover Wilson argues that it does not, because 'it was a convention to convey information to the audience about the general drift of the play, much as a prologue did', and in any case at this stage of the play 'we ought not to be feeling that Falstaff deserves any consideration whatever'. I think this carries the 'sequence' principle rather too far, and most people would know the 'general drift' before they came; but I don't deny, of course, that the placing of this soliloquy is meant to establish Hal as the future hero as firmly as possible. Even so, I do not see that it does anything (whether regarded as a 'convention' or not) to evade the obvious moral reflection, obvious not only to the more moralizing part of the audience but to all of it, that this kind of man made a very unreliable friend. Surely the Elizabethans could follow this simple duality of feeling without getting mixed; it is inevitable that if you enjoy Falstaff you feel a grudge against the eventual swing-over of Hal, even though you agree that the broad plot couldn't be different. The real problems about the rejection do not arise here; we have no reason to presume it will come as a painful shock to his present friends (though 'falsify men's hopes' may be a secret mark of the author's plan). I think a fair amount can be deduced about Shakespeare's own feelings for this kind of condescending patron, but in any case it was a commonplace of his period that the friendships of great men very often were unreliable. The whole thing seems to me in the sunlight, and for that matter the fundamental machinery seems rather crude, and perhaps it had to be to carry such a powerful conflict of judgment. There does not seem much for later critics to disagree about.

Mr Dover Wilson, however, feels that there is, because he wants to build up Hal as a high-minded creature of delicate sensibility. A brief scene with Poins (*Henry IV, Part II*, II ii) is made important for this purpose. We are told about Hal that:

The kind of reserve that springs from absence of self-regard is in point of fact one of his principal characteristics, and such a feature is difficult to represent in dialogue. . . . We have no right to assume that Hal is heartless because he does not, like Richard II, wear his heart on his sleeve. . . . Why not . . . give him a friend like Horatio to reveal himself? . . . Shakespeare gives him Poins, and the discovery of the worthlessness of this friend is the subject of one of the most moving and revealing scenes in which the Prince figures. In view of all this, to assert as Bradley does that Hal is incapable of tenderness or affection except towards members of his own family is surely a quite unwarranted assumption.

Hal begins this scene by treating Poins with insolence, as one of the butts for his habit of contempt, and Poins answers (they have just got back from Wales as part of the civil war):

How ill it follows, after you have laboured so hard, you should talk so idly! Tell me, how many good young princes would do so, their fathers being so sick as yours at this time is?

I can't see that this is an offensive retort; he is expected to keep his end up, and there is not even an obvious insinuation that the Prince wants his father dead – he may be being advised to recover favor. No doubt it could be acted with an offensive leer, but the usual tone in these scenes is merely a rough jeering. The Prince, however, becomes offended and says that his heart bleeds inwardly at his father's illness, but that he can't show it because he keeps bad company such as Poins. It seems a fair answer to this challenge when Poins says he would indeed think the Prince a hypocrite to show sorrow at the prospect of inheriting, 'because you have been so lewd, and so much engrossed to Falstaff'. 'And to thee,' says the gay Prince with his usual brutality. Now of course I agree that the scene is meant to tell the audience that Hal is starting to repent of his bad habits; it could not be more straightforward. It could be acted with a moody sorrow, but I don't think it need be; the main fact is that he is physically tired. But why are we supposed to think that he is 'failed' by his friend in a pathetic manner, or shows affection to anyone not a member of his own family? The whole truth to life of this little scene, in

its surly way, is to be so bare; it does nothing to put Poins in the
wrong, and indeed lets him show a fair amount of dignity and
good-humour; the Prince's feelings are dragging him away from
his old companions, and no new fault of theirs needs to be shown.
Surely Poins has much more difficulty than Hal in expressing
delicate sentiments here; if he tried to condole with the Prince
he would be rebuffed more harshly than ever. A production
which made the Prince disillusioned at not getting sympathy
would have to cut most of the words.

A more important claim of Mr Dover Wilson for Hal is that
it is extremely generous of him to let Falstaff get all the credit for
killing Hotspur, especially because if Hal claimed his due he
might become more acceptable to his father. We are also told
that the sudden fame thus acquired by the previously unknown
Falstaff goes to his head and is the cause of the gradual nemesis
which gathers throughout Part II. This seems to me a valuable
idea, unlike the special pleading about the Poins scene, which
would mislead an actor. The trouble about the death of Hotspur,
it seems to me, is that the story is deliberately left ambiguous,
and we should not allow a learned argument to impose a one-
sided answer. The lyrical language of Mr Dover Wilson about
the native magnanimity and high courtesy of the Prince, 'which
would seem of the very essence of nobility to the Elizabethans',
really does I think bring out part of the intended stage effect
at the end of Part I, though the text is silent. The question is
whether it is meant to go on reverberating all through Part II.
To do the right thing at a dramatic moment is very different
from going on telling an absurd and inconvenient lie indefinitely.
Mr Dover Wilson's view of the matter, I think, really would be
picked on by spectators who preferred it that way, but other
spectators could find quite different pointers. I do not want,
therefore, to refute his view but to show that it is only one
alternative, and I thus give myself an easy task.

The claim of Falstaff to have killed Hotspur is made to Prince
Henry in the presence of Prince John, who says, 'This is the
strangest tale that e'er I heard.' Prince Henry says:

> This is the strangest fellow, brother John.
> Come, bring your luggage nobly on your back.
> For my part, if a lie may do thee grace,
> I'll gild it with the happiest terms I have.

In Mr Dover Wilson's edition, of course, 'aside to Falstaff' has
to introduce the last two lines. But I don't see Hal nipping about
the stage to avoid being overheard by John, whom he despises;
his business here is to stand midcenter and utter fine sentiments
loud and bold. Just what lie was told, and what John made of it,
we don't hear. It seems to me that Part II begins by throwing a
lot of confusion into the matter, and that Mr Dover Wilson
merely selects points that suit him. At the start of the play three
messengers come to the rebel Northumberland; the first with
good news – the Prince has been killed outright and '(his)
brawn,* the hulk Sir John' taken prisoner by Hotspur. Five
other people are mentioned, but it is assumed that Falstaff was
worth attention before he was believed to have killed Hotspur,
and even that Hotspur had done well to capture him. The
second messenger says that Hotspur is dead, the third that he was
killed by the Prince. Mr Dover Wilson admits this shows that
the facts of his death 'had been observed by at least one man', but
adds that no other witness is quoted. But nobody at all, in Part II,
says that Falstaff killed Hotspur. The King himself appears not
to know that the Prince did it, says Mr Dover Wilson; but the
King has other things to talk about whenever we see him, and
never implies that Hal can't fight. 'The Lord Chief Justice
grudgingly praises Falstaff's day's service at Shrewsbury,' says
Mr Dover Wilson, so he must think Falstaff killed Hotspur. He
says that day's service 'hath a little gilded o'er your night's
exploit at Gadshill', which hardly fits a personal triumph over
the chief enemy hero. Certainly people think he fought well

---

* *Brawn* suggests the wild boar, a strong and savage creature,
honorable to hunt, though the fatted hog is not quite out of view. A
similar ambivalence can be felt I think in the incessant metaphors of
heavy meat-eating around Falstaff compared to 'one halfpennyworth
of bread to this intolerable deal of sack', where it is assumed (already
in Part I) that the drunkard has no appetite.

somehow (perhaps because he got his troop killed to keep their pay); the joke of this is driven home in Part II when Coleville surrenders to him on merely hearing his name. But even Coleville does not say, what would be so natural an excuse, that he is surrendering to the man who killed Hotspur. What is more, Falstaff himself does not once say it, and he is not prone to hide his claims. Surely the solution of this puzzle is clear; Shakespeare is deliberately *not* telling us the answer, so that an ingenious argument which forces an answer out of the text only misrepresents his intention.

Consider how difficult it is for a dramatist, especially with a mass audience, to run a second play on the mere assumption that everybody in the audience knows the first one. On Mr Dover Wilson's view, they are assumed to know that all the characters in Part II hold a wrong belief derived from Part I, although Part II begins by letting a man express the right belief and never once lets anybody express the wrong belief. This is incredible. But if some of the audience are expected to *wonder* how the Prince's bit of chivalry worked out, their interest is not rebuffed; they may observe like Mr Dover Wilson that Falstaff is getting above himself. In the main the theme is simply dropped; perhaps because some of the audience would not like the Prince to be so deeply in cahoots with Falstaff, perhaps because Shakespeare did not care to make the Prince so generous, but chiefly because it would only clutter up the new play, which had other material. The puzzle is not beyond resolution; it is natural to guess (if you worry about it) that the Prince waited till the truth came out and then said that Falstaff had been useful to him at the time – thus the claim of Falstaff did not appear a mere lie after the Prince had gilded it in his happiest terms, but had to be modified. This would have been the only sensible lie for the Prince to tell, and indeed Mr Dover Wilson hints at it when he says people thought Falstaff had 'slain, *or helped to slay*' Hotspur, which has no source in the text. You may now feel that I have made a lot of unnecessary fuss, when it turns out that I agree with Mr Dover Wilson; but I think that his treatment ignores the dramatic set-up and the variety of views possible in the audience.

The next step in his argument is that Falstaff only becomes 'a person of consideration in the army' because of the Prince's lies (whatever they were) about the Battle of Shrewsbury; 'in Part I he is Jack Falstaff with his familiars; in Part II he is Sir John with all Europe.' This is why he over-reaches himself; the final effect of the Prince's generosity at the end of Part I is that he is forced to reject Falstaff at the end of Part II. Now, on the general principle that one should accept all theories, however contradictory, which add to the total effect, this must certainly be accepted; it pulls the whole sequence together. But it must not be carried so far as to make Falstaff 'nobody' at the beginning, because that would spoil another effect, equally important for many of the audience. Falstaff is the first major joke by the English against their class system; he is a picture of how badly you can behave, and still get away with it, if you are a gentleman – a mere common rogue would not have been nearly so funny. As to the question of fact, of course, we are told he is a knight the first time he appears, and it is natural to presume he got knighted through influence; Shallow eventually lets drop that he started his career as page to the Duke of Norfolk. The Stage History section of Mr Dover Wilson's edition has some interesting hints, from both the eighteenth and twentieth centuries, to show that he has always been expected to be a gentleman; the dissentient voice is from a nineteenth-century American actor, who wrote a pamphlet claiming that he was right *not* to make the old brute a gentleman. Rather in the same way, I remember some American critic complaining that Evelyn Waugh shows an offensive snobbery about Captain Grimes, since he despises him merely for not being a real gentleman. So far from that, the whole joke about Grimes is that he is an undeniable public school man, and therefore his invariably appalling behavior must always be retrieved, though it always comes as a great shock to the other characters. This English family joke, as from inside an accepted class system, may well not appeal to Americans, but in the case of Falstaff I think English critics have rather tended to wince away from it too.

Maintaining that he was nobody till after the Battle of Shrewsbury, Mr Dover Wilson has to explain his presence at the council of commanders just before it, and says it was simply because Shakespeare needed him on the stage. This lame argument would not apply to the Elizabethan stage. At the actual council he only makes one unneeded joke; he is needed for talk with the Prince afterwards, in what our texts call the same scene, but the back curtain will already have closed on the royal coat-of-arms and so forth; Falstaff could simply walk onto the apron. He is at the council because that adds to the joke about him, or rather because some of the audience will think so. However, it is clear anyhow that the Prince brought him; the battle itself gives a more striking case of this line of argument from Mr Dover Wilson. A. C. Bradley had argued that Falstaff shows courage by hanging around in the battle till the Prince kills Hotspur, and the reply has to be: 'To establish his false claim to the slaying of Hotspur he must be brought into the thick of the fight.' Surely this makes Shakespeare a much less resourceful dramatist than he is; even I could think of a funny device to trick the great coward into his great opportunity, after he had imagined he had found a safe place. Shakespeare does not 'have to' give false impressions; and what we do gather from Falstaff is that he regards a battle as a major occasion for misusing his social position (e.g. 'God be thanked for these rebels; they offend none but the virtuous'). I don't deny that those spectators who would resent the social satire are given an opportunity to evade it, and take him as the 'cowardly swashbuckler' of the Latin tradition; but they aren't given very much. Over the crux at the start of Part II, I think, the indignant special pleading of Mr Dover Wilson reaches actual absurdity:

The special mention of [Falstaff's] capture in the false report of the battle that first reaches the ears of Northumberland . . . are all accounted for by the indecent stab which the dastard gives the corpse of Hotspur as it lies stricken on the bleeding field.

To be sure, Falstaff 'goes a bit too far' when he does that; it is his role. (By the way, the reason why we feel it so strongly is that the rebels have been made to look rather better than the royal family.) But really, how are we to imagine that the sight of Falstaff stabbing a recumbent Hotspur (in another play) made a messenger report that Hotspur was safe and Falstaff captured? No doubt almost any confusion can happen to a real messenger, but how can a dramatist expect his successive audiences to invent the extraordinary subtle confusion imputed here? The fact is, surely, that these pointers represent Falstaff as already a prominent figure, though an embarrassingly scandalous one; they could easily be ignored by members of the audience who were using a different line of assumption, but they would give great assurance to members who started with this one.

The interesting thing here, I think, is that Mr Dover Wilson is partly right; but in the next case I think he is simply wrong. Nobody, whichever way up he took Falstaff, was meant to think him too abject a coward even to be able to bluster. Mr Dover Wilson refuses to let him drive Pistol out of the inn; chiefly, I suppose, because his theory needs Falstaff to be degenerating in Part II. At 11 iv 185 Doll wants Pistol thrown out, so Falstaff says 'Quoit him down, Bardolph,' and Bardolph says 'Come, get you downstairs,' but Pistol makes a threatening harangue; Falstaff then asks for his rapier (196) and himself says 'Get you downstairs,' while Doll says 'I pray thee, Jack, do not draw'; then the Hostess makes a fuss about 'naked weapons', then Doll says 'Jack, be quiet, the rascal's gone. Ah, you whoreson little valiant villain, you,' then the Hostess says 'Are you not hurt i' the groin? Methought a' made a shrewd thrust at your belly'; Falstaff says to Bardolph, who must return, 'Have you turned him out of doors?' and Bardolph says 'Yea, sir, The rascal's drunk, you have hurt him, sir, in the shoulder'; Falstaff says 'A rascal! To brave me!' and Doll in the course of a fond speech says he is as valorous as Hector of Troy. It is unusual to have to copy out so much text to answer a commentator. This is the textual evidence on which Mr Dover Wilson decides that Falstaff dared not fight Pistol at all, and he actually prints as part of the play two stage directions saying that Bardolph has got to do all the work. It must be about the most farcical struggle against the obvious intentions of an author that a modern scholarly editor has ever put up.

This view of Falstaff is supported by a theory about Doll, rather obscure to me: 'We have, I think, to look forward to nineteenth-century French literature to find a match for this study of mingled sentimentality and brutal insentience, characteristic of the prostitute class.' I thought at first, not going further afield than *The Beggar's Opera*, that this meant some criminal plot for gain; but the audience could not know of it (this is the first we hear of Pistol), and I suppose it means that she likes watching fighting. The argument, therefore, is that she jeers at Falstaff for shirking the fight she had encouraged, so this proves he didn't fight. After Pistol has gone he boasts, 'the rogue fled from me like quicksilver' and she answers (on his knee) 'I'faith, and thou followedst him like a church.' Mr Dover Wilson has to push 'aside' into the text before this remark and 'sits on his knee' afterwards, before he can let it go on with her praise of his courage. She does not hide her remarks from him anywhere else. I take it she means that he followed like a massive worthy object, though too fat to do it fast; to find sadism here seems to me wilful. The same trick is used against Mrs Quickly in *Henry V*, II i 36, over the textual crux 'if he be not hewn now', which Mr Dover Wilson refuses to change to 'drawn' – 'as Nym draws, Q screams to her bridegroom to cut the villain down, lest the worst befall'. But this frank blood-thirst is not at all in her style, and if it was she could hardly keep her house open. It seems that this picture of the ladies is drawn from the sombre vignette at the end of Part II, just before the rejection, when they are dragged across the front stage by beadles because 'the man is dead that you and Pistol beat among you'. He is breaking his own rules about the order of scenes, if he makes this imply that they were in a plot with Pistol at his first appearance. What we do gather before his entry is that they are afraid he may kill somebody in the house, and know they will get into trouble if he does. He starts threatening death as soon as he comes, whether as a bawdy joke or not ('I will discharge upon her, sir, with two bullets'). Also Doll had just begun a pathetic farewell to Falstaff, who is going to the wars; she is cross at their being interrupted. Also she came on for this scene already elegantly unwell from too much drink. I need to list the reasons for her anger, because Mr Dover Wilson comments on the line 'Sweet knight, I kiss thy neaf' that Pistol 'is ready to go quietly, but Doll will have him thrown out' – that is, she insists on having a fight. It is hard for Mrs Quickly to turn her own customers out, and Doll will be helping her to avoid serious danger is she can scare the bully away permanently; this, if anything, is what is underlined by the beadle scene, though by the time of *Henry V*, as we needn't be surprised, he has become a valuable protector. Such is what I would call her motive, if I looked for one, but she may well simply be too drunk and cross to realize that he is already going quietly. Either way there is no need to drag in sadism.

Mr Dover Wilson has still another argument from this scene to prove Falstaff's increasing degeneration. After Pistol has been thrown out the Prince arrives and eavesdrops on Falstaff, who is making some rather justified remarks against him, so that Falstaff again has to find a quick excuse; he says he dispraised the Prince before the wicked, that the wicked might not fall in love with him. 'He now whines and cringes on a new note, while he is forced to have recourse to defaming Doll in turn, a shift which is neither witty nor attractive.' To be sure, the words 'corrupt blood' may imply that she has syphilis; it is only the editor's stage direction which makes him point at her, but the idea does give her a professional reason for displaying anger. He has long been saying he has it himself, so there doesn't seem any great betrayal in saying that she has it too (as he does soon after, l. 335). I imagine that the point of the joke is to insinuate that the Prince has it; thus it is too late to save him from the wicked, and too late for him to think he can cure himself by saying he has re-formed – to forestall being laughed at for being found making love, Falstaff welcomes the Prince among his fellow-sufferers. The badinage in these circles is always a bit rough, and I don't deny that it is hard to know how you are expected to take it. But in this case we have an immediate pointer from an 'aside' by Poins, who as usual is in a plot with the Prince against Falstaff.

(By the way, this shows what nonsense it is to suppose that the Prince made a sudden pathetic discovery of the worthlessness of Poins only two scenes before, a decisive step in his life, we are to believe; they are on just the same footing as ever.) Poins says, 'My lord, he will drive you out of your revenge, and turn all to a merriment, if you take not the heat.' How could this be said if Falstaff was only whining and cringing, or even if he were picking a serious quarrel with the ladies? At the end of the scene, when he is called off to the war as an important officer (a dozen captains are knocking at every tavern door for Sir John Falstaff, sweating with eagerness – so says Peto, and Bardolph corroborates about the dozen; and however much the editor insists that this is only 'a summons for neglect of duty' it still treats Falstaff as worth a lot of trouble in an emergency), both the women speak with heartbreaking pathos about how much they love him, and the text requires Doll to shed tears. If we critics are to call this a 'calculated degradation', I do not know what we expect our own old age to be like. The truth is, surely, that we never see the old brute more triumphant; doomed you might already feel him, but not degraded.

However, I do not want simply to defend Falstaff against the reproaches of the virtuous, represented by Mr Dover Wilson; it was always an unrewarding occupation, and even the most patient treatment of detail, in such a case, has often failed to convince a jury. I think, indeed, that Mr Dover Wilson's points are well worth examining, being of great interest in themselves; but, what is more, I think many of them are thrown in with a broadminded indifference as to whether they fit his thesis or not. Some of them seem to me rather too hot on my side of the question, and this may serve to remind us of what is so easily forgotten in a controversy, that the final truth may be complex. For example, he has a fine remark on Mrs Quickly's description of Falstaff's death. She says she felt his feet, and then his knees, and so upward and upward, and all as cold as any stone. The only comment that would occur to me is that this dramatist can continue unflinchingly to insert bawdy jokes while both the

speaker and the audience are meant to be almost in tears. Mr
Dover Wilson, taking a more scholarly view, remarks that the
detail is drawn from the death of Socrates; the symptoms are
those of the gradual death from hemlock. But whatever can he
have intended by this parallel? Surely it has to imply that Falstaff
like Socrates was a wise teacher killed by a false accusation of
corrupting young men; his patient heroism under injustice, and
how right the young men were to love him, are what we have to
reflect on. I hope that somebody pointed out this parallel to
Shakespeare; he did, I believe, feel enough magic about Falstaff
for it to have given him a mixed but keen pleasure; but that seems
as far as speculation can reasonably go. To make it an intentional
irony really would be like Verrall on Euripides, and it would
blow Mr Dover Wilson's picture of Falstaff into smithereens.
And yet, though it seems natural to talk like this, I am not certain;
the idea that Falstaff was a good tutor *somehow* was a quite public
part of the play, and might conceivably have been fitted out with
a learned reference. He has a similar eerie flash of imagination
about a stage direction in *Henry V*, where the heroes of Agincourt
are described as 'poor troops'. He rightly explains that modern
editions omit the epithet, an important guide to the producer;
the story would be mere boasting if it did not emphasize that their
victory was a hairbreadth escape after being gruelled. But then
he goes on, 'Did the "scarecrows" that Falstaff led to Shrewsbury return to the stage?' It seems rather likely, for the convenience of a repertory company, that they did; but what can it mean,
if we suppose it means anything? What is recalled is the most
unbeatable of all Falstaff's retorts to Henry – 'they'll fit a pit as
well as better; tush, man, mortal men, mortal men'. Falstaff has
just boasted that he took bribes to accept such bad recruits ('I
have abused the King's press damnably'), and boasts later that
he got them killed to keep their pay (by the way, it is before his
success has 'degraded' him) but this makes his reply all the more
crashing, as from one murderer to another: 'that is all you
Norman lords want, in your squabbles between cousins over
your loot, which you make an excuse to murder the English
people.' This very strong joke could be implied in *Henry IV*, as

part of a vague protest against civil war, but to recall it over Henry's hereditary claim to France would surely be reckless; besides, the mere return of those stage figures could not carry so much weight. But I believe that thoughts of that kind were somewhere in the ambience of the play, however firmly they were being rebutted; it is conceivable that Mr Dover Wilson here is being wiser than either of us know. . . .

Falstaff is in part simply a 'Vice', that is, an energetic symbol of impulses which most people have to repress, who gives pleasure by at once releasing and externalizing them. His plausibility is amusing, and his incidental satire on the world can be accepted as true, but what he stands for is recognized as wrong, and he must be punished in the end. Also (as a minor version of this type) he is in part the 'cowardly swashbuckler', of the Latin play rather than the Miracle Play, whose absurdity and eventual exposure are to comfort the audience for their frequent anxiety and humiliation from 'swashbucklers'. As part of the historical series, he stands for the social disorder which is sure to be produced by a line of usurpers, therefore he is a parallel to the rebel leaders though very unlike them; the good king must shake him off in the end as part of his work of re-uniting the country. Also I think there is a more timeless element about him, neither tied to his period in the story nor easily called Renaissance or medieval, though it seems to start with Shakespeare; he is the scandalous upper-class man whose behavior embarrasses his class and thereby pleases the lower class in the audience, as an 'exposure'; the faint echoes of upper-class complaints about him, as in the change of his name, are I think evidence that this was felt. For these last two functions, cowardice is not the vice chiefly required of him. But surely we have no reason to doubt that there were other forces at work behind the popularity of the myth, which can more directly be called Renaissance; something to do with greater trust in the natural man or pleasure in contemplating him, which would join on to what so many critics have said about 'the comic idealization of freedom'. I think it needs putting in more specific terms, but I don't see that Mr Dover Wilson can be plausible in denying it altogether.

The most important 'Renaissance' aspects of Falstaff, I think, can be most quickly described as nationalism and Machiavellianism; both of them make him a positively good tutor for a prince, as he regularly claims to be, so that it is not surprising that he produced a good King or that his rejection, though necessary, could be presented as somehow tragic. The Machiavellian view (no more tied to that author then than it is now, but more novel and shocking than it is now) is mainly the familiar one that a young man is better for 'sowing his wild oats', especially if he is being trained to 'handle men'. The sort of ruler you can trust, you being one of the ruled, the sort that can understand his people, can lead them to glory, is one who has learned the world by experience, especially rather low experience; he knows the tricks, he can allow for human failings, and somehow between the two he can gauge the spirit of a situation or a period. The idea is not simply that Falstaff is debauched and tricky, though that in itself made him give Hal experience, and hardly any price was too high to pay for getting a good ruler, but that he had the breadth of mind and of social understanding which the Magnanimous Man needed to acquire. It seems a lower-class rather than upper-class line of thought (it is, of course, militantly anti-puritan, as we can assume the groundlings tended to be), and Falstaff can be regarded as a parody of it rather than a coarse acceptance of it by Shakespeare; but surely it is obviously present; indeed I imagine that previous critics have thought it too obvious to be worth writing down – there was no need to, till Mr Dover Wilson began preaching at us about his Medieval Vice and his Ideal King. After rejecting Falstaff Henry continues to show the popular touch and so forth that Falstaff taught him; indeed, *Henry V* limits itself rather rigidly to describing the good effects of this training, for example in his treatment of the troops and of the Princess (we hear nothing about the longbow-men who actually won the battle). One tends to think of the wooing scene as a sickeningly obvious bit of film dialogue (whereas Dr Johnson thought it implausibly low); but this was *the first time* a good young millionaire democrat had immediately melted a 'foreign aristocrat' by the universal power of his earthly approach; and the idea is that only his wild oats, or only Falstaff, could have taught him that important method of playing to the gallery.*

SOURCE: *Kenyon Review* (Spring, 1953).

* The Hal legend invented this rather than Shakespeare; it comes in a milder form into *The Famous Victories of Henry V*, the pre-Shakespearean stage version, which does give credit to the longbow-men and doesn't to the Scotch, Welsh and Irish.

Harold Jenkins

THE STRUCTURAL PROBLEM IN
SHAKESPEARE'S *HENRY IV* (1956)

THE first problem that confronts one in approaching *Henry IV*, and the one about which I propose to be particular, is, 'Is it one play or two?' Some will dismiss this as an academic question, the sort of thing that only people like professors bother their heads about. Others will look askance at it as a metaphysical question, which in a sense it is. But it is also, surely, a practical question: how satisfactorily can either the first part or the second be shown in the theatre without the other? . . . And thus of course the question becomes a problem of literary criticism. Until it has been answered, how can the dramatic quality of *Henry IV* be fully appreciated, or even defined? Yet the numerous literary critics who have attempted an answer to the question have reached surprisingly opposite conclusions.

Answers began more than two hundred years ago in the *Critical Observations on Shakespeare* by John Upton, a man who deserves our regard for trying to scotch the notion so strangely current in the eighteenth century that 'Shakespeare had no learning'. Far from accepting that Shakespeare's plays were the happy, or the not so happy, products of untutored nature, Upton maintained that they were constructed according to some principles of art; and his examination of *Henry IV* suggested to him that each of its two parts had, what Aristotle of course demanded, its own beginning, middle, and end. Upton held it to be an injury to Shakespeare even to speak of a first and second *part* and thus conceal the fact that there were here two quite independent plays.[1] To this Dr Johnson retorted that these two plays, so far from being independent, are 'two only because they are too long to be one'. They could appear as separate plays, he thought, only to

those who looked at them with the 'ambition of critical dis-
coveries'. . . . Dr Johnson's contemporaries did not all find it as
plain as he did that *Henry IV* was just one continuous composition. It seemed probable to Malone that Part II was not even
'conceived'[2] until Part I had been a roaring success. Capell, on
the other hand, thought that both parts were 'planned at the
same time, and with great judgment'.[3]

Among present-day scholars Professor Dover Wilson is on
Johnson's side. He insists that the two parts of *Henry IV* are 'a
single structure' with the 'normal dramatic curve' stretched over
ten acts instead of five. Professor R. A. Law, however, declares
that *Henry IV* is 'not a single ten-act play', but two organic units
'written with different purposes in view'. On the contrary, says
Dr Tillyard, 'The two parts of the play are a single organism.'
Part I by itself is 'patently incomplete'. 'Each part is a drama
complete in itself', says Kittredge flatly.[4] In short, some two
centuries after Upton and Johnson, scholars are still about equally
divided as to whether *Henry IV* was 'planned' as 'one long drama'
or whether the second part was, as they put it, an 'unpremeditated sequel'. . . .

Words like 'planned' and 'unpremeditated' figure largely in
this controversy; and of course they imply intention or the lack
of it, and will therefore be suspect in those circles which denounce
what is called 'the intentional fallacy'.[5] I am far from belonging
to that school of criticism which holds that an author's own
intention is irrelevant to our reading of his work; yet, as Lascelles
Abercrombie says, aesthetic criticism must ultimately judge by
results: a man's work is evidence of what he did, but you can
never be sure what he intended.[6] This position, with the coming
of the Freudian psychology, is finally inescapable, but in its
extreme form it seems to me unnecessarily defeatist. If we leave
aside for the present all question of Shakespeare's intention, what
does *Henry IV* itself, as it begins and proceeds along its course,
warn us to expect?

The short first scene, filled with reports of wars – wars this
time in which multitudes are 'butchered' – makes an apt beginning for a history play. But its dialogue announces no main

action. Yet certain topics, brought in with apparent casualness, naturally engage our interest. There is talk of two young men who do not yet appear, both called 'young Harry', yet apparently unlike. The first of them, Hotspur, is introduced as 'gallant', an epithet which is very soon repeated when he is said to have won 'a gallant prize'. The prisoners he has taken are, we are told, 'a conquest for a prince to boast of'. Already, before Prince Hal is even named, a contrast is being begun between a man who behaves like a prince though he is not one and another who is in fact a prince but does not act the part. The King makes this explicit. Hotspur, who has gained 'an honourable spoil', is 'a son who is the theme of honour's tongue', while the King's own son is stained with 'riot and dishonour'. In the second and third scenes the two Harries in turn appear. First, the Prince, already associated with dishonour, instead of, like Hotspur, taking prisoners in battle, plans to engage in highway robbery. Then, when he has arranged to sup next night in a tavern, he is followed on the stage by Hotspur telling how, when he took his prisoners, he was 'dry with rage and extreme toil'. This practice of juxtaposing characters who exhibit opposite codes of conduct is a common one in Shakespeare's drama. After the 'unsavoury similes' that Hal swaps with Falstaff, in which a squalling cat and a stinking ditch are prominent, there is Hotspur's hyperbole about plucking 'bright honour from the pale-faced moon'. It may not be a classical construction, but there is enough suggestion here of arrangement to justify Upton's claim for Shakespeare's art. We expect that central to the play will be the antithesis between these two young men and the lives they lead. And we shall find that this antithesis precipitates a moral contest which is an important aspect of the historical action of the drama.

The historical action presents Hotspur's rebellion. It is an action which develops with a fine structural proportion throughout Part I. The act divisions, although they are not Shakespeare's of course, being first found in the Folio, may serve nevertheless as a convenient register of the way the action is disposed. In the first act the rebel plot is hatched, in the second Hotspur prepares to leave home, in the third he joins forces with the other rebel

leaders, in the fourth the rebel army is encamped ready to give
battle, in the fifth it is defeated and Hotspur is killed. Meantime,
along with the military contest between Hotspur and the King,
the moral contest between the Prince and Hotspur proceeds with
an equally perfect balance. The opposition of honour and riot
established in the first act is intensified in the second, where a
scene of Hotspur at home preparing for war is set against one of
Hal revelling in the tavern. The revelry even includes a little
skit by Hal on Hotspur's conversation with his wife, which serves
not only to adjust our view of Hotspur's honour by subjecting
it to ridicule, but also to emphasize that the Prince is – with
gleeful understatement – 'not yet of Percy's mind'. That he is
not of Percy's mind leads the King in the third act to resume his
opening plaint: it is not the Prince but Percy, with his 'never-
dying honour', who is fit to be a king's son. At this point the
Prince vows to outshine his rival. He will meet 'this gallant
Hotspur' – the words echo the opening scene – this 'child of
honour', and overcome him. And so, when the rebels see the
Prince in Act IV, he is 'gallantly arm'd' – Hotspur's word is now
applied to him – and he vaults upon his horse 'as if an angel
dropp'd down from the clouds' – with a glory, that is, already
beyond Hotspur. All that then remains is that the Prince shall
demonstrate his new chivalry in action, which of course he does
in the fifth act, first saving his father's life and finally slaying
Hotspur in single combat. Opposed to one another throughout
the play, constantly spoken of together, these two are nevertheless kept apart till the fifth act, when their first and last encounter
completes in the expected manner the pattern of their rivalry that
began in the opening words. The two have exchanged places.
Supremacy in honour has passed from Hotspur to the Prince,
and the wayward hero of the opening ends by exhibiting his true
princely nature.

What then is one to make of the view of Professor Dover
Wilson that the Battle of Shrewsbury, in which the Prince kills
Hotspur, is not an adequate conclusion but merely the 'nodal
point we expect in a third act'? If we do expect a 'nodal point' in a
third act, then *Henry IV, Part I* will not disappoint us. For there

is a nodal point, and – I am tempted to say this categorically – it is in the third act of Part I that it occurs. In this third act, when the King rebukes his son, the Prince replies, 'I will redeem all this . . .'; in the fifth act he fulfils this vow at Shrewsbury, as is signalized by the King's admission that the Prince has 'redeem'd' his 'lost opinion'. Again, in the third act, the Prince swears that he will take from Hotspur 'every honour sitting on his helm'; in the fifth act Hotspur is brought to confess that the Prince has won 'proud titles' from him.[7] More significantly still, the third act ends with the Prince saying,

> Percy stands on high;
> And either we or they must lower lie;

and then the fifth act shows us the spectacle of the hero looking down upon his rival's prostrate form. The curve of the plot could hardly be more firmly or more symmetrically drawn. It does not seem easy to agree with Dr Johnson and Professor Dover Wilson that *Henry IV, Part I* is only the first half of a play.

If this were all there were to *Henry IV, Part I*, the matter would be simple. But the Prince's conquest of honour is only one aspect of his progress; the other is his break with the companions of his riots. Interwoven with the story of the Prince and Hotspur are the Prince's relations with Falstaff, and these, from Falstaff's first appearance in the second scene of the play, are presented in a way which leads us to expect a similar reversal. The essential thing about Hal is that, scapegrace that he is, he is the future king – the 'true prince', the 'sweet young prince', the 'king's son', the 'heir apparent', as Falstaff variously calls him, with whatever degree of mockery, in their first dialogue together. More than that, this dialogue is constantly pointing forward to the moment when he will come to the throne. 'When thou art king' – Falstaff uses these words four times in the first seventy lines and yet again before the scene is over. 'Shall there be gallows standing in England when thou art king?' 'Do not thou, when thou art king, hang a thief.' And so on. With these words ringing in our ears, then, we are continually being reminded of what is to come. The words seem, however, to refer to some vague time in the distant

future. The Prince's reign will inescapably become reality, but
it is at present apprehended as a dream. Falstaff's irrepressible
fancy blows up a vast gaily-coloured bubble, and as Bradley
recognized,[8] it is because this bubble encloses the dreams of all of
us that we feel for Falstaff so much affection. In our dreams we all
do exactly as we like, and the date of their realization is to be when
Hal is king. Then, everything will be changed – except of course
ourselves. *We* shall go on as before, our friend Falstaff will
continue his nocturnal depredations, but highwaymen will not
be regarded as thieves and punishments will be abolished. Unfortunately, in the real world outside the bubble, it is not the law
but we ourselves that should change, as Falstaff recognizes when
he says, 'I must give over this life, and I will give it over . . . I'll
be damned for never a king's son in Christendom.' The joke of
this is that we know that Falstaff will never give over, nor means
to; but the joke does not quite conceal the seriousness of the
alternatives – give over or be damned; and the idea of damnation
continues to dance before us, now and later, in further jests
about Falstaff's selling his soul to the devil, wishing to repent,
and having to 'give the devil his due'. What Falstaff's eventual
doom is to be could be discerned more than dimly by a mind that
came to this play unfurnished by literature or folk-lore. And none
of us is quite as innocent as that. We cannot help being aware of
an archetypal situation in which a man dallies with a diabolical
tempter whom he either renounces or is destroyed by; and to the
first audience of *Henry IV* this situation was already familiar
in a long line of Christian plays, in some of which man's suc-
cumbing to temptation was symbolized in his selling his soul
to the devil and being carried off to Hell. It is because it is so
familiar that it is readily accepted as matter for jesting, while the
jests give a hint of Falstaff's role in the play. I merely pick out
one or two threads in the very complex fabric of the dialogue: you
will be good enough, I trust, to believe that, in spite of some
dubious precedents in the recent criticism of other plays, I am
not seeking to interpret *Henry IV* as an allegory of sin and damnation. Falstaff is not a type-figure, though within his vast
person several types are contained. And one of them is a sinner

and provokes many piquant allusions to the typical fate of sinners, whether on the earthly gallows or in the infernal fire. There is also an ambiguity, to use the modern jargon, which permits Falstaff to be not only the sinner but the tempter as well. The jokes of a later scene will call him indeed a devil who haunts the Prince, a 'reverend vice', an 'old white-bearded Satan'. What I think the play makes clear from the beginning is that neither as sinner nor as tempter will Falstaff come to triumph. Even as we share his dream of what will happen when Hal is king, we confidently await the bursting of his bubble.

To strengthen our expectation even further is what we know of history, or at least of that traditional world where the territories of history and legend have no clear boundaries. The peculiarity of the history play is that while pursuing its dramatic ends, it must also obey history and steer a course reasonably close to an already known pattern of events. The story of Prince Hal was perfectly familiar to the Elizabethan audience before the play began, and it was the story of a prince who had a madcap youth, including at least one escapade of highway robbery, and then, on succeeding to the throne, banished his riotous companions from court and became the most valorous king England had ever had. Not only was this story vouched for in the chronicles, but it had already found its way on to the stage, as an extant play, *The Famous Victories of Henry the Fifth*, bears witness, in however garbled a text. It is hardly open to *our* play, then, to depart from the accepted pattern, in which the banishment of the tavern friends is an essential feature. Moreover, that they are to be banished the Prince himself assures us at the end of his first scene with Poins and Falstaff in that soliloquy which generations of critics have made notorious.

> I know you all, and will awhile uphold
> The unyoked humour of your idleness.

The word 'awhile' plants its threat of a different time to come when a 'humour' now 'unyoked' will be brought under restraint. The soliloquy tells us as plain as any prologue what the end of the play is to be.

Yet although *Henry IV, Part I* thus from its first act directs
our interest to the time when Hal will be king, it is not of course
until the last act of Part II that Pistol comes to announce, 'Sir
John, thy tender lambkin now is king.' It is not until the last act
of Part II that the Prince is able to institute the new régime which
makes mock of Falstaff's dream-world. And it is not of course till
the final scene of all that the newly crowned king makes his ceremonial entrance and pronounces the words that have threatened
since he and Falstaff first were shown together. 'I banish thee.'
To all that has been said about the rejection of Falstaff I propose
to add very little. The chief of those who objected to it, Bradley
himself, recognized the necessity of it while complaining of how
it was done. Granted that the new king had to drop his former
friend, might he not have spared him the sermon and parted
from him in private?[9] Yet Professor Dover Wilson is surely
right to maintain that the public utterance is the essential thing.[10]
From the first, as I have shown, interest is concentrated on the
prince as the future sovereign and Falstaff builds hopes on the
nature of his rule. Their separation, when it comes, is not then a
reluctant parting between friends, but a royal decree promul-
gated with due solemnity. This is also the perfect moment for it,
when the crown that has hovered over the hero from the beginning is seen, a striking symbol in the theatre, fixed firmly on his
head. The first words of the rejection speech elevate him still
further – 'I know thee not' – for the scriptural overtones here[11]
make the speaker more than a king. The situation presents many
aspects, but one of them shows the tempter vanquished and
another the sinner cast into outer darkness. In either case the
devil, we may say, gets his due.

The last act of Part II thus works out a design which is begun
in the first act of Part I. How then can we agree with Kittredge
that each part is a complete play? Such a pronouncement fits the
text no better than the opposite view of Johnson and Dover
Wilson that Part I, though it ends in Hotspur's death and the
Prince's glory, is yet only the first half of a play. If it were a
question of what Shakespeare intended in the matter, the evidence provided by what he wrote would not suggest either that

the two parts were planned as a single drama or that Part II was an 'unpremeditated sequel'.

An escape from this dilemma has sometimes been sought in a theory, expounded especially by Professor Dover Wilson and Dr Tillyard, that what *Henry IV* shows is one action with two phases. While the whole drama shows the transformation of the madcap youth into the virtuous ruler, the first part, we are told, deals with the chivalric virtues, the second with the civil. In the first part the hero acquires honour, in the second he establishes justice. But I see no solution of the structural problem here. For though it is left to Part II to embody the idea of justice in the upright judge, the interest in justice and law is present from the start. On Falstaff's first appearance in Part I he jibes at the law as 'old father antic'. And he goes further. Included within his bubble is a vision of his future self not simply as a man freed from 'the rusty curb' of the law but as a man who actually administers the law himself. 'By the Lord, I'll be a brave judge', he says, making a mistake about his destined office which provokes Hal's retort, 'Thou judgest false already.' It is in the last act of Part II that we have the completion of this motif. Its climax comes when on Hal's accession Falstaff brags, 'The laws of England are at my commandment', and its resolution when the true judge sends the false judge off to prison. But it begins, we see, in the first act of Part I. The Prince's achievement in justice cannot, then, be regarded simply as the second phase of his progress. Certainly he has two contests: in one he outstrips Hotspur, in the other he puts down Falstaff. But these contests are not distributed at the rate of one per part. The plain fact is that in *Henry IV* two actions, each with the Prince as hero, begin together in the first act of Part I, though one of them ends with the death of Hotspur at the end of Part I, the other with the banishment of Falstaff at the end of Part II.

Now, since the Falstaff plot is to take twice as long to complete its course, it might well be expected to develop from the beginning more slowly than the other. Certainly if it is to keep symmetry, it must come later to its turning-point. But is this in fact what we find? Frankly it is not. On the contrary, through the

first half of Part I the Hotspur plot and the Falstaff plot show
every sign of moving towards their crisis together.

Both plots, for example, are presented, though I think both
are not usually observed, in the Prince's soliloquy in the first act
which I have already quoted as foretelling the banishment of his
tavern companions. It is unfortunate that this speech has usually
been studied for its bearing on Falstaff's rejection; its emphasis is
really elsewhere. It is only the first two lines, with the reference
to the 'unyoked humour' of the Prince's companions, that allude
specifically to them, and what is primarily in question is not
what is to happen to the companions but what is to happen to
the Prince. In the splendid image which follows of the sun breaking through the clouds we recognize a royal emblem and behold
the promise of a radiant king who is to come forth from the 'ugly
mists' which at present obscure the Prince's real self. Since
Falstaff has just been rejoicing at the thought that they 'go by the
moon ... and not by Phœbus', it is apparent that his fortunes will
decline when the Prince emerges like Phoebus himself. It is
equally apparent, or should be, that the brilliant Hotspur will be
outshone.[12] There is certainly no clue at this stage that the catas-
trophes of Hotspur and Falstaff will not be simultaneous.

Our expectation that they will be is indeed encouraged as the
two actions now move forward. While Hotspur in pursuit of
honour is preparing war, Falstaff displays his cowardice (I use
the word advisedly) at Gadshill. While Hotspur rides forth from
home on the journey that will take him to his downfall, the
exposure of Falstaff's makebelieve in the matter of the men in
buckram is the foreshadowing of his. The news of Hotspur's
rebellion brings the Falstaffian revels to a climax at the same time
as it summons the Prince to that interview with his father which
will prove, as we have seen, the crisis of his career and the 'nodal
point' of the drama. That this interview is to be dramatically
momentous is clear enough in advance: before we come to it,
it is twice prefigured by the Prince and Falstaff in burlesque. But
not only do the two mock-interviews excite our interest in the
real one to come; the mock-interviews are in the story of the
Prince and Falstaff what the real interview is in the story of the

Prince and Hotspur. First, Falstaff, whose dream it is that he may one day govern England, basks in the makebelieve that he is king; and then Hal, who, as we have so often been reminded, is presently to be king, performs in masquerade his future part. The question they discuss is central to the play: 'Shall the son of England prove a thief and take purses?' Shall he in fact continue to associate with Falstaff? One should notice that although the two actors exchange roles, they do not really change sides in this debate. Whether he acts the part of king or prince, Falstaff takes the opportunity of pleading for himself. When he is king he instructs the prince to 'keep with' Falstaff; as prince he begs, 'Banish not him thy Harry's company, banish not him thy Harry's company: banish plump Jack, and banish all the world.' Falstaff's relations to the future king, a theme of speculation since the opening of the play, now come to a focus in this repeated word 'banish'. And when the Prince replies, 'I do, I will', he anticipates in jest the sentence he is later to pronounce in earnest. If it were never to be pronounced in earnest, that would rob the masquerade of the dramatic irony from which comes its bouquet: those who accept Part I as a play complete in itself wrongly surrender their legitimate expectations. In this mock-interview the Prince declares his intentions towards Falstaff just as surely as in his real interview with his father he declares his intentions towards Hotspur. One declaration is a solemn vow, the other a glorious piece of fun, but they are equally prophetic and structurally their function is the same. We now approach the turning-point not of one, but of both dramatic actions. Indeed we miss the core of the play if we do not perceive that the two actions are really the same. The moment at the end of the third act when the Prince goes off to challenge Hotspur is also the moment when he leaves Falstaff's favourite tavern for what we well might think would be evermore. It is at the exit from the tavern that the road to Shrewsbury begins; and all the signposts I see indicate one-way traffic only. There should be no return.

The various dooms of Hotspur and Falstaff are now in sight; and we reasonably expect both dooms to be arrived at in Act v.

What we are not at all prepared for is that one of the two will be deferred till five acts later than the other. The symmetry so beautifully preserved in the story of Hotspur is in Falstaff's case abandoned. Statistics are known to be misleading, and nowhere more so than in literary criticism; but it is not without significance that in *Henry IV, Part I* Falstaff's speeches in the first two acts number ninety-six and in the last two acts only twenty-five. As for Falstaff's satellites, with the exception of a single perfunctory appearance on the part of Bardolph, the whole galaxy vanishes altogether in the last two acts, only to reappear with some changes in personnel in Part II. Falstaff, admittedly, goes on without a break, if broken in wind; and his diminished role does show some trace of the expected pattern of development. His going to war on foot while Hal is on horseback marks a separation of these erstwhile companions and a decline in Falstaff's status which was anticipated in jest when his horse was taken from him at Gadshill. When he nevertheless appears at one council of war his sole attempt at a characteristic joke is cut short by the Prince with 'Peace, chewet, peace!' A fine touch, this, which contributes to the picture of the Prince's transformation: the boon companion whose jests he has delighted in is now silenced in a word. There is even the shadow of a rejection of Falstaff; over his supposed corpse the Prince speaks words that, for all their affectionate regret, remind us that he has turned his back on 'vanity'. But these things, however significant, are details, no more than shorthand notes for the degradation of Falstaff that we have so confidently looked for. What it comes to is that after the middle of Part I, *Henry IV* changes its shape. And that, it seems to me, is the root and cause of the structural problem.

Now that this change of shape has been, I hope I may say, demonstrated from within the play itself, it may at this stage be permissible to venture an opinion about the author's plan. I do not of course mean to imply that *Henry IV*, or indeed any other of Shakespeare's plays, ever had a plan precisely laid down for it in advance. But it has to be supposed that when Shakespeare began a play he had some idea of the general direction it would take, however ready he may have been to modify his idea as art or expediency might suggest. Though this is where I shall be told I pass the bounds of literary criticism into the province of biography or worse, I hold it reasonable to infer from the analysis I have given that in the course of writing *Henry IV* Shakespeare changed his mind. I am compelled to believe that the author himself foresaw, I will even say intended, that pattern which evolves through the early acts of Part I and which demands for its completion that the hero's rise to an eminence of valour shall be accompanied, or at least swiftly followed, by the banishment of the riotous friends who hope to profit from his reign. In other words, hard upon the Battle of Shrewsbury there was to come the coronation of the hero as king. This inference from the play is not without support from other evidence. The prince's penitence in the interview with his father in the middle of Part I corresponds to an episode which, both in Holinshed and in the play of *The Famous Victories of Henry the Fifth*, is placed only shortly before the old king's death. And still more remarkable is the sequence of events in a poem which has been shown to be one of Shakespeare's sources.[13] At the historical Battle of Shrewsbury the Prince was only sixteen years old, whereas Hotspur was thirty-nine. But in Samuel Daniel's poem, *The Civil Wars*, Hotspur is made 'young' and 'rash' and encounters a prince of equal age who emerges like a 'new-appearing glorious star'.[14] It is Daniel, that is to say, who sets in opposition these two splendid youths and so provides the germ from which grows the rivalry of the Prince and Hotspur which is structural to Shakespeare's play. And in view of this resemblance between Daniel and Shakespeare, it is significant that Daniel ignores the ten years that in history elapsed between the death of Hotspur and the Prince's accession. Whereas in Holinshed the events of those ten years fill nearly twenty pages, Daniel goes straight from Shrewsbury to the old king's deathbed. This telescoping of events, which confronts the Prince with his kingly responsibilities directly after the slaying of Hotspur, adumbrates the pattern that Shakespeare, as I see it, must have had it in mind to follow out. The progress of a prince was to be presented not in two phases but in a single play of normal length which would show the hero wayward in its first half, pledging reform in the middle, and then in the second half climbing at Shrewsbury the ladder of honour by which, appropriately, he would ascend to the throne.

The exact point at which a new pattern supervenes I should not care to define. But I think the new pattern can be seen emerging during the fourth act. At a corresponding stage the history play of *Richard II* shows the deposition of its king, *Henry V* the victory at Agincourt, even *Henry IV, Part II* the quelling of its rebellion in Gaultree Forest. By contrast *Henry IV, Part I,* postponing any such decisive action, is content with preparation. While the rebels gather, the Prince is arming and Falstaff recruiting to meet them. Until well into the fifth act ambassadors are going back and forth between the rival camps, and we may even hear a message twice over, once when it is despatched and once when it is delivered. True, this is not undramatic: these scenes achieve a fine animation and suspense as well as the lowlier feat of verisimilitude. But the technique is obviously not one of compression. Any thought of crowding into the two-hour traffic of one play the death of the old king and the coronation of the new has by now been relinquished, and instead the Battle of Shrewsbury is being built up into a grand finale in its own right. In our eagerness to come to this battle and our gratification at the exciting climax it provides, we easily lose sight of our previous expectations. Most of us, I suspect, go from the theatre well satisfied with the improvised conclusion. It is not, of course, that we cease to care about the fate of individuals. On the contrary, the battle succeeds so well because amid the crowded tumult of the fighting it keeps the key figures in due prominence. Clearly showing who is killed, who is rescued, and who shams dead, who slays a valiant foe and who only pretends to, it brings each man to a destiny that we perceive to be appropriate. We merely fail to notice that the destiny is not in every case exactly what was promised. There is no room now in Part I to banish Falstaff. A superb comic tact permits him instead the fate of reformation, in fact the alternative of giving over instead of being damned. It is a melancholy fate enough, for it means giving over being Falstaff: we leave him saying that if he is rewarded, he will 'leave sack, and live cleanly as a nobleman should do'. But since this resolution is conditional and need in any case be believed no more than Falstaff has already taught us to believe him, it has the advantage that it leaves the issue open, which, to judge from the outcry there has always been over the ending of Part II, is how most people would prefer to have it left. Shakespeare's brilliant improvisation thus provides a dénouement to Part I which has proved perfectly acceptable, while it still leaves opportunity for what I hope I may call the original ending, if the dramatist should choose to add a second part. I refrain, however, from assuming that a second part was necessarily planned before Part I was acted.

Part II itself does not require extended treatment. For whenever it was 'planned', it is a consequence of Part I. Its freedom is limited by the need to present what Part I so plainly prepared for and then left out. Falstaff cannot be allowed to escape a second time. His opposition to the law, being now the dominant interest, accordingly shapes the plot; and the law, now bodied forth in the half-legendary figure of the Lord Chief Justice, becomes a formidable person in the drama. The opening encounter between these two, in which Falstaff makes believe not to see or hear his reprover, is symbolic of Falstaff's whole attitude to law – he ignores its existence as long as he can. But the voice which he at first refuses to hear is the voice which will pronounce his final sentence. The theme of the individual versus the law proves so fertile that it readily gives rise to subplots. Justice Shallow, of course, claims his place in the play by virtue of the life that is in him, exuberant in the capers of senility itself. He functions all the same as the Lord Chief Justice's antithesis: he is the foolish justice with whom Falstaff has his way and from whom he wrings the thousand pounds that the wise justice has denied him. Even Shallow's servant Davy has his relation to the law; and his view of law is that though a man may be a knave, if he is my friend and I am the justice's servant, it is hard if the knave cannot win. In this humane sentiment Davy takes on full vitality as a person; but he simultaneously brings us back to confront at a different angle the main moral issue of the play. Is he to control the law

or the law him? In fact, shall Falstaff flourish or shall a thief be
hanged?

It has sometimes been objected that Falstaff runs away with
Part II. In truth he has to shoulder the burden of it because a
dead man and a converted one can give him small assistance. Part
II has less opportunity for the integrated double action of Part I.
To be sure, it attempts a double action, and has often been observed to be in some respects a close replica of Part I – 'almost a
carbon copy', Professor Shaaber says. At exactly the same point
in each part, for example, is a little domestic scene where a rebel
leader contemplates leaving home, and in each part this is directly
followed by the big tavern scene in which revelry rises to a
climax. And so on. An article in a recent number of *The Review
of English Studies* has even called *Henry IV* a diptych, finding the
'parallel presentation of incidents' in the two parts the primary
formal feature. I do not wish to deny the aesthetic satisfaction
to be got from a recognition of this rhythmic repetition; yet it is
only the more superficial pattern that can be thus repeated. With
history and Holinshed obliging, rebellion can break out as before;
yet the rebellion of Part II, though it occupies our attention, has
no significance, nor can have, for the principal characters of the
play. The story of the Prince and Hotspur is over, and the King
has only to die.

The one thing about history is that it does not repeat itself.
Hotspur, unlike Sherlock Holmes, cannot come back to life.
But there are degrees in all things; conversion has not quite the
same finality as death. And besides, there is a type of hero whose
adventures always can recur. Robin Hood has no sooner plun-
dered one rich man than another comes along. It is the nature of
Brer Fox, and indeed of Dr Watson, to be incapable of learning
from experience. In folk-lore, that is to say, though not in history,
you can be at the same point twice. And it seems as if Prince Hal
may be sufficient of a folk-lore hero to be permitted to go again
through the cycle of riot and reform. In Part II as in Part I the
King laments his son's unprincely life. Yet this folk-lore hero is
also a historical, and what is more to the point, a dramatic per-
sonage, and it is not tolerable that the victor of Shrewsbury should

do as critics sometimes say he does, relapse into his former wildness and then reform again. The Prince cannot come into Part II
unreclaimed without destroying the dramatic effect of Part I.
Yet if Part II is not to forgo its own dramatic effect, and especially its splendid last-act peripeteia, it requires a prince who
is unreclaimed. This is Part II's dilemma, and the way that it
takes out of it is a bold one. When the King on his deathbed
exclaims against the Prince's 'headstrong riot', he has not forgotten that at Shrewsbury he congratulated the Prince on his
redemption. He has not forgotten it for the simple reason that it
has never taken place. The only man at court who believes in the
Prince's reformation, the Earl of Warwick, believes that it will
happen, not that it has happened already. Even as we watch the
hero repeating his folk-lore cycle, we are positively instructed
that he has not been here before:

> The tide of blood in me
> Hath proudly flow'd in vanity till now.

In the two parts of *Henry IV* there are not two princely reforma-
tions but two versions of a single reformation. And they are
mutually exclusive.[15] Though Part II frequently recalls and
sometimes depends on what has happened in Part I, it also denies
that Part I exists. Accordingly the ideal spectator of either part
must not cry with Shakespeare's Lucio, 'I know what I know.'
He must sometimes remember what he knows and sometimes be
content to forget it. This, however, is a requirement made in
some degree by any work of fiction, or as they used to call it,
feigning. And the feat is not a difficult one for those accustomed
to grant the poet's demand for 'that willing suspension of dis-
belief . . . which constitutes poetic faith'.

Henry IV, then, is both one play and two. Part I begins an
action which it finds it has not scope for but which Part II rounds
off. But with one half of the action already concluded in Part I,
there is danger of a gap in Part II. To stop the gap Part II
expands the unfinished story of Falstaff and reduplicates what is
already finished in the story of the Prince. The two parts are
complementary, they are also independent and even incompatible.

What they are, with their various formal anomalies, I suppose them to have become through what Johnson termed 'the necessity of exhibition'. Though it would be dangerous to dispute Coleridge's view that a work of art must 'contain in itself the reason why it is so', that its form must proceed from within,[16] yet even works of art, like other of man's productions, must submit to the bondage of the finite. Even the unwieldy novels of the Victorians, as recent criticism has been showing, obey the demands of their allotted three volumes of space; and the dramatic masterpieces of any age must acknowledge the dimensions of time.

SOURCE: *The Structural Problem in Shakespeare's 'Henry IV'* (1956).

NOTES

1. *Critical Observations on Shakespeare* (1746). See especially pp. 11, 41–2, 70–1.

2. *Shakespeare*, Johnson-Steevens Variorum, 2nd ed. (1778) I 300.

3. *Notes and Various Readings to Shakespeare* [1775] p. 164.

4. *Henry IV, Part I*, ed. Kittredge (1940) p. viii.

5. This is actually the title of an article by W. K. Wimsatt and M. C. Beardsley in the *Sewanee Review*, LIV (1946) 468 ff, reprinted in Wimsatt's *The Verbal Icon* (1954).

6. *A Plea for the Liberty of Interpreting* (British Academy Shakespeare Lecture: 1930) p. 6.

7. The connection here is reinforced by the Prince's use of his earlier image: 'all the budding honours on thy crest I'll crop'.

8. 'The Rejection of Falstaff', in *Oxford Lectures on Poetry* (1909) pp. 262–3.

9. Ibid. p. 253.

10. *The Fortunes of Falstaff* (1943) pp. 120–1.

11. Cf Luke 13: 25–7.

12. This first-Act soliloquy looks forward not only to the rejection of Falstaff but also to Vernon's vision of the Prince and his company before Shrewsbury, 'gorgeous as the sun at midsummer'.

13. See F. W. Moorman, 'Shakespeare's History Plays and Daniel's "Civile Wars"', in *Shakespeare Jahrbuch*, XL (1904) 77–83.

14. Book III, stanzas 97, 109–10.

15. All this is very well exhibited by H. E. Cain. But his conclusion that the two parts therefore have no continuity is invalidated because, like many others, he is content to isolate particular elements in the problem and does not examine it whole. Except when the views of others are being quoted or discussed, the word 'Falstaff' does not occur in his article.

16. This is a synthesis of several passages in Coleridge. The words in quotation marks are said of whatever can give permanent pleasure; but the context shows Coleridge to be thinking of literary composition. See *Biographia Literaria*, ed. Shawcross (1907) II 9. Also relevant are 'On Poesy or Art', ibid. II 262; and *Coleridge's Shakespearean Criticism*, ed. T. M. Raysor (1930) I 223–4.

L. C. Knights

TIME'S SUBJECTS:
2 HENRY IV (1959)

In Sonnet LXIV, pondering the general instability of things, Shakespeare had instanced the shifting edges of the sea:

> When I have seen the hungry ocean gain
> Advantage on the kingdom of the shore,
> And the firm soil win of the watery main,
> Increasing store with loss and loss with store . . .

The image is repeated, with an added note of irony for men's expectation of stability, in the Second Part of *King Henry IV*:

> O God! that one might read the book of fate,
> And see the revolution of the times
> Make mountains level, and the continent,
> Weary of solid firmness, melt itself
> Into the sea! and, other times, to see
> The beachy girdle of the ocean
> Too wide for Neptune's hips; how chances mock,
> And changes fill the cup of alteration
> With divers liquors![1]   (III i 45–53)

This, so far as any one passage can, suggests the nature of the imaginative vision that is now coming to expression in the plays. *Henry IV, Part II*, a tragi-comedy of human frailty, is about the varied aspects of mutability – age, disappointment and decay. The theme of 'policy' is of course continued from Part I, and sometimes it is presented with similar methods of ironic deflation; but we cannot go far into the play without becoming aware of a change of emphasis and direction, already marked indeed by the words of the dying Hotspur at Shrewsbury,

> But thought's the slave of life, and life time's fool;
> And time, that takes survey of all the world,
> Must have a stop.

Each of the three scenes of the first act gives a particular emphasis to elements present in Part I, though largely subdued there by the brisker tone, by the high-spirited satire. Now the proportions are altered. Act i, scene i is not comic satire: it is a harsh reminder of what is involved in the hard game of power politics – the desperate resolve ('each heart being set On bloody courses . . .') and the penalties for failure; and for some thirty lines, throughout Northumberland's elaborate rhetoric of pro-testation against ill news (i i 67–103), the word 'dead' (or 'death') tolls with monotonous insistence. Now just as the comedy of the first meeting of the conspirators in Part I was in keeping with the Falstaffian mode that so largely determined the tone of that play, so this scene is attuned to the appearance of a Falstaff who seems, at first perplexingly, to be both the same figure as before and yet another: it is as though we had given a further twist to the screw of our binoculars and a figure that we thought we knew had appeared more sharply defined against a background that he no longer dominated. When Falstaff enters with his page ('Sirrah, you giant, what says the doctor to my water?'), through-out his exchange with the Lord Chief Justice, and in his conclud-ing soliloquy, it is impossible to turn the almost obsessive references to age and disease, as the references to Falstaff's corpulence are turned in Part I, in the direction of comedy.[2] Later, Falstaff will try again his familiar tactics of evasion – 'Peace, good Doll! do not speak like a death's-head; do not bid me remember mine end' (ii iv 229–30); but from the scene of his first appearance the well-known *memento mori*, if not – as in *The Revenger's Tragedy* – actually present on the stage, has certainly been present to the minds of the audience. 'Is not . . . every part about you blasted with antiquity?' – to that question wit in its wantonness must make what reply it can.

Scene iii, where some of the principal rebels discuss their resources and prospects, is short but significant. As in the pre-ceding scenes the significance is found not in any precisely con-trolled minute particulars of the poetry but simply in a certain expansiveness and insistence at key points; what our thoughts are directed towards is the lack of certainty in human affairs and the

consequent precariousness of those hopes that are so often referred to (seven times in sixty-one lines, to be exact). Hastings
is for going ahead and trusting that things will turn out well;
Lord Bardolph urges caution.

> *Hastings.* But, by your leave, it never yet did hurt
>   To lay down likelihoods and forms of hope.
> *L. Bardolph.* Yes, if this present quality of war,
>   Indeed the instant action, a cause on foot,
>   Lives so in hope, as in an early spring
>   We see the appearing buds; which to prove fruit,
>   Hope gives not so much warrant as despair
>   That frosts will bite them.[3]

This is followed by an elaboration of the parable of the man who
began to build and, because he had not counted the cost, was not
able to finish (Luke, XIV 28–30):

> Like one that draws the model of a house
> Beyond his power to build it; who, half through,
> Gives o'er and leaves his part-created cost
> A naked subject to the weeping clouds,
> And waste for churlish winter's tyranny.

The Archbishop of York then intervenes on the side of immediate action –

> The commonwealth is sick of their own choice;
> Their over-greedy love hath surfeited:
> An habitation giddy and unsure
> Hath he that buildeth on the vulgar heart . . .

and it is characteristic of this play that the very fickleness of the
common people, dwelt on at some length, should be used to
point an obvious moral – 'What trust is in these times?' – and,
simultaneously, adduced as a ground for optimism. It is the
impetuous Hastings who carries his policy and, with unintended
irony, hustles off his fellows to try their chance:

> We are time's subjects, and time bids be gone.

The world of *King Henry IV, Part II* – the world we are
introduced to in the first Act – is a world where men are only too

plainly time's subjects, yet persist in planning and contriving and attempting by hook or by crook to further their own interests. Most of them, drawing a model of a desirable future beyond their power to build, are, in the course of the play, disappointed. Since there is no close poetic texture lengthy quotation is unnecessary, but it is worth remarking how often the pattern of hope and disappointment is repeated. Hotspur at Shrewsbury – so we are reminded early in the play – had 'lined himself with hope',

> Eating the air on promise of supply,
> Flattering himself in project of a power
> Much smaller than the smallest of his thoughts.
> And so, with great imagination
> Proper to madmen, led his powers to death,
> And winking leap'd into destruction.   (I iii 27–33)

The news of Hotspur's death reaches Northumberland hard on the heels of 'certain news' ('As good as heart can wish') of rebel victory. In the very scene in which Hotspur's folly is recalled the rebel leaders allow themselves an over-optimistic estimate of their resources, as we see when, before the encounter with the royal forces, Northumberland again defaults, sending 'hearty prayers' for their success instead of men: 'Thus do the hopes we have in him touch ground' (IV i 17). When the king's generals offer to negotiate, Hastings (who might indeed adopt Pistol's somewhat travel-stained motto, 'Si fortune me tormente, sperato me contento') finds fresh grounds for optimism: 'Our peace shall stand as firm as rocky mountains' (IV i 188) – and on that note the rebel generals walk into the prepared trap. It may of course be said that a play about an unsuccessful rebellion was bound to put some emphasis on frustrated hopes; but it is not only the Northumberland faction who provide examples of the ironic discrepancy between what is planned for and what is achieved. Henry Bolingbroke, caught in the toils of 'necessity' (for 'to end one doubt by death Revives two greater in the heirs of life' (IV i 199–200)), spends his powers seeking an elusive stability. It is when this is almost achieved, the long-planned crusade about to be embarked on – 'And every thing lies level to our wish' (IV iv 7) – that his own strength fails him. The scene in which he hears of the rebel overthrow is indeed an obvious parallel to that in which Northumberland declared that ill tidings 'have in some measure made me well' (I i 139):

> And wherefore should these good news make me sick?
> Will Fortune never come with both hands full,
> But write her fair words still in foulest letters? . . .
> I should rejoice now at this happy news;
> And now my sight fails, and my brain is giddy . . .
>
> (IV iv 102–10)

It is of course true that Henry has the satisfaction of a reconciliation with his eldest son, and dies hoping that the reign of Henry V will be quieter than his own,

> for what in me was purchased,
> Falls upon thee in a more fairer sort.

But in the imaginative impact of the play as a whole Hal's robust assertion of *de facto* sovereignty

> – My gracious liege,
> You won it [the crown], wore it, kept it, gave it me;
> Then plain and right must my possession be –

counts for little beside the bleak and disillusioned summary of his reign that the elder Henry has just given his son (IV v 183 ff). As for Falstaff, there is the superb comedy of the scene where he and his companions indulge themselves in what, to any sober view, is the most imbecile bit of wishful thinking that ever deluded poor mortals.

> *Pistol.* Sir John, thy tender lambkin now is king; Harry the fifth's the man. . . .
> *Falstaff.* What, is the old king dead?
> *Pistol.* As nail in door: the things I speak are just.
> *Falstaff.* Away, Bardolph! saddle my horse. Master Robert Shallow, choose what office thou wilt in the land, 'tis thine. Pistol! I will double-charge thee with dignities.

Bardolph. O joyful day!
   I would not take a knighthood for my fortune.
Pistol. What! I do bring good news.
Falstaff. Carry Master Silence to bed. Master Shallow, my
   Lord Shallow, – be what thou wilt; I am fortune's
   steward – get on thy boots: we'll ride all night. O
   sweet Pistol! Away Bardolph! [*Exit Bardolph*] Come,
   Pistol, utter more to me; and withal devise something
   to do thyself good. Boot, boot, Master Shallow! I
   know the young king is sick for me. Let us take any
   man's horses; the laws of England are at my commandment. Blessed are they that have been my friends;
   and woe to my lord chief justice!
Pistol. Let vultures vile seize on his lungs also!
   'Where is the life that late I led?' say they:
   Why, here it is; welcome these pleasant days!

In this context it is plain that the King's mutability speech
already quoted (p. 174, above) is not just a bit of moralizing
appropriate to a sick and disappointed man. It is not merely 'in
character'; it is an explicit formulation of feelings and attitudes
deeply embedded in the play. Act III, the central act, has only two
scenes, one at court, one in Gloucestershire, and the second
succeeds the first without a break. With the King's words still
in our ears we are given (among other things) one of the most
superb variations in English literature on the theme of *le temps
perdu*. Act III, scene ii, like the later Cotswold scenes, is firmly
rooted in the actual. Life is going on in this little bit of rural
England, and will go on, for all the wars and civil wars now and
to come – the smith must be paid, the hade land sown with red
wheat, and the well-chain mended.[4] That life is vividly present
to us, built up little by little with unobtrusive art. But the scene is
drenched in memory. In the first fifty lines, as Shallow recalls the
poor pranks of his mad days at Clement's Inn, the exploits of
young Jack Falstaff who is now old, and of old Double who is
dead, we are at least as much aware of the past (and of the fact
that it *is* the past) as of anything in the present. There follows the
arrival of Bardolph and Falstaff and the play with the conscripts:
Mouldy, whose old mother has no one else to do 'her husbandry

and her drudgery', the thin Shadow, the ragged Wart, Feeble the
woman's taylor, who has a stout heart and – like Hamlet – a
philosophic mind,[5] Bullcalf who has a cough 'caught with ringing
in the king's affairs upon his coronation-day' – all of them, though
two escape the press, 'mortal men' who 'owe God a death'. Then
the theme of times past – part memory, part make-believe – is
taken up again. 'Doth she hold her own well?' Shallow asks
Falstaff of Jane Nightwork.

> *Falstaff.* Old, old, Master Shallow.
> *Shallow.* Nay, she must be old; she cannot choose but be old;
>   certain she's old; and had Robin Nightwork by old
>   Nightwork before I came to Clement's Inn.
> *Silence.* That's fifty-five year ago.
> *Shallow.* Ha, cousin Silence, that thou hadst seen that that this
>   knight and I have seen! Ha, Sir John, said I well?
> *Falstaff.* We have heard the chimes at midnight, Master
>   Shallow.
> *Shallow.* That we have, that we have, that we have; in faith,
>   Sir John, we have: our watch-word was 'Hem boys!'
>   Come, let's to dinner; come, let's to dinner: Jesus, the
>   days that we have seen! Come, come.   (III ii 200–15)

Now there are obvious ways in which the dominant mood of the
play can be related to the mood of so many of the Sonnets; for
here before us we

> perceive that men as plants increase,
> Cheered and check'd even by the self-same sky,
> Vaunt in their youthful sap, at height decrease,
> And wear their brave state out of memory.

Henry IV, Part II, like the Sonnets, is permeated by 'the conceit
of this inconstant stay', and for an understanding of the play
itself, as for any attempt to understand the Shakespearean progress, it is necessary to see how the constant sense of time – of
time as mere sequence, bringing change – shapes the matter before
us. Yet to put the matter thus, necessary as it is, is to give a partial
and one-sided impression. Unqualified, the account so far given
falsifies the imaginative impact of a play that is more lively, more

complex, and more far-reaching in its implications than I have so
far been able to suggest.

The tone of the play is sombre; but it could not possibly be
called pessimistic or depressed. Not only is there the vigour of
mind with which the political theme is grasped and presented,
there is, in the Falstaff scenes, a familiar comic verve together
with an outgoing sympathy – even, at times, liking – for what is
so firmly judged. It is important, here, to say neither more nor
less than one means, and humour is of all literary qualities the
most difficult to handle. Where, as in Shakespeare or Jonson or
Molière, humour serves a serious, a truly imaginative purpose,
the commentator who tries to define the purpose is likely to cut
an odd figure in the eyes of those whose gusto prefers to dwell
exclusively on the fun. And indeed there is something comic in a
pedagogic or literary-critical handling of things that make you
laugh. In *King Henry IV, Part II*, there is nothing, to my taste,
so funny as the scene of the mock-kings in Part I; but there is the
superb incoherence of Mrs Quickly, there is Pistol's constant
re-creation of the dramatic part in which he lives,[6] there is the
exquisite absence of positive presence in Silence; and Falstaff,
though he can sometimes go through the motions of wit without
the reality (a failure that seems, on Shakespeare's part, deliberate)
can still sometimes surprise us with the sheer agility of his self-
defence. These things are there, and we can only suppose that the
mind that created them enjoyed them. But in relation to our larger
themes the significance for us is this: we know that we are dealing
with a free mind – one that is neither driven by, nor bent on
driving, an 'idea'; the sombre preoccupations are not obsessions.

And Shakespeare shows a further characteristic of great
genius: he can feel for, can even invest with dignity, those representative human types who, in the complex play of attitudes that
constitute his dramatic statement, are judged and found wanting.
When Falstaff celebrates with Doll Tearsheet, at the Boar's Head
Tavern, his departure for the wars (II iv), there is nothing comic
in the exhibition of senile lechery. Yet the tipsy Doll can move
us with, 'Come, I'll be friends with thee, Jack: thou art going to
the wars; and whether I shall ever see thee again or no, there is

nobody cares'. And at the end of the scene Mrs Quickly too has
her moment, when sentimentality itself is transformed simply by
looking towards those human decencies and affections for which
– the realities being absent – it must do duty:

> Well, fare thee well: I have known thee these twenty nine
> years, come peascod time; but an honester and truer-hearted
> man, – well, fare thee well.

There is nothing facile in Shakespeare's charity; it is simply that
Shakespeare, like Chaucer, is not afraid of his spontaneous
feelings, and his feelings are not – so to speak – afraid of each
other.

Here, then, is one way in which the insistent elegiac note is
both qualified and deepened. There is yet another. We have
already noticed the repeated references to Falstaff's age and
diseases. But it is not only Falstaff who is diseased. Northumberland is sick, or 'crafty-sick'; the King is dying; and the imagery
of disease links the individuals to the general action.

> Then you perceive the body of our kingdom
> How foul it is; what rank diseases grow,
> And with what danger, near the heart of it.
>
> (III i 38–40)

The King speaks here the same language as the Archbishop who
opposes him:

> . . . we are all diseased,
> And with our surfeiting and wanton hours
> Have brought ourselves into a burning fever,
> And we must bleed for it.   (IV i 54–7)

Now disease is not simply, like old age, an inevitable result of
time. Disease, in this play as in others, is associated with disorder
originating in the will. The land is sick because of an original act
of usurpation, and because of the further self-seeking of those
who helped Bolingbroke to the throne, and because people like
Falstaff think that 'the law of nature'[7] is different from and can
override the law of justice.

In the light of this we can understand why the feelings associated with time in this play are not simply feelings of pathos ('And is old Double dead?'). As Mr Traversi has remarked in an excellent essay,[8] 'allied to the idea of Time in this play is the conception of over-ruling necessity. . . . *Necessity* is a fact generally accepted by all the political characters . . . All are "time's subjects".' Now it is certainly true that we are very much aware of time's power; all the strivings of the characters are shadowed by it. But the word 'time' (or 'times'), so frequently appearing, more often than not means the present age, the present state of affairs; and it is with 'the times' in this sense that, again and again, there is associated the compulsion or 'necessity' invoked by both sides in the political quarrel:

> We see which way the stream of time doth run,
> And are enforced from our most quiet shore
> By the rough torrent of occasion.

> The time misorder'd doth, in common sense,
> Crowd us and crush us to this monstrous form,
> To hold our safety up.[9]

'Time's subjects', in short, are men compelled because they are followers of that policy, or self-interest, which works, and can only work, 'on leases of short-number'd hours'.[10] And it is because they accept the times – the world's standards, the shifting pattern of warring interests – that they are ruled by Time, that it is impossible for them to see the temporal process as other than absolute: 'Let time shape, and there an end'.

I hope this does not seem like putting Shakespeare on the rack of a demand for a moral at any price. Shakespeare never explicitly points a moral; and it will be some years before he fully reveals in terms of the awakened imagination why those that follow their noses are led by their eyes, or what it really means to be the fool of time. For the moment we are only concerned with the direction that his developing insight is taking; and it seems to me that what is coming into consciousness is nothing less than an awareness of how men make the world that they inhabit, an understanding of the relation between what men are and the kind of perceptions they have about the nature of things. It is this growing awareness, linking the overt social criticism with the more deep-lying and pervasive concern with time's power, that explains our sense of fundamental issues coming to expression. It explains why the tone of *Henry IV, Part II* is entirely different from the tone of detached observation of the earlier plays. In Act I, scene i, Northumberland, finding physic in the poison of ill news, throws away his crutch and 'sickly quoif'.

> Now bind my brows with iron; and approach
> The ragged'st hour that time and spite dare bring
> To frown upon the enraged Northumberland!
> Let heaven kiss earth! now let not Nature's hand
> Keep the wild flood confined! let order die!
> And let this world no longer be a stage
> To feed contention in a lingering act;
> But let one spirit of the first-born Cain
> Reign in all bosoms, that, each heart being set
> On bloody courses, the rude scene may end,
> And darkness be the burier of the dead!

These lines, placed as they are at the climax of the first scene of the play, are intended to be taken with deadly seriousness: this is what is implied in Northumberland's 'aptest way for safety and revenge'. If the note of horror seems momentarily to go beyond the prevailing mood of the play (it is a note more appropriate to *Lear* or *Macbeth*),[11] it is not discordant with that mood which, even without this vision of anarchy, is sombre enough.

Henry IV, Part II, is markedly a transitional play. It looks back to the Sonnets and the earlier history plays, and it looks forward to the great tragedies. In technique too we are beginning to find that more complete permeation of the material by the shaping imagination which distinguishes the plays that follow it from those that went before.[12] The words do not yet strike to unsuspected depths (it is significant that some of the most vividly realized scenes are in prose); but in the manner of its working the play is nearer to *Macbeth* than to *Richard III*; the imagery is organic to the whole, and the verse and prose alike are beginning to promote that associative activity that I have tried to define as the distinguishing mark of great poetic drama.

It is this imaginative wholeness that allows us to say that Shakespeare is now wholly *within* his material. As a result the play has
that doubleness which, as T. S. Eliot says, is a characteristic of
the greatest poetry,[13] and the more obvious qualities of action,
satire, humour and pathos are informed and integrated by a
serious vision of life subjected to time.

SOURCE: *Some Shakespearean Themes* (1959).

NOTES

1. In each instance Shakespeare is drawing on the passage from book
xv of Ovid's *Metamorphoses*, which so haunted his imagination. See
Knox Pooler's Arden edition of the Sonnets (1918) p. 66, and, more
especially, J. W. Lever, *The Elizabethan Love Sonnet* (1956) pp. 248 ff.

2. The Scriptural references in which both parts of this play abound
(see Richmond Noble, *Shakespeare's Biblical Knowledge* (1935) pp.
169–81) seem to me to take on a more severe significance in Part II; in
the scene under consideration the references to Job, in particular –
'and your bodies like the clay' (13: 12), 'his candle shall be put out with
him' (18: 6), and 'Among old persons there is wisdom, and in age is
understanding' (12: 12) – seem to point a sombre irony. Noble (p.
65 and p. 174) says that *Henry IV, Part II* 'is the earliest play in which
Genevan readings show a decided preponderance over Bishops'',
which suggests a comparatively fresh re-reading of considerable parts
of the Bible at this time.

3. The very slight alteration of the Folio punctuation that I have
made here seems to me to give excellent sense to a passage usually
labelled corrupt. Lord Bardolph says, in effect, 'Yes, it does do harm,
if (as in the present case) a military enterprise relies on hope prematurely
aroused, as when we see buds appear in a too early spring etc.' The line
'Indeed the instant action, a cause on foot,' is emphatic repetition as
Bardolph tries to impress Hastings with his own sense of the desperate
importance of seeing their present enterprise as an example of the
general rule about not counting your chickens, etc.

4. Dr Tillyard (*Shakespeare's History Plays* (1944) p. 303) aptly
quotes Hardy's 'In a Time of the Breaking of Nations'.

5. 'By my troth, I care not; a man can die but once: we owe God a
death: I'll ne'er bear a base mind: an't be my destiny, so; an't be not,
so: no man's too good to serve his prince; and let it go which way it
will, he that dies this year is quit for the next' (III ii 230–4).

6. See Leslie Hotson's essay, 'Ancient Pistol', in *Shakespeare's Sonnets Dated and Other Essays* (1949).

7. 'If the young dace be a bate for the old pike, I see no reason in the law of nature but I may snap at him [Shallow]' (III ii 325–7).

8. *Scrutiny*, XV, no. 2 (Spring 1948). This essay is incorporated in Mr Traversi's *Shakespeare from 'Richard II' to 'Henry V'* (1957).

9. IV i 70–3 (Vaughan's 'shore' – Folio, 'there' – is adopted by Professor Dover Wilson in the New Cambridge edition), IV ii 33–5. Both these passages are spoken by the Archbishop of York. Bolingbroke's version of affairs is similar: he had no intention of taking the throne from Richard, 'But that necessity so bow'd the state, That I and greatness were compell'd to kiss' (III i 73–4); and of the rebellion against himself, 'Are these things then necessities? Then let us meet them like necessities' (III i 92–3).

10.   [Love] fears not policy, that heretic,
       Which works on leases of short-number'd hours . . .

                                             (Sonnet CXXIV)

11. There are the obvious parallels – *King Lear*, IV ii 29–50, *Macbeth*, IV i 50–60; also of course *Sir Thomas More*, II iv and *Troilus and Cressida*, I iii 108–24. Of the passage quoted in the text Professor Dover Wilson aptly asks, 'What does not Pope's famous conclusion to *The Dunciad* owe to it?'

12. See D. A. Traversi's essay already referred to.

13. Introduction to G. Wilson Knight, *The Wheel of Fire* (1930), p. xiv.

W. H. Auden

THE PRINCE'S DOG (1959)

Whoever takes up the sword shall perish by the sword. And
whoever does not take up the sword (or lets it drop) shall perish
on the cross.
(SIMONE WEIL)

IT has been observed that critics who write about Shakespeare
reveal more about themselves than about Shakespeare, but
perhaps that is the great value of drama of the Shakespearian
kind, namely, that whatever he may see taking place on stage, its
final effect upon each spectator is a self-revelation.

Shakespeare holds the position in our literature of Top Bard,
but this deserved priority has one unfortunate consequence; we
generally make our first acquaintance with his plays, not in the
theatre, but in the classroom or study, so that, when we do attend
a performance, we have lost that naïve openness to surprise which
is the proper frame of mind in which to witness any drama. The
experience of reading a play and the experience of watching it
performed are never identical, but in the case of *Henry IV* the
difference between the two is particularly great.

At a performance, my immediate reaction is to wonder what
Falstaff is doing in this play at all. At the end of *Richard II*, we
were told that the Heir Apparent has taken up with a dissolute
crew of 'unrestrained loose companions'. What sort of bad
company would one expect to find Prince Hal keeping when the
curtain rises on *Henry IV*? Surely, one could expect to see him
surrounded by daring, rather sinister juvenile delinquents and
beautiful gold-digging whores. But whom do we meet in the
Boar's Head? A fat, cowardly tosspot, old enough to be his father,
two down-at-heel hangers-on, a slatternly hostess and only one
whore, who is not in her earliest youth either; all of them seedy,
and, by any worldly standards, including those of the criminal

classes, all of them *failures*. Surely, one thinks, an Heir Apparent, sowing his wild oats, could have picked himself a more exciting crew than that. As the play proceeds, our surprise is replaced by another kind of puzzle, for the better we come to know Falstaff, the clearer it becomes that the world of historical reality which a Chronicle Play claims to imitate is not a world which he can inhabit.

If it really was Queen Elizabeth who demanded to see Falstaff in a comedy, then she showed herself a very perceptive critic. But even in *The Merry Wives of Windsor*, Falstaff has not and could not have found his true home because Shakespeare was only a poet. For that he was to wait nearly two hundred years till Verdi wrote his last opera. Falstaff is not the only case of a character whose true home is the world of music; others are Tristan, Isolde, and Don Giovanni.[1]

Though they each call for a different kind of music, Tristan, Don Giovanni, and Falstaff have certain traits in common. They do not belong to the temporal world of change. One cannot imagine any of them as babies, for a Tristan who is not in love, a Don Giovanni who has no name on his list, a Falstaff who is not old and fat, are inconceivable. When Falstaff says, 'When I was about their years, Hal, I was not an eagle's talent in the waist; I could have crept into an alderman's thumb-ring' – we take it as a typical Falstaffian fib, but we believe him when he says, 'I was born about three in the afternoon, with a white head and something of a round belly.'

Time, for Tristan, is a single moment stretched out tighter and tighter until it snaps. Time, for Don Giovanni, is an infinite arithmetical series of unrelated moments which has no beginning and would have no end if Heaven did not intervene and cut it short. For Falstaff, time does not exist, since he belongs to the *opera buffa* world of play and mock action governed not by will or desire, but by innocent wish, a world where no one can suffer because everything he says and does is only a pretense.

Thus, while we must see Tristan die in Isolde's arms and we must see Don Giovanni sink into the earth, because being doomed to die and to go to hell are essential to their beings, we cannot see Falstaff die on stage because, if we did, we should not believe it; we should know that, as at the battle of Shrewsbury, he was only shamming. I am not even quite sure that we believe it when we are told of his death in *Henry V*; I think we accept it, as we accept the death of Sherlock Holmes, as his creator's way of saying, 'I am getting tired of this character'; we feel sure that, if the public pleads with him strongly enough, Shakespeare will find some way to bring him to life again. The only kind of funeral music we can associate with him is the mock-requiem in the last act of Verdi's opera.

Domine fallo casto

　　　　　　　　　　　　　Ma salvaggi l'addomine

Domine fallo guasto.

　　　　　　　　　　　　　Ma salvaggi l'addomine.

There are at least two places in the play where the incongruity of the *opera buffa* world with the historical world is too much, even for Shakespeare, and a patently false note is struck. The first occurs when, on the battlefield of Shrewsbury, Falstaff thrusts his sword into Hotspur's corpse. Within his own world, Falstaff could stab a corpse because, there, all battles are mock battles, all corpses straw dummies; but we, the audience, are too conscious that this battle has been a real battle and that this corpse is the real dead body of a brave and noble young man. Pistol could do it, because Pistol is a contemptible character, but Falstaff cannot; that is to say, there is no way in which an actor can play the scene convincingly. So, too, with the surrender of Colevile to Falstaff in Part II. In his conversation, first with Colevile and then with Prince John, Falstaff talks exactly as we expect – to him, the whole business is a huge joke. But then he is present during a scene when we are shown that it is no joke at all. How is any actor to behave and speak his lines during the following?

Lancaster. Is thy name Colevile?
Colevile. It is, my lord.
Lancaster. A famous rebel art thou, Colevile.
Falstaff. And a famous true subject took him.

Colevile. I am, my lord, but as my betters are,
   That led me hither. Had they been ruled by me,
   You should have won them dearer than you have.
Falstaff. I know not how they sold themselves: but thou,
      like a kind fellow, gavest thyself away gratis; and I
      thank thee for thee.
Lancaster. Now have you left pursuit?
Westmoreland. Retreat is made and execution stay'd.
Lancaster. Send Colevile, with his confederates,
   To York, to present execution.

The Falstaffian frivolity and the headsman's axe cannot so
directly confront each other.

Reading *Henry IV*, we can easily give our full attention to
the historical-political scenes, but, when watching a performance,
attention is distracted by our eagerness to see Falstaff reappear.
Short of cutting him out of the play altogether, no producer can
prevent him stealing the show. From an actor's point of view,
the role of Falstaff has the enormous advantage that he has only
to think of one thing – playing to an audience. Since he lives in an
eternal present and the historical world does not exist for him,
there is no difference for Falstaff between those on stage and
those out front, and if the actor were to appear in one scene in
Elizabethan costume and in the next in top hat and morning coat,
no one would be bewildered. The speech of all the other characters is, like our own, conditioned by two factors, the external
situation with its questions, answers, and commands, and the
inner need of each character to disclose himself to others. But
Falstaff's speech has only one cause, his absolute insistence, at
every moment and at all costs, upon disclosing himself. Half his
lines could be moved from one speech to another without our
noticing, for nearly everything he says is a variant upon one
theme – 'I am that I am.'

Moreover, Shakespeare has so written his part that it cannot
be played unsympathetically. A good actor can make us admire
Prince Hal, but he cannot hope to make us like him as much as
even a second-rate actor will make us like Falstaff. Sober reflection in the study may tell us that Falstaff is not, after all, a

very admirable person, but Falstaff on the stage gives us no time
for sober reflection. When Hal or the Chief Justice or any others
indicate that they are not bewitched by Falstaff, reason might tell
us that they are in the right, but we ourselves are already bewitched, so that their disenchantment seems out of place, like the
presence of teetotalers at a drunken party.

Suppose, then, that a producer were to cut the Falstaff scenes
altogether, what would *Henry IV* become? The middle section
of a political trilogy which could be entitled *Looking for the Doctor*.

The body politic of England catches an infection from its
family physician. An able but unqualified practitioner throws
him out of the sickroom and takes over. The patient's tempera-
ture continues to rise. But then, to everybody's amazement, the
son of the unqualified practitioner whom, though he has taken
his degree, everyone has hitherto believed to be a hopeless
invalid, effects a cure. Not only is the patient restored to health
but also, at the doctor's orders, takes another body politic, France,
to wife.

The theme of this trilogy is, that is to say, the question: What
combination of qualities is needed in the Ruler whose function is
the establishment and maintenance of Temporal Justice? According to Shakespeare, the ideal Ruler must satisfy five conditions.
(1) He must know what is just and what is unjust. (2) He must
himself be just. (3) He must be strong enough to compel those
who would like to be unjust to behave justly. (4) He must have
the capacity both by nature and by art of making others loyal to
his person. (5) He must be the legitimate ruler by whatever
standard legitimacy is determined in the society to which he
belongs.

Richard II fails to satisfy the first four of these. He does not
know what Justice is, for he follows the advice of foolish flatterers.
He is himself unjust, for he spends the money he obtains by
taxing the Commons and fining the Nobility, not on defending
England against her foes, but upon maintaining a lavish and
frivolous court, so that, when he really does need money for a
patriotic purpose, the war with Ireland, his exchequer is empty

and in desperation he commits a gross act of injustice by con-
fiscating Bolingbroke's estates.

It would seem that at one time he had been popular but he has
now lost his popularity, partly on account of his actions, but also
because he lacks the art of winning hearts. According to his
successor, he had made the mistake of being overfamiliar – the
ruler should not let himself be seen too often as 'human' – and in
addition, he is not by nature the athletic, physically brave warrior
who is the type most admired by the feudal society he is called
upon to rule.

In consequence, Richard II is a weak ruler who cannot keep
the great nobles in order or even command the loyalty of his
soldiers, and weakness in a ruler is the worst defect of all. A
cruel, even an unjust king, who is strong, is preferable to the
most saintly weakling because most men will behave unjustly if
they discover that they can with impunity; tyranny, the injustice
of one, is less unjust than anarchy, the injustice of many.

But there remains the fifth condition: whatever his defects,
Richard II is the legitimate King of England. Since all men
are mortal, and many men are ambitious, unless there is some
impersonal principle by which, when the present ruler dies, the
choice of his successor can be decided, there will be a risk of
civil war in every generation. It is better to endure the injustice
of the legitimate ruler, who will die anyway sooner or later, than
allow a usurper to take his place by force.

As a potential ruler, Bolingbroke possesses many of the right
qualities. He is a strong man, he knows how to make himself
popular, and he would like to be just. We never hear, even from
the rebels, of any specific actions of Henry IV which are unjust,
only of suspicions which may be just or unjust. But in yielding
to the temptation, when the opportunity unexpectedly offers
itself, of deposing his lawful sovereign, he commits an act of
injustice for which he and his kingdom have to pay a heavy price.
Because of it, though he is strong enough to crush rebellion, he
is not strong or popular enough to prevent rebellion breaking out.

Once Richard has been murdered, however, the rule of Henry
IV is better than any alternative. Though, legally, Mortimer may

have a good or better right to the throne, the scene at Bangor
between Hotspur, Worcester, Mortimer, and Glendower, convinces us that Henry's victory is a victory for justice since we
learn that the rebels have no concern for the interests of the
Kingdom, only for their own. Their plan, if they succeed, is to
carve up England into three petty states. Henry may wish that
Hotspur, not Hal, were his heir, because Hotspur is a brave
warrior ready to risk his life in battle against England's foes,
while Hal appears to be dissipated and frivolous, but we know
better. Hotspur is indeed brave, but that is all. A man who can
say

> I'll give thrice so much land
> To any well-deserving friend;
> But in the way of bargain, mark ye me,
> I'll cavil on the ninth part of a hair

is clearly unfitted to be a ruler because his actions are based, not
on justice, but on personal whim. Moreover, he is not interested
in political power; all he desires is military glory.

Thirdly, there is Prince Hal, Henry V-to-be. To everyone
except himself, he seems at first to be another Richard, unjust,
lacking in self-control but, unfortunately, the legitimate heir.
By the time the curtain falls on *Henry V*, however, he is recognized by all to be the Ideal Ruler. Like his father in his youth, he
is brave and personable. In addition, he is a much cleverer politician. While his father was an improviser, he is a master of the
art of timing. His first soliloquy reveals him as a person who always sees several steps ahead and has the patience to wait, even
though waiting means temporary misunderstanding and un-
popularity, until the right moment for action comes; he will
never, if he can help it, leave anything to chance. Last but not
least, he is blessed by luck. His father had foreseen that internal
dissension could only be cured if some common cause could be
found which would unite all parties but he was too old and ill,
the internal quarrels too violent. But when Hal succeeds as
Henry V, most of his enemies are dead or powerless – Cambridge
and Scroop have no armies at their back – and his possible right

to the throne of France provides the common cause required to unite both the nobles and the commons, and gives him the opportunity, at Agincourt, to show his true mettle.

One of Falstaff's dramatic functions is to be the means by which Hal is revealed to be the Just Ruler, not the dissolute and frivolous young man everybody has thought him; but, so far as the audience is concerned, Falstaff has fulfilled his function by Act III, scene ii of the First Part, when the King entrusts Hal with a military command. Up to this point the Falstaff scenes have kept us in suspense. In Act I, scene ii, we hear Hal promise

> I'll so offend, to make offense a skill,
> Redeeming time when men think least I will.

But then we watch the rebellion being prepared while he does nothing but amuse himself with Falstaff, so that we are left wondering whether he meant what he said or was only play acting. But from the moment he engages in the political action of the play, we have no doubts whatsoever as to his ambition, capacity, and ultimate triumph for, however often henceforward we may see him with Falstaff, it is never at a time when his advice and arms are needed by the State; he visits the Boar's Head in leisure hours when there is nothing serious for him to do.

For those in the play, the decisive moment of revelation is, of course, his first public act as Henry V, his rejection of Falstaff and company. For his subjects who have not, as we have, watched him with Falstaff, it is necessary to allay their fears that, though they already know him to be brave and capable, he may still be unjust and put his personal friendships before the impartial justice which it is his duty as king to maintain. But we, who have watched his private life, have no such fears. We have long known that his first soliloquy meant what it said, that he has never been under any false illusions about Falstaff or anyone else and that when the right moment comes to reject Falstaff, that is to say, when such a rejection will make the maximum political effect, he will do so without hesitation. Even the magnanimity he shows in granting his old companion a life competence, which so impresses those about him, cannot impress us because, knowing Falstaff as they do not, we know what the effect on him of such a rejection must be, that his heart will be 'fracted and corroborate' and no life competence can mend that. It is Hal's company he wants, not a pension from the Civil List.

The essential Falstaff is the Falstaff of *The Merry Wives* and Verdi's opera, the comic hero of the world of play, the unkillable self-sufficient immortal whose verdict on existence is

> *Tutto nel mondo è burla. . . .*
> *Tutti gabbàti. Irridè*
> *L'un l'altro ogni mortal.*
> *Ma ride ben chi ride*
> *La risata final*

In *Henry IV*, however, something has happened to this immortal which draws him out of his proper world into the historical world of suffering and death. He has become capable of serious emotion. He continues to employ the speech of his comic world:

I have forsworn his company hourly any time this two-and-twenty years, and yet I am bewitched with the rogue's company. If the rascal have not given me medicines to make me love him, I'll be hanged. It could not be else. I have drunk medicines.

But the emotion so flippantly expressed could equally well be expressed thus:

> If my dear love were but the child of state
> It might for Fortune's bastard be unfathered,
> As subject to Time's love or to Time's hate,
> Weeds among weeds, or flowers with flowers gathered.
> No, it was builded far from accident;
> It suffers not in smiling pomp, nor falls
> Under the blow of thralled discontent,
> Whereto th' inviting time our fashion calls.
> It fears not Policy, that heretic
> Which works on leases of short-numbered hours,
> But all alone stands hugely politic.

As the play proceeds, we become aware, behind all the fun, of something tragic. Falstaff loves Hal with an absolute devotion.

'The lovely bully' is the son he has never had, the youth pre-
destined to the success and worldly glory which he will never
enjoy. He believes that his love is returned, that the Prince is
indeed his other self, so he is happy, despite old age and poverty.
We, however, can see that he is living in a fool's paradise, for the
Prince cares no more for him as a person than he would care for
the King's Jester. He finds Falstaff amusing but no more. If we
could warn Falstaff of what he is too blind to see, we might well
say: Beware, before it is too late, of becoming involved with one
of those mortals

> That do not do the thing they most do show,
> Who, moving others, are themselves as stone. . . .

Falstaff's story, in fact, is not unlike one of those folk tales in
which a mermaid falls in love with a mortal prince: the price she
pays for her infatuation is the loss of her immortality without the
compensation of temporal happiness.

Let us now suppose, not only that Falstaff takes no part in the
play, but is also allowed to sit in the audience as a spectator. How
much will he understand of what he sees going on?

He will see a number of Englishmen divided into two parties
who finally come to blows. That they should come to blows will
in itself be no proof to him that they are enemies because they
might, like boxers, have agreed to fight for fun. In Falstaff's
world there are two causes of friendship and enmity. My friend
may be someone whose appearance and manner I like at this
moment, my enemy someone whose appearance and manner I
dislike. Thus, he will understand Hotspur's objection to Bolingbroke perfectly well.

> Why, what a candy deal of courtesy
> This fawning greyhound then did proffer me.
> 'Look, when his infant fortune came to age,'
> And 'gentle Harry Percy' and 'kind cousin'.
> O the devil take such cozeners.

To Falstaff, 'my friend' can also mean he whose wish at this
moment coincides with mine, 'my enemy' he whose wish contra-

dicts mine. He will see the civil war, therefore, as a clash between Henry and Mortimer who both wish to wear the crown. What will perplex him is any argument as to who has the better right to wear it.

Anger and fear he can understand, because they are immediate emotions, but not nursing a grievance or planning revenge or apprehension, for these presuppose that the future inherits from the past. He will not, therefore, be able to make head or tail of Warwick's speech, 'There is a history in all men's lives . . .', nor any reasons the rebels give for their actions which are based upon anything Bolingbroke did before he became king, nor the reason given by Worcester for concealing the king's peace offer from Hotspur:

> It is not possible, it cannot be
> The King should keep his word in loving us.
> He will suspect us still and find a time
> To punish this offence in other faults.

To *keep his word* is a phrase outside Falstaff's comprehension, for a promise means that at some future moment I might have to refuse to do what I wish, and, in Falstaff's world to wish and to do are synonymous. For the same reason, when, by promising them redress, Prince John tricks the rebels into disbanding their armies and then arrests them, Falstaff will not understand why they and all the audience except himself are shocked.

The first words Shakespeare puts into Falstaff's mouth are, 'Now Hal, what time of day is it, lad?' to which the Prince quite rightly replies, 'What the devil hast thou to do with the time of day?' In Falstaff's world, every moment is one of infinite possibility when anything can be wished. As a spectator, he will keep hearing the characters use the words *time* and *occasion* in a sense which will stump him.

> What I know
> Is ruminated, plotted, and set down
> And only stays but to behold the face
> Of that occasion that shall bring it on.

The purpose you undertake is dangerous . . . the time itself unsorted. . . .

> . . . I will resolve for Scotland. There am I
> Till time and vantage crave my company.

Of all the characters in the play, the one he will think he understands best is the least Falstaff-like of them all, Hotspur, for Hotspur, like himself, appears to obey the impulse of the moment and say exactly what he thinks without prudent calculation. Both conceal nothing from others, Falstaff because he has no mask to put on, Hotspur because he has so become his mask that he has no face beneath it. Falstaff says, as it were, 'I am I. Whatever I do, however outrageous, is of infinite importance because I do it.' Hotspur says: 'I am Hotspur, the fearless, the honest, plain-spoken warrior. If I should ever show fear or tell lies, even white ones, I should cease to exist.' If Falstaff belonged to the same world as Hotspur, one could call him a liar, but, in his own eyes, he is perfectly truthful, for, to him, fact is subjective fact, 'what I am actually feeling and thinking at this moment'. To call him a liar is as ridiculous as if, in a play, a character should say, 'I am Napoleon,' and a member of the audience should cry, 'You're not. You're Sir John Gielgud.'

In Ibsen's *Peer Gynt*, there is a remarkable scene in which Peer visits the Troll King. At the entertainment given in his honor, animals dance to hideous noises, but Peer behaves to them with perfect manners as if they were beautiful girls and the music ravishing. After it is over, the Troll King asks him: 'Now, frankly, tell me what you saw.' Peer replies: 'What I saw was impossibly ugly' – and then describes the scene as the audience had seen it. The Troll King who has taken a fancy to him, suggests that Peer would be happier as a troll. All that is needed is a little eye operation, after which he will really see a cow as a beautiful girl. Peer indignantly refuses. He is perfectly willing, he says, to swear that a cow is a girl, but to surrender his humanity so that he can no longer lie, because he cannot distinguish between fact and fiction, that he will never do. By this criterion, neither Falstaff nor Hotspur is quite human, Falstaff because he is pure troll, Hotspur because he is so lacking in imagination that the troll kingdom is invisible to him.

At first, then, Falstaff will believe that Hotspur is one of his own kind, who like himself enjoys putting on an act, but then he will hear Hotspur say words which he cannot comprehend.

> . . . time serves wherein you may redeem
> Your banished honours and restore yourselves
> Into the good thoughts of the world again.

In Falstaff's world, the only value standard is importance, that is to say, all he demands from others is attention, all he fears is being ignored. Whether others applaud or hiss does not matter; what matters is the volume of the hissing or the applause.

Hence, in his soliloquy about honor, his reasoning runs something like this: if the consequence of demanding moral approval from others is dying, it is better to win their disapproval; a dead man has no audience.

Since the Prince is a personal friend, Falstaff is, of course, a King's man who thinks it a shame to be on any side but one, but his loyalty is like that of those who, out of local pride, support one football team rather than another. As a member of the audience, his final comment upon the political action of the play will be the same as he makes from behind the footlights.

> Well, God be thanked for these rebels: they offend none but the virtuous. . . .

A young knave and begging! Is there not employment? Doth not the King lack subjects? Do not the rebels need soldiers?

Once upon a time we were all Falstaffs: then we became social beings with super-egos. Most of us learn to accept this, but there are some in whom the nostalgia for the state of innocent self-importance is so strong that they refuse to accept adult life and responsibilities and seek some means to become again the Falstaffs they once were. The commonest technique adopted is the bottle, and, curiously enough, the male drinker reveals his intention by developing a drinker's belly.

If one visits a bathing beach, one can observe that men and

women grow fat in different ways. A fat woman exaggerates her femininity; her breasts and buttocks enlarge till she comes to look like the Venus of Willendorf. A fat man, on the other hand, looks like a cross between a very young child and a pregnant mother. There have been cultures in which obesity in women was considered the ideal of sexual attraction, but in no culture, so far as I know, has a fat man been considered more attractive than a thin one. If my own weight and experience give me any authority, I would say that fatness in the male is the physical expression of a psychological wish to withdraw from sexual competition and, by combining mother and child in his own person, to become emotionally self-sufficient. The Greeks thought of Narcissus as a slender youth but I think they were wrong. I see him as a middle-aged man with a corporation, for, however ashamed he may be of displaying it in public, in private a man with a belly loves it dearly; it may be an unprepossessing child to look at, but he has borne it all by himself.

I do here walk before thee like a sow that hath overwhelmed all her litter but one. . . .

I have a whole school of tongues in this belly of mine, and not a tongue of them all speaks any other word but my name. . . . My womb, my womb undoes me.

Not all fat men are heavy drinkers, but all males who drink heavily become fat.* At the same time, the more they drink, the less they eat. 'O monstrous! But one halfpenny worth of bread to this intolerable deal of sack!' exclaims Hal on looking at Falstaff's bill, but he cannot have expected anything else. Drunkards die, not from the liquid alcohol they take so much of, but from their refusal to eat solid food, and anyone who had to look after a drunk knows that the only way to get enough nourishment into him is to give him liquid or mashed-up foods, for he will reject any dish that needs chewing. Solid food is to the drunkard a symbolic reminder of the loss of the mother's breast and his ejection from Eden.

* All the women I have met who drank heavily were lighter and thinner than average.

A plague of sighing and grief. It blows a man up like a bladder. . . .

So Falstaff, and popular idiom identifies the kind of griefs which have this fattening effect – eating humble pie, swallowing insults, etc.

In a recent number of the *Paris Review*, Mr Nicholas Tucci writes:

The death song of the drunkard – it may go on for thirty years – goes more or less like this. 'I was born a god, with the whole world in reach of my hands, lie now defeated in the gutter. Come and listen: hear what the world has done to me.'

In Vino Veritas is an old saying that has nothing to do with the drunkard's own truth. He has no secrets – that is true – but it is not true that his truth may be found under the skin of his moral reserve or of his sober lies, so that the moment he begins to cross his eyes and pour out his heart, anyone may come in and get his fill of truth. What happens is exactly the opposite. When the drunkard confesses, he makes a careful choice of his pet sins: and these are nonexistent. He may be unable to distinguish a person from a chair, but never an unprofitable lie from a profitable one. How could he see himself as a very insignificant entity in a huge world of others, when he sees nothing but himself spread over the whole universe. 'I am alone' is indeed a true cry, but it should not be taken literally.

The drunk is unlovely to look at, intolerable to listen to, and his self-pity is contemptible. Nevertheless, as not merely a worldly failure but also a willful failure, he is a disturbing image for the sober citizen. His refusal to accept the realities of this world, babyish as it may be, compels us to take another look at this world and reflect upon our motives for accepting it. The drunkard's suffering may be self-inflicted, but it is real suffering and reminds us of all the suffering in this world which we prefer not to think about because, from the moment we accepted this world, we acquired our share of responsibility for everything that happens in it.

When we see Falstaff's gross paunch and red face, we are

reminded that the body politic of England is not so healthy, either.

> The Commonwealth is sick of their own choice.
> Their over-greedy love hath surfeited. . . .
> Thou (beastly feeder) art so full of him
> That thou provokest thyself to cast him up.
> So, so, thou common dog, didst thou disgorge
> Thy glutton bosom of the royal Richard. . . .

> Then you perceive the body of our kingdom
> How foul it is: what rank diseases grow,
> And with what danger near the heart of it.

It might be expected that we would be revolted at the sight and turn our eyes with relief and admiration to the Hero Prince. But in fact we aren't and we don't. Whenever Falstaff is on stage, we have no eyes for Hal. If Shakespeare did originally write a part for Falstaff in *Henry V*, it would not have taken pressure from the Cobhams to make him cut it out; his own dramatic instinct would have told him that, if Henry was to be shown in his full glory, the presence of Falstaff would diminish it.

Seeking for an explanation of why Falstaff affects us as he does, I find myself compelled to see *Henry IV* as possessing, in addition to its overt meaning, a parabolic significance. Overtly, Falstaff is a Lord of Misrule; parabolically, he is a comic symbol for the supernatural order of Charity as contrasted with the temporal order of Justice symbolized by Henry of Monmouth.

Such readings are only possible with drama which, like Shakespeare's, is secular, concerned directly, not with the relation of man and God, but with the relations between men. Greek tragedy, at least before Euripides, is directly religious, concerned with what the gods do to men rather than what men do to each other: it presents a picture of human events, the causes of which are divine actions. In consequence, a Greek tragedy does not demand that we 'read' it in the sense that we speak of 'reading' a face. The way of the gods may be mysterious to human beings but they are not ambiguous.

There can be no secular drama of any depth or importance except in a culture which recognizes that man has an internal history as well as an external; that his actions are partly in response to an objective situation created by his past acts and the acts of others, and partly initiated by his subjective need to recreate, redefine, and rechoose himself. Surprise and revelation are the essence of drama. In Greek tragedy these are supplied by the gods; no mortal can foresee how and when they will act. But the conduct of men has no element of surprise, that is to say, the way in which they react to the surprising events which befall them is exactly what one would expect.

A secular drama presupposes that in all which men say and do there is a gratuitous element which makes their conduct ambiguous and unpredictable. Secular drama, therefore, demands a much more active role from its audience than a Greek tragedy. The audience has to be at one and the same time a witness to what is occurring on stage and a subjective participant who interprets what he sees and hears. And a secular dramatist like Shakespeare who attempts to project the inner history of human beings into objective stage action is faced with problems which Aeschylus and Sophocles were spared, for there are aspects of this inner history which resist and sometimes defy manifestation.

Humility is represented with difficulty – when it is shown in its ideal moment, the beholder senses the lack of something because he feels that its true ideality does not consist in the fact that it is ideal in the moment but that it is constant. Romantic love can very well be represented in the moment, but conjugal love cannot, because an ideal husband is not one who is such once in his life but one who every day is such. Courage can very well be concentrated in the moment, but not patience, precisely for the reason that patience strives with time. A king who conquers kingdoms can be represented in the moment, but a cross bearer who every day takes up his cross cannot be represented in art because the point is that he does it every day. (Kierkegaard)

Let us suppose, then, that a dramatist wishes to show a character acting out of the spirit of charity or agape. At first this looks easy. Agape requires that we love our enemies, do good to those that hate us and forgive those who injure us, and this command is unconditional. Surely, all a dramatist has to do is to show one human being forgiving an enemy.

In *Measure for Measure*, Angelo has wronged Isabella and Mariana, and the facts of the wrong become public. Angelo repents and demands that the just sentence of death be passed on him by the Duke. Isabella and Mariana implore the Duke to show mercy. The Duke yields to their prayers and all ends happily. I agree with Professor Coghill's interpretation of *Measure for Measure* as a parable in which Isabella is an image for the redeemed Christian Soul, perfectly chaste and loving, whose reward is to become the bride of God; but, to my mind, the parable does not quite work because it is impossible to distinguish in dramatic action between the spirit of forgiveness and the act of pardon.

The command to forgive is unconditional: whether my enemy harden his heart or repent and beg forgiveness is irrelevant. If he hardens his heart, he does not care whether I forgive him or not and it would be impertinent of me to say, 'I forgive you.' If he repents and asks, 'Will you forgive me?' the answer, 'Yes,' should not express a decision on my part but describe a state of feeling which has always existed. On the stage, however, it is impossible to show one person forgiving another, unless the wrongdoer asks for forgiveness, because silence and inaction are undramatic. The Isabella we are shown in earlier scenes of *Measure for Measure* is certainly not in a forgiving spirit – she is in a passion of rage and despair at Angelo's injustice – and dramatically she could not be otherwise, for then there would be no play. Again, on the stage, forgiveness requires manifestation in action, that is to say, the one who forgives must be in a position to do something for the other which, if he were not forgiving, he would not do. This means that my enemy must be at my mercy; but, to the spirit of charity, it is irrelevant whether I am at my enemy's mercy or he at mine. So long as he is at my mercy, forgiveness is indistinguishable from judicial pardon.

The law cannot forgive, for the law has not been wronged, only broken; only persons can be wronged. The law can pardon, but it can only pardon what it has the power to punish. If the lawbreaker is stronger than the legal authorities, they are powerless to do either. The decision to grant or refuse pardon must be governed by prudent calculation – if the wrongdoer is pardoned, he will behave better in the future than if he were punished, etc. But charity is forbidden to calculate in this way: I am required to forgive my enemy whatever the effect on him may be.

One may say that Isabella forgives Angelo and the Duke pardons him. But, on the stage, this distinction is invisible because, there, power, justice and love are all on the same side. Justice is able to pardon what love is commanded to forgive. But to love, it is an accident that the power of temporal justice should be on its side; indeed, the Gospels assure us that, sooner or later, they will find themselves in opposition and that love must suffer at the hands of justice.

In *King Lear*, Shakespeare attempts to show absolute love and goodness, in the person of Cordelia, destroyed by the powers of this world, but the price he pays is that Cordelia, as a dramatic character, is a bore.

If she is not to be a fake, what she says cannot be poetically very impressive nor what she does dramatically very exciting.

What shall Cordelia do? Love and be silent.

In a play with twenty-six scenes, Shakespeare allows her to appear in only four, and from a total of over three thousand three hundred lines, he allots to her less than ninety.

Temporal Justice demands the use of force to quell the unjust; it demands prudence, a practical reckoning with time and place; and it demands publicity for its laws and its penalties. But Charity forbids all three – we are not to resist evil, if a man demand our coat we are to give him our cloak also, we are to take no thought for the morrow and, while secretly fasting and giving alms, we are to appear in public as persons who do neither.

A direct manifestation of charity in secular terms is, therefore, impossible. One form of indirect manifestation employed by religious teachers has been through parables in which actions which are ethically immoral are made to stand as a sign for that

which transcends ethics. The Gospel parable of the Unjust
Steward is one example. These words by a Hasidic Rabbi are
another:

I cannot teach you the ten principles of service but a little
child and a thief can show you what they are. From the child you
can learn three things;
He is merry for no particular reason.
Never for a moment is he idle.
When he wants something, he demands it vigorously.
The thief can instruct you in many things.
He does his service by night.
If he does not finish what he has set out to do in one night,
    he devotes the next night to it.
He and all those who work for him, love one another.
He risks his life for slight gains.
What he takes has so little value for him that he gives it up for
    a very small coin.
He endures blows and hardships and it matters nothing to him.
He likes his trade and would not exchange it for any other.

If a parable of this kind is dramatized, the action must be comic,
that is to say, the apparently immoral actions of the hero must not
inflict, as in the actual world they would, real suffering upon
others.

Thus, Falstaff speaks of himself as if he were always robbing
travelers. We see him do this once – incidentally, it is not Falstaff
but the Prince who is the instigator – and the sight convinces
us that he never has been and never could be a successful highwayman. The money is restolen from him and returned to its
proper owners; the only sufferer is Falstaff himself who has
been made a fool of. He lives shamelessly on credit, but none of
his creditors seems to be in serious trouble as a result. The Hostess may swear that if he does not pay his bill, she will have to
pawn her plate and tapestries, but this is shown to be the kind of
exaggeration habitual to landladies, for in the next scene they are
still there. What, overtly, is dishonesty becomes, parabolically,
a sign for a lack of pride, humility which acknowledges its unim-
portance and dependence upon others.

Then he rejoices in his reputation as a fornicator with whom no woman is safe alone, but the Falstaff on stage is too old to fornicate, and it is impossible to imagine him younger. All we see him do is defend a whore against a bully, set her on his knee and make her cry out of affection and pity. What in the real world is promiscuous lust, the treatment of other persons as objects of sexual greed, becomes in the comic world of play a symbol for the charity that loves all neighbours without distinction.

Living off other people's money and indiscriminate fornication are acts of injustice towards private individuals; Falstaff is also guilty of injustice to others in their public character as citizens. In any war it is not the justice or injustice of either side that decides who is to be the victor but the force each can command. It is therefore the duty of all who believe in the justice of the King's side to supply him with the best soldiers possible. Falstaff makes no attempt to fulfill this duty. Before the battle of Shrewsbury, he first conscripts those who have most money and least will to fight and then allows them to buy their way out, so that he is finally left with a sorry regiment of 'discarded unjust serving men, younger sons to younger brothers, revolted tapsters and ostlers trade-fallen. . . .' Before the battle of Gaultree Forest, the two most sturdy young men, Mouldy and Bullcalf, offer him money and are let off, and the weakest, Shadow, Feeble and Wart, taken.

From the point of view of society this is unjust, but if the villagers who are subject to conscription were to be asked, as private individuals, whether they would rather be treated justly or as Falstaff treats them, there is no doubt as to their answer. What their betters call just and unjust means nothing to them; all they know is that conscription will tear them away from their homes and livelihoods with a good chance of getting killed or returning maimed 'to beg at the town's end'. Those whom Falstaff selects are those with least to lose, derelicts without home or livelihood to whom soldiering at least offers a chance of loot. Bullcalf wants to stay with his friends, Mouldy has an old mother to look after, but Feeble is quite ready to go if his friend Wart can go with him.

Falstaff's neglect of the public interest in favor of private concerns is an image for the justice of charity which treats each person, not as a cipher, but as a unique person. The Prince may justly complain:

I did never see such pitiful rascals

but Falstaff's retort speaks for all the insulted and injured of this world:

Tut tut – good enough to toss, food for powder, food for powder. They'll fit a pit as well as better. Tush, man, mortal men, mortal men. . . .

These are Falstaff's only acts: for the rest, he fritters away his time, swigging at the bottle and taking no thought for the morrow. As a parable, both the idleness and the drinking, the surrender to immediacy and the refusal to accept reality, become signs for the Unworldly Man as contrasted with Prince Hal who represents worldliness at its best.

At his best, the worldly man is one who dedicates his life to some public end, politics, science, industry, art, etc. The end is outside himself, but the choice of end is determined by the particular talents with which nature has endowed him, and the proof that he has chosen rightly is worldly success. To dedicate one's life to an end for which one is not endowed is madness, the madness of Don Quixote. Strictly speaking, he does not desire fame for himself, but to achieve something which merits fame. Because his end is worldly, that is, in the public domain – to marry the girl of one's choice, or to become a good parent, are private, not worldly, ends – the personal life and its satisfactions are, for the worldly man, of secondary importance and, should they ever conflict with his vocation, must be sacrificed. The worldly man at his best knows that other persons exist and desires that they should – a statesman has no wish to establish justice among tables and chairs – but if it is necessary to the achievement of his end to treat certain persons as if they were things, then, callously or regretfully, he will. What distinguishes him from the ordinary criminal is that the criminal lacks the imagination to conceive of others as being persons like himself; when he sacrifices others, he feels no guilt because, to the criminal, he is the only person in a world of things. What distinguishes both the worldly man and the criminal from the wicked man is their lack of malice. The wicked man is not worldly, but anti-worldly. His conscious end is nothing less than the destruction of others. He is obsessed by hatred at his knowledge that other persons exist besides himself and cannot rest until he has reduced them all to the status of things.

But it is not always easy to distinguish the worldly man from the criminal or the wicked man by observing their behavior and its results. It can happen, for instance, that, despite his intention, a wicked man does good. Don John in *Much Ado About Nothing* certainly means nothing but harm to Claudio and Hero, yet it is thanks to him that Claudio obtains insight into his own shortcomings and becomes, what previously he was not, a fit husband for Hero. To the outward eye, however different their subjective intentions, both Harry of Monmouth and Iago deceive and destroy. Even in their speech one cannot help noticing a certain resemblance between

> So when this loose behaviour I throw off
> And pay the debt I never promised,
> By how much better than my word I am. . . .
> I'll so offend, to make offence a skill
> Redeeming time when men think least I will.

and:

> For when my outward action doth demonstrate
> The native act and figure of my heart
> In compliment extern, 'tis not long after
> But I will wear my heart upon my sleeve
> For daws to peck at. I am not what I am. . . .

and the contrast of both to Sonnet 121:

> No, I am that I am; and they that level
> At my abuses reckon up their own.
> I may be straight though they themselves be bevel.

Falstaff is perfectly willing to tell the world: 'I am that I am, a drunken old failure.' Hal cannot jeopardize his career by such careless disclosure but must always assume whatever manner is politic at the moment. To the degree that we have worldly ambitions, Falstaff's verdict on the Prince strikes home.

Thou art essentially mad without seeming so.

Falstaff never really does anything, but he never stops talking, so that the impression he makes on the audience is not of idleness but of infinite energy. He is never tired, never bored, and until he is rejected he radiates happiness as Hal radiates power, and this happiness without apparent cause, this untiring devotion to making others laugh, becomes a comic image for a love which is absolutely self-giving.

Laughing and loving have certain properties in common. Laughter is contagious but not, like physical force, irresistible. A man in a passion of any kind cannot be made to laugh; if he laughs, it is a proof that he has already mastered his passion. Laughter is an action only in a special sense. Many kinds of action can cause laughter, but the only kind of action that laughter causes is more laughter; while we laugh, time stops and no other kind of action can be contemplated. In rage or hysteria people sometimes are said to 'laugh' but no one can confuse the noises they make with the sound of real laughter. Real laughter is absolutely unaggressive; we cannot wish people or things we find amusing to be other than they are; we do not desire to change them, far less hurt or destroy them. An angry and dangerous mob is rendered harmless by the orator who can succeed in making it laugh. Real laughter is always, as we say, 'disarming'.

Falstaff makes the same impression on us that the Sinner of Lublin made upon his rabbi.

In Lublin lived a great sinner. Whenever he went to talk to the rabbi, the rabbi readily consented and conversed with him as if he were a man of integrity and one who was a close friend. Many of the hassidim were annoyed at this and one said to the other: 'Is it possible that our rabbi who has only to look once into a man's face to know his life from first to last, to know the very origin of his soul, does not see that this fellow is a sinner? And if he does see it, that he considers him worthy to speak to and associate with?' Finally they summoned up courage to go to the rabbi himself with their question. He answered them: 'I know all about him as well as you. But you know how I love gaiety and hate dejection. And this man is so great a sinner. Others repent the moment they have sinned, are sorry for a moment, and then return to their folly. But he knows no regrets and no doldrums, and lives in his happiness as in a tower. And it is the radiance of his happiness that overwhelms my heart.'

Falstaff's happiness is almost an impregnable tower, but not quite. 'I am that I am' is not a complete self-description; he must also add – 'The young prince hath misled me. I am the fellow with the great belly, and he my dog.'

The Christian God is not a self-sufficient being like Aristotle's First Cause, but a God who creates a world which he continues to love although it refuses to love him in return. He appears in this world, not as Apollo or Aphrodite might appear, disguised as man so that no mortal should recognize his divinity, but as a real man who openly claims to be God. And the consequence is inevitable. The highest religious and temporal authorities condemn Him as a blasphemer and a Lord of Misrule, as a Bad Companion for mankind. Inevitable because, as Richelieu said, 'The salvation of States is in this world,' and history has not as yet provided us with any evidence that the Prince of this world has changed his character.

SOURCE: 'The Fallen City', from *Encounter*, XIII (1959).

NOTE

1. If Verdi's *Macbetto* fails to come off, the main reason is that the proper world for Macbeth is poetry, not song; he won't go into notes.

C. L. Barber

RULE AND MISRULE
IN *HENRY IV* (1959)

If all the year were playing holidays,
To sport would be as tedious as to work . . .

THE two parts of *Henry IV*, written probably in 1597 and 1598,
are an astonishing development of drama in the direction of in-
clusiveness, a development possible because of the range of the
traditional culture and the popular theater, but realized only
because Shakespeare's genius for construction matched his re-
ceptivity. Early in his career Shakespeare made brilliant use of the
long standing tradition of comic accompaniment and counter-
statement by the clown. Now suddenly he takes the diverse
elements in the potpourri of the popular chronicle play and
composes a structure in which they draw each other out. The
Falstaff comedy, far from being forced into an alien environment
of historical drama, is begotten by that environment, giving and
taking meaning as it grows. The implications of the saturnalian
attitude are more drastically and inclusively expressed here than
anywhere else, because here misrule is presented along with rule
and along with the tensions that challenge rule. Shakespeare
dramatizes not only holiday but also the need for holiday and the
need to limit holiday.

It is in the Henry IV plays that we can consider most fruitfully
general questions concerning the relation of comedy to analogous
forms of symbolic action in folk rituals: not only the likenesses of
comedy to ritual, but the differences, the features of comic form
which make it comedy and not ritual. Such analogies, I think,
prove to be useful critical tools: they lead us to see structure in
the drama. And they also raise fascinating historical and theoretical questions about the relation of drama to other products of
culture. One way in which our time has been seeing the universal

in literature has been to find in complex literary works patterns which are analogous to myths and rituals and which can be regarded as archetypes, in some sense primitive or fundamental. I have found this approach very exciting indeed. But at the same time, such analysis can be misleading if it results in equating the literary form with primitive analogues. When we are dealing with so developed an art as Shakespeare's, in so complex an epoch as the Renaissance, primitive patterns may be seen in literature mainly because literary imagination, exploiting the heritage of literary form, disengages them from the suggestions of a complex culture. And the primitive levels are articulated in the course of reunderstanding their nature – indeed, the primitive can be fully expressed only on condition that the artist can deal with it in a most civilized way. Shakespeare presents patterns analogous to magic and ritual in the process of redefining magic as imagination, ritual as social action.

Shakespeare was the opposite of primitivistic, for in his culture what we search out and call primitive was in the blood and bone as a matter of course; the problem was to deal with it, to master it. The Renaissance, moreover, was a moment when educated men were modifying a ceremonial conception of human life to create a historical conception. The ceremonial view, which assumed that names and meanings are fixed and final, expressed experience as pageant and ritual – pageant where the right names could march in proper order, or ritual where names could be changed in the right, the proper way. The historical view expresses life as drama. People in drama are not identical with their names, for they gain and lose their names, their status and meaning – and not by settled ritual: the gaining and losing of names, of meaning, is beyond the control of any set ritual sequence. Shakespeare's plays are full of pageantry and of action patterned in a ritualistic way. But the pageants are regularly interrupted; the rituals are abortive or perverted; or if they succeed, they succeed against odds or in an unexpected fashion. The people in the plays try to organize their lives by pageant and ritual, but the plays are dramatic precisely because the effort fails. This failure drama presents as history and personality; in the largest perspective, as destiny.

At the heart of the plays there is, I think, a fascination with the individualistic use or abuse of ritual – with magic. There is an intoxication with the possibility of an omnipotence of mind by which words might become things, by which a man might 'gain a deity', might achieve, by making his own ritual, an unlimited power to incarnate meaning.* This fascination is expressed in the poetry by which Shakespeare's people envisage their ideal selves. But his drama also expresses an equal and complementary awareness that magic is delusory, that words can become things or lead to deeds only within a social group, by virtue of a historical, social situation beyond the mind and discourse of any one man. This awareness of limitations is expressed by the ironies, whether comic or tragic, which Shakespeare embodies in the dramatic situations of his speakers, the ironies which bring down the meanings which fly high in winged words.

In using an analogy with temporary king and scapegoat to bring out patterns of symbolic action in Falstaff's role, it will be important to keep it clear that the analogy is one we make now, that it is not Shakespeare's analogy; otherwise we falsify his relation to tradition.† He did not need to discriminate consciously,

---

* Fascination with the abuse of ritual is nowhere clearer than in Marlowe's *Tamburlaine* and *Dr Faustus*.

† The use of analogies like the scapegoat rituals can be misleading, or merely amusing, if the pattern is not rigorously related to the imaginative process in the play. Janet Spens, a student of Gilbert Murray's, wrote in 1916 a brief study which attempted to establish the presence of ritual patterns in Shakespeare's work (*An Essay on Shakespeare's Relation to Tradition*, Oxford, 1916). She throws out some brilliant suggestions. But her method for the most part consists of leaping intuitively from folklore to the plots of the plays, via the hypothesis of lost intermediary folk plays; and the plots, abstracted from the concrete emphasis of their dramatic realization, can be adjusted to square with an almost unlimited range of analogies. Miss Spens argues, for example, that because Antonio in *The Merchant of Venice* is enigmatically detached from personal concerns, and because in accepting the prospect of death at Shylock's hands he says 'I am the tainted wether of the flock,' he 'is' the Scapegoat. To be sure, at a very general level there is a partial analogy to scapegoat rituals, since Antonio is undertaking to bear the consequence of Bassanio's extravagance; and perhaps the pound of flesh motif goes back ultimately, through the

in our way, underlying configurations which came to him with his themes and materials. His way of extending consciousness of such patterns was the drama. In creating the Falstaff comedy, he fused two main saturnalian traditions, the clowning customary on the stage and the folly customary on holiday, and produced something unprecedented. He was working out attitudes towards chivalry, the state and crown in history, in response to the challenge posed by the fate he had dramatized in *Richard II*. The fact that we find analogies to the ritual interregnum relevant to what Shakespeare produced is not the consequence of a direct influence; his power of dramatic statement, in developing saturnalian comedy, reached to modes of organizing experience which primitive cultures have developed with a clarity of outline comparable to that of his drama. The large and profound relations he expressed were developed from the relatively simple dramatic method of composing with statement and counter-statement, elevated action and burlesque. The Henry IV plays are masterpieces of the popular theater whose plays were, in Sidney's words, 'neither right tragedies nor right comedies, mingling kings and clowns'.

Mingling Kings and Clowns

The fascination of Falstaff as a dramatic figure has led criticism, from Morgann's essay onward, to center *Henry IV, Part I* on him, and to treat the rest of the play merely as a setting for him. But despite his predominating imaginative significance, the play

---

tangle of legend and story tradition, to some such ceremonial. But there is no controlling such analogies if we go after them by catching at fragments of narrative; and one can understand, on that basis, the impulse to give up the whole approach as hopelessly capricious.

The case is altered, however, if attention is focused, not on this or that group of people in this or that story, but on the roles the persons are given in the play. When we are concerned to describe dramatic form – the rhythm of feeling and awareness in the audience which is focused through complementary roles in the fable and implemented by concrete patterns of language and gesture – then the form of rituals is relevant to the form of the plays as a parallel expression of the same kind of organization of experience.

is centered on Prince Hal, developing in such a way as to exhibit
in the prince an inclusive, sovereign nature fitted for kingship.
The relation of the Prince to Falstaff can be summarized fairly
adequately in terms of the relation of holiday to everyday. As
the non-historical material came to Shakespeare in *The Famous
Victories of Henry the Fifth*, the prince was cast in the traditional
role of the prodigal son, while his disreputable companions
functioned as tempters in the same general fashion as the Vice
of the morality plays. At one level Shakespeare keeps this pattern,
but he shifts the emphasis away from simple moral terms. The
issue, in his hands, is not whether Hal will be good or bad but
whether he will be noble or degenerate, whether his holiday will
become his everyday. The interregnum of a Lord of Misrule,
delightful in its moment, might develop into the anarchic reign
of a favorite dominating a dissolute king. Hal's secret, which he
confides early to the audience, is that for him Falstaff is merely a
pastime, to be dismissed in due course:

> If all the year were playing holidays,
> To sport would be as tedious as to work;
> But when they seldom come, they wish'd-for come . . .
> (I ii 228–30)

The prince's sports, accordingly, express not dissoluteness but
a fine excess of vitality – 'as full of spirit as the month of May' –
together with a capacity for occasionally looking at the world as
though it were upside down. His energy is controlled by an
inclusive awareness of the rhythm in which he is living: despite
appearances, he will not make the mistake which undid Richard
II, who played at saturnalia until it caught up with him in earnest.
During the battle of Shrewsbury (when, in Hotspur's phrase,
'Doomsday is near'), Hal dismisses Falstaff with 'What! is it a
time to jest and dally now?' (v iii 57) This sense of timing, of
the relation of holiday to everyday and doomsday, contributes
to establishing the prince as a sovereign nature.

But the way Hal sees the relations is not the way other people
see them, nor indeed the way the audience sees them until the
end. The holiday-everyday antithesis is his resource for control,

and in the end he makes it stick. But before that, the only clear-cut definition of relations in these terms is in his single soliloquy, after his first appearance with Falstaff. Indeed, it is remarkable how little satisfactory formulation there is of the relationships which the play explores dramatically. It is essential to the play that the prince should be misconstrued, that the king should see 'riot and dishonor stain' (I i 85) his brow, that Percy should patronize him as a 'nimble-footed madcap' (IV ii 95) who might easily be poisoned with a pot of ale if it were worth the trouble. But the absence of adequate summary also reflects the fact that Shakespeare was doing something which he could not summarize, which only the whole resources of his dramatic art could convey.

It is an open question, throughout Part I, as to just who or what Falstaff is. At the very end, when Prince John observes 'This is the strangest tale that ever I heard,' Hal responds with 'This is the strangest fellow, brother John' (V iv 158–9). From the beginning, Falstaff is constantly renaming himself:

Marry, then, sweet wag, when thou art king, let not us that are squires of the night's body be called thieves of the day's beauty. Let us be Diana's Foresters, Gentlemen of the Shade, Minions of the Moon; and let men say we be men of good government . . .
(I ii 26–31)

Here Misrule is asking to be called Good Government, as it is his role to do – though he does so with a wink which sets real good government at naught, concluding with 'steal':

. . . men of good government, being governed as the sea is, by our noble and chaste mistress the moon, under whose countenance we steal.   (I ii 31–3)

The witty equivocation Falstaff practises, like that of Nashe's Bacchus and other apologists for folly and vice, alludes to the very morality it is flouting. Such 'damnable iteration' is a sport that implies a rolling-eyed awareness of both sides of the moral medal; the Prince summarizes it in saying that Sir John 'was never yet a breaker of proverbs. He will give the devil his due' (I ii 131–3). It is also a game to be played with cards close to the chest. A Lord of Misrule naturally does not call himself Lord of Misrule in setting out to reign, but takes some title with the life of pretense in it. Falstaff's pretensions, moreover, are not limited to one occasion, for he is not properly a holiday lord, but a *de facto* buffoon who makes his way by continually seizing, catch as catch can, on what names and meanings the moment offers. He is not a professed buffoon – few buffoons, in life, are apt to be. In Renaissance courts, the role of buffoon was recognized but not necessarily formalized, not necessarily altogether distinct from the role of favorite. And he is a highwayman: Shakespeare draws on the euphemistic, mock-chivalric cant by which 'the profession' grace themselves. Falstaff in Part I plays it that he is Hal's friend, a gentleman, a 'gentleman of the shade', and a soldier; he even enjoys turning the tables with 'Thou hast done much harm upon me, Hal . . . I must give over this life, and I will give it over . . . I'll be damn'd for never a king's son in Christendom' (1 ii 102–9). It is the essence of his character, and his role, in Part I, that he never comes to rest where we can see him for what he 'is'. He is always in motion, always adopting postures, assuming characters.

That he does indeed care for Hal can be conveyed in performance without imposing sentimental tableaux on the action, provided that actors and producer recognize that he cares for the prince after his own fashion. It is from the prince that he chiefly gets his meaning, as it is from real kings that mock kings always get their meaning. We can believe it when we hear in *Henry V* that banishment has 'killed his heart' (11 i 92). But to make much of a personal affection for the prince is a misconceived way to find meaning in Falstaff. His extraordinary meaningfulness comes from the way he manages to live 'out of all order, out of all compass' by his wit and his wits; and from the way he keeps reflecting on the rest of the action, at first indirectly by the mock roles that he plays, at the end directly by his comments at the battle. Through this burlesque and mockery an intelligence of the highest order is expressed. It is not always clear whether the intelligence is Falstaff's or the dramatist's; often the question need not arise. Romantic criticism went the limit in ascribing a Godlike superiority to the character, to the point of insisting that he tells the lies about the multiplying men in buckram merely to amuse, that he knew all the time at Gadshill that it was with Hal and Poins that he fought. To go so far in that direction obviously destroys the drama – spoils the joke in the case of the 'incomprehensible lies', a joke which, as E. E. Stoll abundantly demonstrates, must be a joke *on* Falstaff.[1] On the other hand, I see no reason why actor and producer should not do all they can to make us enjoy the intellectual mastery involved in Falstaff's comic resource and power of humorous redefinition. It is crucial that he should not be made so superior that he is never in predicaments, for his genius is expressed in getting out of them. But he does have genius, as Maurice Morgann rightly insisted though in a misconceived way. Through his part Shakespeare expressed attitudes towards experience which, grounded in a saturnalian reversal of values, went beyond that to include a radical challenge to received ideas.

Throughout the first three acts of Part I, the Falstaff comedy is continuously responsive to the serious action. There are constant parallels and contrasts with what happens at court or with the rebels. And yet these parallels are not explicitly noticed; the relations are presented, not formulated. So the first scene ends in a mood of urgency, with the tired king urging haste: 'come yourself with speed to us again.' The second scene opens with Hal asking Falstaff 'What a devil hast thou to do with the time of day?' The prose in which he explains why time is nothing to Sir John is wonderfully leisurely and abundant, an elegant sort of talk that has all the time in the world to enjoy the completion of its schematized patterns:

Unless hours were cups of sack, and minutes capons, and clocks the tongues of bawds, and dials the signs of leaping houses, and the blessed sun himself a fair hot wench in flame-colored taffeta, I see no reason why thou shouldst be so superfluous to demand the time of the day.   (I ii 7–13)

The same difference in the attitude towards time runs throughout and goes with the difference between verse and prose

mediums. A similar contrast obtains about lese majesty. Thus at
their first appearance Falstaff insults Hal's majesty with casual,
off-hand wit which the prince tolerates (while getting his own
back by jibing at Falstaff's girth):

> And I prithee, sweet wag, when thou art king, as God
> save thy Grace – Majesty I should say, for grace thou
> wilt have none –
> *Prince.* What, none?
> *Falstaff.* No, by my troth; not so much as will serve to be
> prologue to an egg and butter.
> *Prince.* Well, how then? Come, roundly, roundly. (i ii 17–25)

In the next scene, we see Worcester calling into question the
grace of Bolingbroke, 'that same greatness too which our own
hands / Have holp to make so portly' (i iii 12–13). The King's
response is immediate and drastic, and his lines point a moral
that Hal seems to be ignoring:

> Worcester, get thee gone; for I do see
> Danger and disobedience in thine eye.
> O, sir, your presence is too bold and peremptory,
> And majesty might never yet endure
> The moody frontier of a servant brow.   (i iii 15–19)

Similar parallels run between Hotspur's heroics and Falstaff's
mock-heroics. In the third scene we hear Hotspur talking of 'an
easy leap / To pluck bright honor from the pale-face'd moon'
(i iii 201–2). Then in the robbery, Falstaff is complaining that
'Eight yards of uneven ground is threescore and ten miles afoot
for me,' and asking 'Have you any levers to lift me up again,
being down?' (ii ii 25–8, 36) After Hotspur enters exclaiming
against the cowardly lord who has written that he will not join
the rebellion, we have Falstaff's entrance to the tune of 'A plague
of all cowards' (ii iv 127). And so on, and so on. Shakespeare's
art has reached the point where he makes everything foil to
everything else. Hal's imagery, in his soliloquy, shows the dramatist thinking about such relations: 'like bright metal on a sullen
ground, / My reformation, glitt'ring o'er my fault' (i ii 236–7).

Now it is not true that Falstaff's impudence about Hal's grace

undercuts Bolingbroke's majesty, nor that Sir John's posturing
as a hero among cowards invalidates the heroic commitment
Hotspur expresses when he says 'but I tell you, my lord fool, out
of this nettle, danger, we pluck this flower, safety' (II iii 11–12).
The relationship is not one of a mocking echo. Instead, there is a
certain distance between the comic and serious strains which
leaves room for a complex interaction, organized by the crucial
role of the prince. We are invited, by the King's unfavorable
comparison in the opening scene, to see the Prince in relation to
Hotspur. And Hal himself, in the midst of his Boars Head revel,
compares himself with Hotspur. In telling Poins of his encounter
with the drawers among the hogsheads of the wine-cellar, he says
'I have sounded the very bass-string of humility,' goes on to
note what he has gained by it, 'I can drink with any tinker in his
own language during my life,' and concludes with 'I tell thee,
Ned, thou hast lost much honour that thou wert not with me in
this action' (II iv 5, 20–4). His mock-heroic way of talking
about 'this action' shows how well he knows how to value it
from a princely vantage. But the remark cuts two ways. For
running the gamut of society *is* an important action: after their
experiment with Francis and his 'Anon, anon, sir,' the Prince
exclaims

> That ever this fellow should have fewer words than a parrot,
> and yet the son of a woman! . . . I am not yet of Percy's mind,
> the Hotspur of the North; he that kills me some six or seven dozen
> of Scots at a breakfast, washes his hands, and says to his wife,
> 'Fie upon this quiet life! I want work.' 'O my sweet Harry,' says
> she, 'how many hast thou kill'd to-day?' 'Give my roan horse a
> drench,' says he, and answers 'Some fourteen,' an hour after, 'a
> trifle, a trifle.' I prithee call in Falstaff. I'll play Percy, and that
> damn'd brawn shall play Dame Mortimer his wife.
>
> (II iv 110–24)

It is the narrowness and obliviousness of the martial hero that
Hal's mockery brings out; here his awareness explicitly spans the
distance between the separate strains of the action; indeed, the
distance is made the measure of the kingliness of his nature. His
'I am not *yet* of Percy's mind' implies what he later promises his

father (the commercial image he employs reflects his ability to use, after his father's fashion, the politician's calculation and indirection):

> Percy is but my factor, good my lord,
> To engross up glorious deeds on my behalf . . .
>
> (III ii 147–8)

In the Boars Head Tavern scene, Hal never carries out the plan of playing Percy to Falstaff's Dame Mortimer; in effect he has played both their parts already in his snatch of mimicry. But Falstaff provides him with a continuous exercise in the consciousness that comes from playing at being what one is not, and from seeing through such playing.

Even here, where one world does comment on another explicitly, Hotspur's quality is not invalidated; rather, his achievement is *placed*. It is included within a wider field which contains also the drawers, mine host, Mistress Quickly, and by implication, not only 'all the good lads of Eastcheap' but all the estates of England.[2] When we saw Hotspur and his Lady, he was not foolish, but delightful in his headlong, spontaneous way. His Lady has a certain pathos in the complaints which serve to convey how all absorbing his battle passion is. But the joke is with him as he mocks her:

> Love? I love thee not;
> I care not for thee, Kate. This is no world
> To play with mammets and to tilt with lips.
> We must have bloody noses and crack'd crowns,
> And pass them current, too. Gods me, my horse!
>
> (II iii 93–7)

One could make some very broad fun of Hotspur's preference for his horse over his wife. But there is nothing of the kind in Shakespeare: here and later, his treatment values the conversion of love into war as one of the important human powers. Hotspur has the fullness of life and the unforced integrity of the great aristocrat who has never known what it is to cramp his own style. His style shows it; he speaks the richest, freshest poetry of the

play, in lines that take all the scope they need to fulfill feeling and
perception:

> oft the teeming earth
> Is with a kind of colic pinch'd and vex'd
> By the imprisoning of unruly wind
> Within her womb, which, for enlargement striving,
> Shakes the old beldame earth and topples down
> Steeples and mossgrown towers. At your birth
> Our grandam earth, having this distemp'rature,
> In passion shook.
> *Glendower.* Cousin, of many men
> I do not bear these crossings. Give me leave
> To tell you once again that at my birth
> The front of heaven was full of fiery shapes,
> The goats ran from the mountains, and the herds
> Were strangely clamorous to the frighted fields.
>
> (III i 28–40)

The established life of moss-grown towers is in Percy's poetic
speech, as the grazed-over Welsh mountains are in Glendower's.
They are both strong; everybody in this play is strong in his own
way. Hotspur's humour is untrammeled, like his verse, based on
the heedless empiricism of an active, secure nobleman:

> *Glendower.* I can call spirits from the vasty deep.
> *Hotspur.* Why, so can I, or so can any man;
> But will they come when you do call for them?
>
> (III i 53–55)

His unconsciousness makes him, at other moments, a comic if
winning figure, as the limitations of his feudal virtues are brought
out: his want of tact and judgment, his choleric man's forgetfulness, his sudden boyish habit of leaping to conclusions, the
noble but also comical way he can be carried away by 'imagination of some great exploit' (I iii 199), or by indignation at 'this
vile politician, Bolingbroke' (I iii 241). Professor Lily B. Campbell has demonstrated that the rebellion of the Northern Earls in
1570 was present for Shakespeare's audience in watching the
Percy family in the play.[3] The remoteness of this rough north

country life from the London world of his audience, as well as its
aristocratic charm, are conveyed when Hotspur tells his wife that
she swears 'like a comfit-maker's wife',

> As if thou ne'er walk'st further than Finsbury.
> Swear me, Kate, like a lady as thou art,
> A good mouth-filling oath; and leave 'in sooth'
> And such protest of pepper gingerbread
> To velvet guards and Sunday citizens.   (III i 255–9)

It is the various strengths of a stirring world, not deficiencies,
which make the conflict in *Henry IV, Part I*. Even the humble
carriers, and the professional thieves, are full of themselves and
their business:

I am joined with no foot land-rakers, no long-staff sixpenny
strikers, none of these mad mustachio purple-hued maltworms;
but with nobility and tranquillity, burgomasters and great
oneyers, such as can hold in, such as will strike sooner than
speak, and speak sooner than drink, and drink sooner than pray;
and yet, zounds, I lie; for they pray continually to their saint,
the commonwealth, or rather, not pray to her, but prey on her,
for they ride up and down on her and make her their boots.

                                                    (II i 81–91)

In his early history play, *Henry VI, Part II*, Shakespeare used
his clowns to present the Jack Cade rebellion as a saturnalia
ignorantly undertaken in earnest, a highly-stylized piece of
dramaturgy, which he brings off triumphantly. In this more
complex play the underworld is presented as endemic disorder
alongside the crisis of noble rebellion: the king's lines are apposite
when he says that insurrection can always mobilize

> moody beggars, starving for a time
> Of pell-mell havoc and confusion.   (v i 81–2)

Falstaff places himself in saying 'Well, God be thanked for these
rebels. They offend none but the virtuous. I laud them, I praise
them.'

The whole effect, in the opening acts, when there is little
commentary on the spectacle as a whole, is of life overflowing its

bounds by sheer vitality. Thieves and rebels and honest men – 'one that hath abundance of charge too, God knows what' (II i 64) – ride up and down on the commonwealth, pray to her and prey on her. Hotspur exults that 'That roan shall be my throne' (II iii 73). Falstaff exclaims, 'Shall I? Content. This chair shall be my state' (II iv 415). Hal summarizes the effect, after Hotspur is dead, with

> When that this body did contain a spirit,
> A kingdom for it was too small a bound.
>
> (v iv 89–90)

The stillness when he says this, at the close of the battle, is the moment when his royalty is made manifest. When he stands poised above the prostrate bodies of Hotspur and Falstaff, his position on the stage and his lines about the two heroes express a nature which includes within a larger order the now subordinated parts of life which are represented in those two: in Hotspur, honor, the social obligation to courage and self-sacrifice, a value which has been isolated in this magnificently anarchical feudal lord to become almost everything; and in Falstaff, the complementary *joie de vivre* which rejects all social obligations with 'I like not such grinning honour as Sir Walter hath. Give me life' (v iii 61).

Getting Rid of Bad Luck by Comedy

But Falstaff does not stay dead. He jumps up in a triumph which, like Bottom coming alive after Pyramus is dead, reminds one of the comic resurrections in the St George plays. He comes back to life because he is still relevant. His apology for counterfeiting cuts deeply indeed, because it does not apply merely to himself; we can relate it, as William Empson has shown, to the counterfeiting of the king. Bolingbroke too knows when it is time to counterfeit, both in this battle, where he survives because he has many marching in his coats, and throughout a political career where, as he acknowledges to Hal, he manipulates the symbols of majesty with a calculating concern for ulterior results.

L. C. Knights, noticing this relation and the burlesque, elsewhere in Falstaff's part, of the attitudes of chivalry, concluded with nineteenth-century critics like Ulrici and Victor Hugo that the comedy should be taken as a devastating satire on war and government.[4] But this is obviously an impossible, anachronistic view, based on the assumption of the age of individualism that politics and war are unnatural activities that can be done without. Mr Knights would have it that the audience should feel a jeering response when Henry sonorously declares, after Shrewsbury: 'Thus ever did rebellion find rebuke.' This interpretation makes a shambles of the heroic moments of the play – makes them clearly impossible to act. My own view, as will be clear, is that the dynamic relation of comedy and serious action is saturnalian rather than satiric, that the misrule works, through the whole dramatic rhythm, to consolidate rule. But it is also true, as Mr Empson remarks, that 'the double plot is carrying a fearful strain here'.[5] Shakespeare is putting an enormous pressure on the comedy to resolve the challenge posed by the ironic perceptions presented in his historical action.

The process at work, here and earlier in the play, can be made clearer, I hope, by reference now to the carrying off of bad luck by the scapegoat of saturnalian ritual. We do not need to assume that Shakespeare had any such ritual patterns consciously in mind; whatever his conscious intention, it seems to me that these analogues illuminate patterns which his poetic drama presents concretely and dramatically. After such figures as the Mardi Gras or Carnival have presided over a revel, they are frequently turned on by their followers, tried in some sort of court, convicted of sins notorious in the village during the last year, and burned or buried in effigy to signify a new start. In other ceremonies described in *The Golden Bough*, mockery kings appear as recognizable substitutes for real kings, stand trial in their stead, and carry away the evils of their realms into exile or death. One such scapegoat figure, as remote historically as could be from Shakespeare, is the Tibetan King of the Years, who enjoyed ten days' misrule during the annual holiday of Buddhist monks at Lhasa. At the climax of his ceremony, after doing what he liked while collecting bad luck by shaking a black yak's tail over the people, he mounted the temple steps and ridiculed the representative of the Grand Llama, proclaiming heresies like 'What we perceive through the five senses is no illusion. All you teach is untrue.' A few minutes later, discredited by a cast of loaded dice, he was chased off to exile and possible death in the mountains.[6] One cannot help thinking of Falstaff's catechism on honor, spoken just before another valuation of honor is expressed in the elevated blank verse of a hero confronting death: 'Can honour . . . take away the grief of a wound? No. . . . What is honour? a word. What is that word, honour? Air.' Hal's final expulsion of Falstaff appears in the light of these analogies to carry out an impersonal pattern, not merely political but ritual in character. After the guilty reign of Bolingbroke, the prince is making a fresh start as the new king. At a level beneath the moral notions of a personal reform, we can see a nonlogical process of purification by sacrifice – the sacrifice of Falstaff. The career of the old king, a successful usurper whose conduct of affairs has been sceptical and opportunistic, has cast doubt on the validity of the whole conception of a divinely-ordained and chivalrous kingship to which Shakespeare and his society were committed. And before Bolingbroke, Richard II had given occasion for doubts about the rituals of kingship in an opposite way, by trying to use them magically. Shakespeare had shown Richard assuming that the symbols of majesty should be absolutes, that the names of legitimate power should be transcendently effective regardless of social forces. Now both these attitudes have been projected also in Falstaff; he carries to comically delightful and degraded extremes both a magical use of moral sanctions and the complementary opportunistic manipulation and scepticism. So the ritual analogy suggests that by turning on Falstaff as a scapegoat, as the villagers turned on their Mardi Gras, the prince can free himself from the sins, the 'bad luck', of Richard's reign and of his father's reign, to become a king in whom chivalry and a sense of divine ordination are restored.

But this process of carrying off bad luck, if it is to be made *dramatically* cogent, as a symbolic action accomplished in and by dramatic form, cannot take place magically in Shakespeare's play. When it happens magically in the play, we have, I think, a failure to transform ritual into comedy. In dealing with fully successful comedy, the magical analogy is only a useful way of organizing our awareness of a complex symbolic action. The expulsion of evil works as dramatic form only in so far as it is realized in a movement from participation to rejection which happens, moment by moment, in our response to Falstaff's clowning misrule. We watch Falstaff adopt one posture after another, in the effort to give himself meaning at no cost; and moment by moment we see that the meaning is specious. So our participation is repeatedly diverted to laughter. The laughter, disbursing energy originally mobilized to respond to a valid meaning, signalizes our mastery by understanding of the tendency which has been misapplied or carried to an extreme.

Consider, for example, the use of magical notions of royal power in the most famous of all Falstaff's burlesques:

By the Lord, I knew ye as well as he that made ye. . . . Was it for me to kill the heir apparent? Should I turn upon the true prince? Why, thou knowest I am as valiant as Hercules; but beware instinct. The lion will not touch the true prince. Instinct is a great matter. I was now a coward on instinct. I shall think the better of myself, and thee, during my life – I for a valiant lion, and thou for a true prince. But, by the Lord, lads, I am glad you have the money. Hostess, clap to the doors: watch to-night, pray to-morrow.   (II iv 295–306)

Here Falstaff has recourse to the brave conception that legitimate kingship has a magical potency. This is the sort of absolutist appeal to sanctions which Richard II keeps falling back on in his desperate 'conjuration' (*Richard II*, III ii 23) by hyperbole:

> So when this thief, this traitor, Bolingbroke . . .
> Shall see us rising in our throne, the East,
> His treasons will sit blushing in his face,
> Not able to endure the sight of day . . .
> The breath of worldly men cannot depose
> The deputy elected by the Lord.

> For every man that Bolingbroke hath press'd
> To lift shrewd steel against our golden crown,
> God for his Richard hath in heavenly pay
> A glorious angel.   (*Richard II*, III ii 47–61)

In Richard's case, a tragic irony enforces the fact that heavenly angels are of no avail if one's coffers are empty of golden angels and the Welsh army have dispersed. In Falstaff's case, the irony is comically obvious, the 'lies are like their father that begets them; gross as a mountain, open, palpable' (II iv 249–50). Hal stands for the judgment side of our response, while Falstaff embodies the enthusiastic, irrepressible conviction of fantasy's omnipotence. The Prince keeps returning to Falstaff's bogus 'instinct'; 'Now, sirs . . . You are lions too, you ran away upon instinct, you will not touch the true prince; no – fie!' (II iv 329–34) After enjoying the experience of seeing through such notions of magical majesty, he is never apt to make the mistake of assuming that, just because he is king, lions like Northumberland will not touch him. King Richard's bad luck came precisely from such an assumption – unexamined, of course, as fatal assumptions always are. Freud's account of bad luck, in *The Psychopathology of Everyday Life*, sees it as the expression of unconscious motives which resist the conscious goals of the personality. This view helps to explain how the acting out of disruptive motives in saturnalia or in comedy can serve to master potential aberration by revaluing it in relation to the whole of experience. So Falstaff, in acting out this absolutist aberration, is taking away what might have been Hal's bad luck, taking it away not in a magical way, but by extending the sphere of conscious control. The comedy is a civilized equivalent of the primitive rite. A similar mastery of potential aberration is promoted by the experience of seeing through Falstaff's burlesque of the sort of headlong chivalry presented seriously in Hotspur.

SOURCE: *Shakespeare's Festive Comedy* (1959).

NOTES

1. E. E. Stoll, *Shakespeare Studies* (New York, 1927) pp. 403–33.

2. William Empson, *Some Versions of Pastoral* (1935) pp. 42 ff.

3. Lily B. Campbell, *Shakespeare's Histories, Mirrors of Elizabethan Policy* (San Marino, 1947) pp. 229–38.

4. L. C. Knights, 'A Note on Comedy', in *Determinations*, ed. F. R. Leavis (1934).

5. Empson, *Pastoral*, p. 46.

6. See James G. Frazer, *The Scapegoat* (1914) pp. 218–23 and passim.

Paul A. Jorgensen

'REDEEMING TIME' IN
SHAKESPEARE'S *HENRY IV* (1960)

As a result of close attention given recently to Shakespeare's language, it has been increasingly recognized that there are more subtle clues to his meaning in a play, and perhaps to his original intention, than the surface meaning of plot and dialogue. Imagery, in particular, has led us to appreciate the fullness with which Shakespeare's mind conveyed its dramatic message. To the study of imagery – which usually implies the dominant image – I would add for certain plays another clue: thematic word or phrase. I would add this with special confidence when it can be demonstrated (1) that the word appears frequently and pivotally in the play (as does *honesty* in *Othello*) and (2) that there is a considerable body of contemporary writing which gave the word a ready connotativeness for any dramatist who would use it.

In *Henry IV*, particularly Part I, the word that is most commonly assumed to have central importance is *honor*; three of the major characters speak interestingly about it, and it serves to differentiate their personalities. *Honor* is an important word in the play, and it also was a word figuring prominently in English life and literature about the time *Henry IV* was written. Nevertheless although *honor* (including derivatives) appears twenty-nine times in *Henry IV, Part I* and eight times in *Henry IV, Part II*, the word *time* (*excluding* derivatives)[1] has forty-one appearances in the first part and thirty-four appearances in the second. It has the added distinction of being talked about in crucial episodes.

Hal in his famous soliloquy promises:

> I'll so offend, to make offence a skill,
> Redeeming time when men think least I will.

Falstaff, significantly, says little about time, except for reluctant acknowledgments that he is growing old. He tries futilely, in what I think is his only real mental conflict, to ignore time. But it catches up with him humiliatingly when Hal rejects him as 'old man' and remarks 'how ill white hairs become a fool and jester' (*2 Henry IV*, v v 51–2). Hotspur, in sharp contrast, is driven by a passionate time-consciousness. He wonders how his father has the leisure to be sick. He pleads with his fellow rebels: 'yet time serves wherein you may redeem / Your banish'd honours' (*1 Henry IV*, 1 iii 180–1). As he approaches the moment of his death he achieves some of the finest perceptions in the play on the subject of time. There is his anguished, but theologically warranted, exclamation:

> O gentlemen, the time of life is short!
> To spend that shortness basely were too long
> If life did ride upon a dial's point,
> Still ending at the arrival of the hour.
>
> (*1 Henry IV*, v ii 82–5)

And in his dying speech there occurs what Aldous Huxley has called one of the most profound observations on life ever made by Shakespeare:

> But thoughts, the slaves of life, and life, time's fool,
> And time, that takes survey of all the world,
> Must have a stop.   (*1 Henry IV*, v iv 81–3)

So important, in fact, is time in *Henry IV* that one might accept as the motto for the two parts the observation made by Hastings: 'We are Time's subjects, and Time bids be gone' (*2 Henry IV*, 1 iii 109).

The emphasis on the concept of time was not, of course, unique with *Henry IV*. Viewed against the background of Shakespeare's other plays written within a few years of *Henry IV*, this emphasis appears to be part of a long-range concern with the meaning and wise use of time. It is noticeable in the antecedent play, *Richard II*, where, as apparently in *Henry IV*, the central character wastes time. Richard laments that because he has wasted time, time wastes him. But the play itself does not justify Richard's own view of his tragedy. The concept of time remains external to the play and does no more than testify to the fact that it was beginning to engage the dramatist's own mind. However, in *As You Like It*, *Hamlet*, and *Troilus and Cressida*, time is not merely talked about; it becomes a part of the dramatic action. A book might very well be devoted to the growing meaningfulness of time in Shakespeare's stories. Here, it must suffice that I acknowledge a greater significance in the subject than is to be found in any one play.

The primary emphasis given to time in *Henry IV* is the problem of its redemption. Hal promises in his soliloquy to redeem time when men think least he will. Since this soliloquy is commonly accepted as Shakespeare's vehicle for telling the audience directly about the play, the ringing couplet concluding it is of thematic importance. Unfortunately, as though the soliloquy in its own right were not perplexing enough, critics have enriched the difficulty by failing to give any real thought to what Hal (and Shakespeare) meant by 'redeeming time'. As a result, the soliloquy and, inevitably, the play as a whole have been misinterpreted.

It is indicative of the casual editorial treatment of the phrase, and also a clue to the way editors avoid precise plagiarism, that every editor has said essentially the same thing in glossing the passage, but has taken the pains only to change a word or so from the gloss used by his predecessors. The English Arden edition has 'making amends for time misspent'; Kittredge, 'making up for time wasted'; Dover Wilson, 'making up for time misspent'; O. J. Campbell, 'making amends for the time I have lost'; and M. A. Shaaber, 'atoning for time misspent'. No two are quite identical; all, I am convinced, are essentially wrong.

What editors of the play have failed to notice – even though one or two refer the reader to *Ephesians*, v 16 for clarification – is that there was a considerable body of contemporary religious literature illuminating the expression and underlining its importance for Shakespeare and his audience. There was even a

sermon by one William Whately (whom Shakespeare may well
have known) called *The Redemption of Time*. Reference to only
a few of these religious works would have preserved editors from
the pitfall of believing that redeeming time meant the making
up for lost time. I have found only one Elizabethan writer who
seemed to believe this feat possible. The others indicate not only
that it was impossible but that the expression had quite a different
meaning.

Let us first examine the evidence showing that time lost was
considered hopeless of redemption. John Carpenter, in a typical
monitory work called *Time Complaining* (1588), says this of
those who have misspent their time (sig. A 5):

The benefit of their time also they either doe not knowe, or have
forgotten it: for they endevor not to use her, but every way to
abuse her, and wast out the time in their worldlie vanities, which
being once let gon is never recalled againe.

William Jewel, in *The Golden Cabinet of True Treasure* (1612),
says that those of us who waste our minutes 'shal find them to be
a great diminution of our dayes; whose redemption being
hoplesse, they doe leave in our soules a wofull remembrance that
they once past by' (p. 64). And Roger Matthew, in another dis-
comfiting work called *The Flight of Time* (1634), offers the only
advice possible to those who have misspent time (p. 10): to
'plucke our selves by the eare for every lost day, and redeeme the
next'. This last quotation in particular makes it clear that 'redeeming' a day meant something quite distinct from making
amends for it and that Prince Hal cannot, as the future 'mirror
of all Christian kings', be hoping to make atonement for months
of debauchery by a sudden reform.

What, then, was the widely understood meaning of 'redeeming
time'? Clearly it had some reference to the passage from *Ephesians*. And there were two popular means of disseminating this
source. One was through the religiously directed drama. In
Lusty Juventus, a crude precursor of *Henry IV*, Good Counsel
tells Lusty Juventus:

Saint Paul unto the Ephesians giveth good exhortation,
Saying, walk circumspectly, redeeming the time,
That is, to spend it well, and not to wickedness incline.[2]

It is worth noting, however, that Lusty Juventus has failed
principally – with a significance which shall appear later – to
expend his time in the pursuit of wisdom. He is not, any more
than Hal, guilty of 'wickedness'. Another vehicle of wide popular
dissemination was the Homilies. Whether or not Shakespeare's
audience ever read a single book of religious exhortation, they
could not have escaped the following instruction included in 'The
Third Part of the Homily for Rogation Week': 'St Paul willeth
us *to redeem the time, because the days are evil*. It is not the counsel
of St Paul only, but of all other that ever gave precepts of wisdom.' 'There is', concludes the Homily, 'no precept more
seriously given and commanded.'[3]

The passage from *Lusty Juventus* is typical in pointing to the
meaning of spending present time well, not trying to recover or
atone for the time of days past. This meaning is clarified by a
passage from a sermon by the popular preacher Henry Smith:
'Let us redeeme the day which wee have foreslowed, so many
dayes, wherein we have so long hardned our hearts: let us take
up this day and make it the day of our repentance.'[4] Matthew
speaks to similar purpose in *The Flight of Time* (p. 10): 'Labour
we by prayer and repentance and new obedience, to make our
evill daies good daies, and so to rescue and recover our time into
its liberty again.' It should be observed that by 'evill daies'
Matthew does not mean past days, but rather the inherently
sinful days of this life, which he refers to on the title page as 'the
sad time of this mortalitie'.

To redeem (or 'rescue') time was to take full advantage of the
time that man is given here on earth for salvation. The godly, said
Adam Hill in a sermon at Paul's Cross in 1593, 'labour earnestly
in their vocations in this precious, short, and irrevocable time
of their life, because after death there is no daye, but night, no
time accepted, but the daye of vengeance'.[5] The wicked, according to the Homily already cited, abuse this short period of life,

and 'therefore do the godly take the better hold of the time, to redeem it out of such use as it is spoiled in by the wicked'.[6] Shakespeare had earlier, in *The Two Gentlemen of Verona*, stated through the mouth of Valentine the potential tragedy of a youth who does as Prince Hal seems to do,

> Omitting the sweet benefit of time
> To clothe mine age with angel-like perfection.
>
> (II iv 65–6)

It may be objected that although Shakespeare must have known and probably accepted the orthodox concept of time given for redemption, *Henry IV* does not strike us today as a play with much religious meaning. It is true that Falstaff quotes the Bible probably more than any other Shakespearian character and that he repeatedly raises the question of repentance. But the idleness of Prince Hal does not seem to be a character trait imperiling his soul. This is, indeed, the point made most ably by Dover Wilson, the only critic who gives serious attention to the theological meaning of the play.

Wilson rightly turns for possible theological meaning to the speculations about Hal's reform made by the bishops in *Henry V*. Shakespeare has given the bishops a lengthy and, to us, rather tedious prominence. Yet, according to Wilson, the prelates 'say nothing about religion except that he is "a true lover of the holy church" and can "reason in divinity"; the rest of their talk, some seventy lines, is concerned with learning and statecraft. . . . If Hal had sinned, it was not against God, but against Chivalry, against Justice, against his father, against the interests of the crown. . . . Instead of educating himself for the burden of kingship, he had been frittering away his time.' Wilson concludes that 'repentance in the theological sense, repentance for sin, is not relevant to his case at all'.[7]

It can, however, be demonstrated that if he were 'frittering away his time' Hal was courting – whether he seems so to us or not – a serious theological hazard, that in fact his very soul was in jeopardy. Editors have too genially dismissed the implication of Hal's statement in his soliloquy:

> I know you all, and will awhile uphold
> The unyok'd humour of your idleness.

Shaaber, for instance, glosses *idleness* as 'frivolity'. An instructive parallel is that of Spenser's Guyon, and one is not surprised to find a similarly amiable interpretation given by critics to this hero's dallying on the Lake of Idleness. According to De Selincourt, for example, after Guyon has manfully resisted the 'violent passions of anger and malignity', he is seduced for a while by idle pleasures. 'But Spenser clearly regards his defection with sympathetic tolerance; and Sir Guyon suffers no great hurt from his short passage with irresponsible Mirth upon the Lake of Idleness.'[8] However much we may today be inclined to treat indulgently the hazard of idleness in the two cases, dismissing it as a rather attractive frivolity, for the Renaissance 'idleness' had as rigorous a religious connotation as 'redeeming time'. In Guevara's very popular work *The Golden Book of Marcus Aurelius* (1586), idleness is referred to as 'the greatest signe of a lost man'. Further, 'the filth of secret chambers, the stinch of the pump in ships, nor the ordures of cities, do not corrupt the aire so much as idle folke doe the people' (sig. K 1). The Church and government felt the subject important enough to warrant 'An Homily against Idleness'. This Homily announced that it is a sign of man's 'corruption of nature through sin' that 'he taketh idleness to be no evil at all, but rather a commendable thing'. Idleness, in actuality, is a 'grievous sin'.[9] Wilson is therefore mistaken in assuming that because Hal is not being actually criminal, his 'frittering away' of time had no religious import.

But I would especially disagree with Wilson in his dismissing of Hal's new learned qualities as nontheological accomplishments. Those Renaissance theologians who tell how to redeem the time pay particular attention to self-searching, meditation, and learning as essential means to salvation. Hardin Craig has pointed out that the Reformation brought 'the idea that learning was necessary for the hereafter as well as for the here and now. Men were suddenly made responsible for the achievement of their salvation, not a salvation resting on virtue and obedience only, but resting also on comprehension.'[10] The pious individual, according to Matthew (p. 11), in order that he shall lose no opportunity for redeeming time, will always be devising 'how to imploy the smallest mites of time, some about his. honest vocation, other some in hearing, reading, meditating, conferring. . . .' Mr Ezechiel Culverwell, 'worthy Man of God', began sometime about 1595 to compile his volume called *Time Well Spent in Sacred Meditations* (1635), which contains models of the sort of reading or meditation that the individual should enjoy when alone. William Whately, in *The Redemption of Time* (1606), designated wisdom as the principal aim of those who would redeem their time. Typical of the growing attempt to make this redemption attractive to all people, Whately advertised in the title of his sermon that he was showing men how to redeem time 'comfortably'. What he did was to make the redemption seem possible for men who, engaged in the bustling life of the era, had little chance for reading and meditation.

The 'comfortable' method of redeeming time brings us back to the applicability of the theological treatises to what Hal actually does in *Henry IV*. He seldom seems very uncomfortable in his pensiveness and, as the bishops perplexedly observe, he seems not to have spent much time in private meditation or study. Now, they agree, 'he weighs time / Even to the utmost grain'. But in his youth, his companies were 'unletter'd, rude, and shallow',

> His hours fill'd up with riots, banquets, sports,
> And never noted in him any study,
> Any retirement, any sequestration
> From open haunts and popularity. (*Henry V*, 1 i 55–8)

Hal's addiction to 'open haunts' and his failure to spend time in private meditation remind one of what Whateley says of certain worldlings. Isaiah, he notes (p. 13), cries out on those who used their days in banqueting, good cheer, and merrymaking, 'so that there was no time to meditate and thinke on those afflictions whereby God did warne them to repentance and amendement, which is most contrary to the duty of redeeming the time, for all this time is even lost and cast away'.

I consider it significant that Shakespeare devotes so much attention to the bishops and to their analysis of Hal's change. They were introduced, I think, to represent the very important clerical view of the subject. Hal's method of redeeming time is disturbingly unorthodox and, with the partial exception of Whately, not the kind that the bishops and their brethren were wont to thunder from Elizabethan pulpits. Shakespeare must have delighted in their discomfiture in this respect as much as in their labored proof that Hal had a claim to the throne of France. But the conclusions they reach are, in both cases, obviously meant to be right. Henry did, in Shakespeare's eyes, have a claim to France and he did, in his own way, redeem the time. It was, moreover, a way that was becoming increasingly popular in an age of business and public activity.

Marveling that 'never was such a sudden scholar made', the prelates observe that 'the art and practic part of life / Must be the mistress to this theoric' (1 i 32, 51–2). In other words, Hal acquired the fruits of meditation by means of a studiously public life. This observation agrees with almost all the facts of *Henry IV*. Warwick, in Part II, emphasizes the studious nature of Hal's participation in the ugly world:

> The Prince but *studies* his companions
> Like a strange tongue, wherein, to gain the language,
> 'Tis needful that the most immodest word
> Be look'd upon and learn'd; when once attain'd
> Your Highness knows, comes to no further use
> But to be known and hated.

He has been a fast learner. He was so proficient in mingling with tinkers and other commoners that in only a quarter of an hour he learned to drink with any one of them 'in his own language' for the rest of his life (*1 Henry IV*, II iv 18–21). Within a short while he achieved the point of view 'of all humours that have showed themselves humours since the old days of goodman Adam to the pupil age of this present twelve o'clock at midnight' (*1 Henry IV*, II iv 104–7). When, as King, he is insulted by a message from the Dauphin about his frivolity in youth, he shows one of his rare moments of genuine anger; he is enraged at the way the Dauphin 'comes o'er us with our wilder days, / Not measuring what use we made of them' (*Henry V*, I ii 267). The Dauphin, like other conventional souls, had misjudged his plainly announced intention of so offending as to make offense a skill. Hal had, in actuality, been expending time with a purpose. He was redeeming the time in much the same educational manner as that described by Sir William Cornwallis three years later:

I Come now from discoursing with an Husband-man, an excellent stiffe slave, without observation, respect, or civilitie. . . . I have sold him an houre of my time and have ware for it, good sound principles, in truth, becomming a better fortune. This time hath not beene lost, for his experience, his learning of Tradition, and his naturall witte hath enformed me of many things. I have picked out of him good Philosophy and Astronomy and other observations of Time and of the worlde; all which, though hee imployes about durt and allotteth to that end, hinders not me from making a more worthy use of them.[11]

The churchmen, however incapable they may be of understanding the unconventionality of Hal's personality, are not entirely unaware that he has prospered spiritually in his own way. They even give him credit for having 'obscur'd his contemplation / Under the veil of wildness' (*Henry V*, I i 59–60). Through this explanation they ultimately reject – and so I think should we – the idea that his reformation came suddenly, that by any single act he made up for lost time. He grew spiritually, they agree; like the strawberry underneath the nettle, unseen but 'crescive', and growing best by night.

Many critics, I know, believe that Hal has redeemed time when, in Part I, he defeats Hotspur or when, in Part II, he casts off his followers and becomes a responsible king. These critics make the mistake of which the Prince repeatedly accuses those who do not know him well – writing him down after his 'seeming'. They fail to realize, moreover, that his redeeming of time is going on almost constantly. The spectacular moves would not have been recognized as adequate by the audience. For in both of them, he has, in the words of his father, 'redeemed [his] lost opinion', not his time; that is to say, he has merely changed the way people look at him, corrected their false impression given by his 'seeming'. He has not radically changed his status in the eyes of God. This distinction is well pointed by his statement, 'For God doth know, so shall the world perceive' (2 *Henry IV*, v v 61). God, like the audience, has known from the beginning; it is only the other characters who are surprised by their later perceptions.

But while agreeing with those critics (Shaaber is one of the best of them) who argue that Hal undergoes no radical reform, I do not believe that a correct interpretation of 'redeeming time' permits us to accept the notion of a static Hal who is perfect from the beginning and is merely enjoying a period of deceiving people, or, even less palatable, a Hal who can immerse himself daintily in a world of idle pleasure and emerge the same as he was before. Hal grows as a result of his experiences and not despite them. What is more, although he is no Hamlet, he undergoes tension and doubt as to the rightness of what he is doing. Occasionally, like Hamlet, he finds himself guilty of purposeless idleness. These are his worst moments. He confesses to Poins, 'Well, thus we play the fools with the time and the spirits of the wise sit in the clouds and mock us' (2 *Henry IV*, II ii 155–7). And again, 'I feel me much to blame / So idly to profane the precious time' (2 *Henry IV*, II iv 390–1). That he was poignantly conscious of occasionally wasting time was theologically in his favor. He never grew callous to idleness as Antony was to do.

But on the other hand, he repudiated the terror and limited dogma of the pulpit. To sixteenth-century audiences, both the drama and the humanity in Hal's method of redeeming time must have been far more instructive than the sermons on the subject which, though frightening, doubtless came to be looked on as little more than mere necessities. First audiences would have recognized *Henry IV* as an essay on the subject of redeeming time, but they would have been more aware that it was a refreshingly different essay. They would have accepted gratefully, with a relaxation of tension that must have been the primary appeal of the play, the realization that time could be redeemed

sociably, actively, and interestingly. Their favorite prince had
done so.

SOURCE: *Tennessee Studies in Literature*, ed. Alwin Thaler and
Richard Beale Davis (1960).

NOTES

1. There are also some sixty-four references to units of time in the
two plays.

2. In Robert Dodsley, *A Select Collection of Old English Plays*,
4th ed. (1874–6) II 49–50.

3. *Certain Sermons Appointed by the Queen's Majesty to be declared
and read by all parsons, vicars, and curates, every Sunday and holiday in
their churches. . . . Newly Imprinted in Parts according as is mentioned
in the book of Common Prayers*, 1574, ed. G. E. Corrie (Cambridge,
1850) p. 492. Henceforth cited as Corrie.

4. *Ten Sermons Preached by Maister Henry Smith* (1596) sig. R 3*v*.

5. *The Crie of England* (1595) p. 67. This sermon was published at
the request of the Lord Mayor.

6. Corrie, p. 492. See also Thomas Becon, 'A New-Year's Gift',
in *Early Writings* (Parker Society: Cambridge, 1843) p. 326.

7. *The Fortunes of Falstaff* (Cambridge, 1944) pp. 24, 33.

8. *The Poetical Works of Edmund Spenser*, ed. J. C. Smith and E.
De Selincourt (1950) p. xliv.

9. Corrie, p. 516.

10. *The Enchanted Glass* (Oxford, 1950) p. 143.

11. Essay 15. 'Of the observation, and use of things', in *Essayes*, ed.
Don Cameron Allen (Baltimore, 1946) p. 50.

SELECT BIBLIOGRAPHY

1. Editions: there are excellent modern Variorum editions (stunningly profuse), Part I edited by S. B. Hemingway (Lippincott, 1936), Part II edited by M. A. Shaaber (Lippincott, 1940); good new Arden editions by A. R. Humphreys, Part I (1960), Part II (1966), both published by Methuen and Harvard. There are also smaller paperback editions; Part II has been edited by Norman Holland for the 'Signet Shakespeare' (New American Library, 1965), and Part I edited by Peter Davison for the 'New Penguin Shakespeare' (Penguin Books, 1968).

2. Wyndham Lewis, *The Lion and the Fox* (Grant Richards, 1927; Harper and Brothers, 1927). Part VI, chapters 3 and 4: 'Falstaff and Don Quixote' and 'Falstaff' deal with Falstaff as the *shaman* of chivalric society.

3. E. M. W. Tillyard, *The Elizabethan World Picture* (Chatto & Windus, 1943; Vintage Books, 1959). Preconceptions about man, nature and 'order' that are involved in the History Plays – written as a prolegomenon to his book on *Shakespeare's History Plays* (1944).

4. J. Dover Wilson, *The Fortunes of Falstaff* (Cambridge U.P., 1943; The Macmillan Co., 1943).

5. Una Ellis-Fermor, *The Frontiers of Drama* (Methuen, 1945). Chapter 3, 'Shakespeare's political plays', deals with the role of the 'public man' in the histories and the later plays.

6. A. J. A. Waldock, 'The men in buckram', in *Review of English Studies*, XXIII (1947) 16–23. Falstaff when he describes the men he fought with on Gadshill is not speaking in character but as a vaudeville comedian.

7. Lily B. Campbell, *Shakespeare's Histories, Mirrors of Elizabethan Policy* (Huntington Library, 1947). An extreme historicist approach to the plays. The plays were written as comments on statecraft and were intended to be seen in this light.

8. J. F. Danby, *Shakespeare's Doctrine of Nature* (Faber & Faber, 1949). Part 2, chapter 1(c) discusses *Henry IV* as a politically true 'world without pity' in which dignity and decency are submerged either in brutality and riot or in heartlessness and frigidity.

9. G. K. Hunter, '*Henry IV* and the Elizabethan two-part play', in *Review of English Studies*, v (1954) 236–48. The point-by-point resemblances between the structure of Part I and that of Part II link these plays with other Elizabethan two-part plays.

10. Irving Ribner, *The English History Play in the Age of Shakespeare* (Princeton U.P., 1957).

11. Brian Vickers, *The Artistry of Shakespeare's Prose* (Methuen, 1968). Chapter 4, 'the world of Falstaff', discusses the elaborate prose which Falstaff uses to escape from the constant challenges of Hal.

NOTES ON CONTRIBUTORS

W. H. AUDEN (1907–73), the most original and influential poet of his generation. *The Dyer's Hand*, a collection of critical essays, was published in 1963.

CESAR L. BARBER, Professor of English, State University of New York at Buffalo. Author of *Shakespeare's Festive Comedy* (1959).

A. C. BRADLEY (1851–1935), author of *Shakespearean Tragedy* (1904), *Oxford Lectures on Poetry* (1909).

H. B. CHARLTON (1890–1961), Professor of English at Manchester 1921–57. His books include *Shakespearian Comedy* (1938) and *Shakespearian Tragedy* (1948).

WILLIAM EMPSON, poet and critic, formerly Professor of English at Sheffield. Author of *Seven Types of Ambiguity* (1930), *Some Versions of Pastoral* (1935), *The Structure of Complex Words* (1951).

HAROLD JENKINS, formerly Professor of English at Edinburgh. General Editor of the New Arden Shakespeare. Author of *Edward Benlowes* (1952).

PAUL A. JORGENSEN, Professor of English in the University of California at Los Angeles. Author of *Shakespeare's Military World* (1956) and *Redeeming Shakespeare's Words* (1962).

L. C. KNIGHTS, formerly Professor of English Literature at the University of Cambridge. Author of *Drama and Society in the Age of Jonson* (1937), *Explorations* (1946), *Some Shakespearean Themes* (1959) and *Further Explorations* (1965).

J. I. M. STEWART, formerly Student of Christ Church and lecturer in English at Oxford. Author of *Character and Motive in Shakespeare* (1949), *Eight Modern Writers* (1963), and many novels under the pen-name of 'Michael Innes'.

E. M. W. TILLYARD (1889–1962), Fellow and later Master of Jesus College, Cambridge. His books include *Shakespeare's Last Plays* (1938), *The Elizabethan World Picture* (1943), *Shakespeare's History Plays* (1944).

JOHN DOVER WILSON (1881–1969), general editor of the New Cambridge Shakespeare. Author of *The Essential Shakespeare* (1932), *What Happens in Hamlet* (1935), *The Fortunes of Falstaff* (1943).

INDEX